KT-103-825

BATTLEFIELD DETECTIVES

THIS IS A CARLTON BOOK

First published in 2003

Text copyright © Granada Media Group Ltd 2003

This edition published in 2014 by
Carlton Books Ltd
A division of the Carlton Publishing Group
20 Mortimer Street
London W1T 3JW

This book was originally published to accompany the Granada Television Production
Battlefield Detectives for Five and The Learning Channel.

All rights reserved. This book is sold subject to the condition that it may not be
reproduced, stored in a retrieval system or transmitted in any form or by any means,
electronic, mechanical, photocopying, recording or otherwise without the publisher's
prior consent.

David Wason is the author of this work and has asserted his right, under the Copyright,
Designs and Patents Act 1988, to be identified as the author of this work.

A catalogue record of this book is available from the British Library.

1 3 5 7 9 10 8 6 4 2

ISBN 978 1 78097 490 3

Printed and bound in Great Britain by CPI Group (UK) Ltd, Croydon CR0 4YY

BATTLEFIELD DETECTIVES

UNEARTHING NEW EVIDENCE ON THE WORLD'S MOST FAMOUS BATTLEFIELDS

DAVID WASON

CARLTON
BOOKS

The publishers would like to thank the following sources for their kind permission to reproduce the pictures in this book:

Paul Cooper: 3t, 3b, 4t.
Grenville Charles: 7t, 10b.
Ken Douglas: 5t.
Jo Walker/GTV: 5b, 6t, 6b.
Louise Say/GTV: 7b, 8bl, 8br, 9t, 9b, 10t.
Chris Malone/GTV: 11, 12t, 13t.
Brian Machin/GTV: 12bl, 12br, 13cr, 13b.
Julian Hartley: 14t, 15b, 16t.
Mary Evans Picture Library: 16b.
Public Record Office: (E101/47/20) 4b.
Martin Schaefer and Dominic Fontana, University of Portsmouth: 2t, 2b.
Topham Picturepoint: 1t, 1bl, 14b, 15t.
Waterloo Panorama, Belgium: 8t.

Every effort has been made to acknowledge correctly and contact the source and/or copyright holder of each picture, and Carlton Publishing Group apologises for any unintentional errors or omissions which will be corrected in future editions of this book.

The Author would like to thank the following for their permission to quote from their books:

Page 4
The Spanish Armada: The Experience of War in 1588 by Felipe Fernandez-Armesto (1988). Reprinted by permission of Oxford University Press.

Pages 38, 47, 54, 67
The Battle of Hastings by Stephen Morillo (1996). Reprinted by permission of Boydell & Brewer.
The Battle of Agincourt: Sources and Interpretations by Anne Curry (2000). Reprinted by permission of Boydell and Brewer.

Page 114
Extract from *Europe: A History* by Norman Davies (1997) published by Pimlico. Used by permission of The Random House Group Limited.

Pages 118 &123
The Charge by Mark Adkin (2000). Used by permission of Pen & Sword Books Ltd

Pages 65 & 74
Extract from *The Face of Battle* by John Keegan (1991), published by Jonathan Cape. Used by permission of The Random House Group Limited.

Pages 78 & 85
Waterloo – A Near Run Thing by David Howarth (1997). Permission granted by The Windrush Press/Phoenix Press.

Contents

Acknowledgements   6
Introduction   9
The Battle of Hastings – 1066   11
Agincourt – 1415   45
The Spanish Armada – 1588   77
Waterloo – 1815   116
Balaklava – 1854   150
The Battle of the Little Bighorn – 1876   180
Gallipoli – 1915   219
Notes   247
Further Reading   252

Acknowledgements

Any book based on a television series relies on a team – the people actually making the programmes, and the contributors without whom the programmes could not be made. This is doubly so in a case such as this, when the book is being written at the same time as the programmes are being made. I'm immensely grateful for the understanding of harassed programme makers to whom I've often had to turn.

To Liz McLeod, Series Editor, friend and colleague for many years, and who suggested I write this book, I'm especially grateful.

My thanks to all those at Granada Television who gave me advice, lent me their draft scripts, sent me their transcripts and shared with me their knowledge: Jo Walker, Karen Stockton, Clare Smith, Louise Say, Georgina Pye, Chris Malone, Brian Machin, Bill Lyons, Jeremy Freeston, Mark Elliott, and Ross Charnock, and to long-suffering friends elsewhere, particularly Peter Whiteley, David Turton, and Bob Stacy.

I'm grateful to Susanna Wadeson at Granada Media and Roland Hall at Carlton Books for their guidance.

I'd like to thank all those contributors whose thoughts, theories and experiments I've used and who are listed below, as well as the Friends of Waterloo Committee, the Crimean War Research Society and the Institute of Classical Archaeology at the University of Texas at Austin. Any mistakes, of course, are my own.

Battle of Hastings
Stephen Carver, Management Consultant, Cranfield School of Management; Colonel Paul Budd, Head of Army Food Service

Acknowledgements

Training; Jan Messent, Embroiderer; Gerald and Christine Grainge, Maritime Archaeologist and Historian; Dr Dominic Fontana, Geographer, University of Portsmouth; Martin Schaefer, Head of GIS Support, University of Portsmouth; Dr Simon Jennings, Environmental Scientist, London Metropolitan University; Paul Hill, Landscape Archaeologist; Pete Seymour, Armourer; Professor David Bernstein, Professor of European and English History, Sarah Lawrence College.

Battle of Agincourt
Tim Sutherland, Archaeological Geophysicist, University of Bradford; Simon Richardson, Artefact Location Surveyor; Matthew Bennett, Military Historian, Royal Military Academy, Sandhurst; Professor Anne Curry, Historian, University of Reading; Dr Alan Williams, Department of Engineering, University of Reading; Dr David Sim, Department of Engineering, University of Reading; Professor Tony Atkins, Mechanical Engineering, University of Reading; Professor Andrew Palmer, Research Professor of Petroleum Engineering, University of Cambridge; Keith Still, Mathematician and Crowd Behaviour Consultant;

The Armada
Professor Colin Martin, Marine Archaeologist; Mark Corby, Military Historian; Ken Douglas, Amateur Historian and Meteorologist; Jon Adams, Archaeologist, Southampton University; Professor Nicholas Rodgers, Naval Historian, Exeter University; Steve Hall, Oceanographer, University of Southampton; Dr Roger Proctor, Proudman Oceanographic Laboratory; Nick Hall, Curator, Royal Armouries, Fort Nelson, Portsmouth; Alex Hildred, The Mary Rose Trust.

Battle of Waterloo
Dr Duncan Anderson, Head of War Studies, Royal Military Academy, Sandhurst; Major Gordon Corrigan MBE, Author and Military Historian; James Kavanagh, Head of Geomatics, Royal Institute of

Chartered Surveyors; Dan Schnurr MSc MRICS, Chartered Land Surveyor; Paul Hill, Landscape and Battlefield Archaeologist; Major Simon West, Royal Artillery; David Paget, Napoleonic Artillery Expert; Mike Robinson, Military Historian; Dr Morgan O'Connell, Chief Consultant Psychiatrist, Combat Stress; Dr Stephen Davies, Consultant Clinical Psychologist, Princess Alexandra Hospital; Colonel Ian Palmer, Head of Psychiatry for the Armed Services; Mick Crumplin, Surgeon; Dr Dennis Wheeler, Climatologist, Department of Geography, University of Sunderland.

Battle of Balaklava

The late Ken Horton, Major Colin Robins and Michael Hargrave Mawson of the Crimean War Research Association; Dr Feroze Yasamee, Department of Middle Eastern Studies, University of Manchester; Dr Phil Freeman, Department of Archaeology, University of Liverpool; Lorraine McEwan, Department of Archaeology, University of Glasgow; Lea Meistrup-Larsen, Archaeological Field Technician; Simon Richardson, Metal Detector Specialist; Richard Rutherford-Moore, Battlefield Tour Guide; Jessica Trelogan, Researcher, Department of Classical Archaeology, University of Texas.

Battle of the Little Bighorn

Melissa A Connor, Forensic Archaeologist, Nebraska State University; P. Willey, Forensic Archaeologist, California State University, Chico; Douglas D. Scott; Archaeologist, Mid-Western Archaeological Center, Lincoln, Nebraska; Richard Allan Fox Jr, Department of Anthropology, University of South Dakota; Mark Bohaty, Firearms Examiner, Nebraska State Police; Joe Medicine Crow, Crow Tribal Historian; Betty Pat Gatliff, Forensic Artist.

Gallipoli

Nigel Steel, Head of Research and Information, Imperial War Museum; Professor Peter Doyle, Geologist, Greenwich University; Colonel Alan Hawley OBE, RAMC, Royal Army Medical Corps; Bill Sellars, Journalist and Author; Kenan Çelik, Battlefield Guide.

Introduction

Battlefield Detectives looks at some of the most famous battles of history in an entirely new way – drawing on the latest scientific techniques to piece together the stories battlefields can tell, and bit by bit uncovering, with the help of historians, what we think really happened.

When I was at school, history was a different subject.

I learned – or rather I was taught – about the Kings and Queens of England – and sometimes Scotland – and the triumph of good over evil. The British tended to be the good guys and everyone else the evil ones. History was entirely based on documents, and events were presumed to have either happened, or not happened. There was no in-between. The English longbow defeated the French. Brave little English ships harried the Spanish Armada to a watery end. The noble Six Hundred rode into glory.

I'm not suggesting that what I was taught was necessarily wrong, just that it was different. It was as different as A.J.P. Taylor's television lectures are from today's popular television approach. Did A.J.P. Taylor really illustrate his programmes with a blackboard?

I did garner some chronological building blocks – Julius Caesar invaded Britain in 55BC as did William the Conqueror in 1066. I knew that Edward III fought at Crécy (with arrows and bows) and built Windsor Castle. My history featured people like the Black Prince, Robert the Bruce, and the proper order of things – 'James and Charles and Charles and James' helped me learn the order of kings. History stopped, I think, in the 19th century.

Introduction

I can still remember the shock, some years later, of being given a copy of a list of the goods owned by some early European settlers in 17th-century North America, and being asked what – given that evidence and no other – I might be able to deduce about their difficult lives. I'm ashamed to say it was probably the first time I realized that history could be about ordinary people.

It was the first time I grasped the notion that learning about history was really detective work.

Battlefield Detectives is about detective work. Land battles usually leave some kind of scar on the landscape, from the visible wounds of terrible trench warfare to the slugs and bullets of Little Bighorn. Even sea battles can leave evidence – the records of time and tide, underwater wrecks, contemporary correspondence. And for battles which seem to have left no physical evidence at all, modern science can still suggest solutions to historic puzzles.

We can learn a lot from these fields of death. Filled with horror they may have been, they form a sort of punctuation mark in history – specific points in time where kings and leaders and ordinary people lived and died in the same place. They left evidence behind, in their bones and their weapons, their orders and records.

With the aid of new sciences like geomatics and oceanography, and old sciences like physics and psychiatry, *Battlefield Detectives* sheds new light on old history.

The Battle of Hastings – 1066

Introduction

1066 was a momentous year for England. It was a year in which three English kings were crowned, two major battles were fought and one man emerged victorious.

It was the year which marked the last true invasion of England.

On 14 October, King Harold II of England met William, Duke of Normandy. The clash of arms lasted nine or ten hours. It was one of the longest battles in mediaeval history.

The Battle of Hastings was a defining moment: it resulted in new laws, a new language, a new aristocracy, a new architecture, a virtually new church and a new system of government. Perhaps because it produced such extraordinary change, we tend to think that the outcome must have been inevitable.

But maybe it wasn't.

William of Normandy – nicknamed William the Bastard, crowned William I of England and remembered as William the Conqueror – had taken the most enormous gamble. He had sailed across the dangerous waters of the English Channel, at night, with a huge and unwieldy fleet of some 700 boats which were crammed with thousands of horses and up to 8,000 men.

And on Saturday, 14 October, his Norman army fought

the Anglo-Saxons – the English – almost to a standstill. At the end of the day, he had won. But only just.

Was the Battle of Hastings the culmination of a brilliantly executed plan? Or was it a hair's-breadth victory which could have gone either way?

It had been, as a later scribe put it, 'a strange kind of battle', fought between infantry on one side and cavalry on the other. It was a day which pitted two very different styles of fighting against each other: ferocious horsemen against powerful axes, repeated charges against an immovable shield wall. It was to be the last time that an army of infantry was to take on cavalry – in Europe, at least. The two armies were as different in their tactics and their formation as their two leaders were different in style, and – as we shall see – management.

Historians have said that William was the better general; that he was wily and shrewd; that he managed his campaign better than Harold; and that his use of a more advanced military technology – the cavalry – made all the difference.

Experts have argued over the centuries as to whether the Norman Conquest, as it was to become known, was a 'good thing' for England. And they have argued that there was more continuity than there was change between the Anglo-Saxon and Norman worlds.

The Conquest was to lead to a realignment of the relationship with Europe and the virtual destruction of England's links with Scandinavia.

Most historians claim that the battle was extraordinarily well documented, even if many of the documents were written a generation – or two, or even three generations – after the event. It is, of course, recorded in fascinating detail in the extraordinary Bayeux Tapestry. This unique work is actually an embroidery, worked on a linen cloth which measures 231 feet long by 20 inches wide. Commissioned almost immediately after the battle, it was probably completed before 1070.

One of the mysteries about the battle site itself is that although there is incredible precision about certain things – such as where Harold actually died – practically no proof has ever been found that a battle actually took place there.

Why not?

If this was a 'well-documented' battle, surely the evidence should lie in the archives?

Perhaps the answer lies in the immediate aftermath of the battle, and in what then happened to the people of England.

The Anglo-Saxons became a subject race dominated by an occupying army. The historian Elisabeth Van-Houts, against the trend, argues that there is in fact a great lack of contemporary literature, which she believes may indicate the traumatized state of the people. She recounts the harrowing aftermath of invasion, when 'apart from the loss of lives of the Anglo-Saxon aristocracy – estimated at between half and three-quarters of the men – many of their widows and daughters fled to nunneries in order to avoid being forced into marriage with William's soldiers'.[1] She writes of punitive expeditions, the demolition of whole areas of cities, the extensive laying to waste of the country-side and a famine of such devastation that it even led to cannibalism. She shows that many were sent into exile, executed and dispossessed. She discovered that even William's ally, Pope Alexander II, wrote to him referring to 'so great a sacrifice of human life'.

The silence of the English she ascribes to the 'shock following the complete surprise of the defeat and surrender that autumn'.

The English then, were stunned into silence. They have left behind many questions.

- Was William a better general than Harold?
- Was William's victory a foregone conclusion?
- How was William able to mount a full-scale amphibious invasion of an island nation which was expecting his arrival?
- Is the Bayeux Tapestry a faithful account of the events of that year, or is it simply Norman propaganda?
- And was Harold really killed when an arrow struck him in the eye?

In *Battlefield Detectives*, experts from a wide variety of backgrounds – in management and archaeology, geography and geology, sailing, the military and embroidery – investigate the clues and search for the answers. Their evidence suggests that the outcome of the battle might easily have been otherwise; in which case the history, language and culture of England, Western Europe – and the world – would have been totally different.

The Campaign and the Battle

King Edward, later to be known as Edward the Confessor, was the last of a long line of Saxon kings of England. Born into turbulent times, and seeking to escape Danish invaders, he had grown up in Normandy, an independent duchy in what is now northern France.

The England he came to rule was a fractious and divided country, dominated by powerful earls. The king was childless, and many contenders believed they had a claim to inherit his throne. Norman chroniclers were later to claim that in about 1051 Edward had agreed that William of Normandy would be his successor.

In 1064, Harold – then the Earl of Wessex – went to Normandy, possibly on Edward's instructions. He landed in the wrong place, was wrecked and – in the spirit of the times – was taken hostage. Soon, however, he joined William on a military campaign against the Bretons. The Bayeux Tapestry records that he helped to save two Norman soldiers who were in danger of being drowned, and that he swore an oath of fealty to William, paying him homage and swearing on holy relics that he would support William's claim to the English throne.

Harold was allowed to return to England: but when the old king, Edward, was on his death-bed, he named Harold as his successor. Edward died on 5 January 1066, and the very next day Harold was crowned king.

Back in Normandy, William was unsurprisingly furious. Both Edward's change of mind and Harold's repudiation of his sacred oath were condemned. There were to be other claimants to the English throne, too, including Harald Hardrada, King of Norway, and Tostig, Harold's own brother, then in exile in Flanders.

It was against this background of rumour, intrigue and ambition for the throne of a country which, in spite of its troubles, was becoming increasingly prosperous, that serious preparations for war began. A comet sped across the skies – we now know it to have been Halley's Comet – regarded as an ominous portent for troubled times ahead. In Normandy, William began to plan an invasion. In England, Harold set up his defences.

Throughout the summer of 1066 Harold, assuming that the greatest danger to his throne came from Normandy rather than from Norway, stationed his army along the south coast of England, and his navy off the Isle of Wight.

The core of his army was a small élite bodyguard of *house-carls*; the rest were raised by the Anglo-Saxon military mobilization system of the *fyrd*, the obligation to perform military duties in return for land held. A complex system governed the length of time a *fyrd* had to serve. Additionally, every able-bodied *freeman* was required to serve within his own shire. The wealthy would ride to battle on horseback, but then dismount and fight on foot.

Harold assembled his forces and he waited – and waited. He was waiting for a Norman invasion.

Across the Channel, William had assembled a vast army of 8,000 or so troops at Dives-sur-Mer, to the west of Honfleur by the Seine estuary. They were a multi-ethnic force of Normans, Bretons and Flemings. To transport them and their horses, William accumulated a fleet which may have numbered well over 700 ships.

It has been estimated that, including support, up to 14,000 men would have been mustered in that camp near Dives. William waited as well – all through the summer.

Historians have argued ever since whether he was waiting because the winds were unfavourable, or whether he was waiting for Harold to run out of the money and supplies which were necessary to support the *fyrd*.

Whatever the reason, on 8 September Harold finally gave up: his army was disbanded and his fleet dispersed.

Four days later William set sail along the coast, reaching St Valery at the mouth of the Somme. At about the same time, Harold – now back in London – heard that Harald Hardrada had sailed with a completely different invasion fleet of 300 ships, and had joined forces with Tostig. Together, on 20 September, Harald and Tostig defeated a northern English army near York.

With astonishing speed King Harold, in London, scrambled to assemble a new *fyrd* and, in five days, had marched 190 miles north towards York – a march without parallel or precedent in its own time.

On 25 September, achieving total surprise, King Harold and his army smashed into the Norsemen at Stamford Bridge, killing both Hardrada and Tostig in the process, before allowing so few shocked survivors to sail away that they needed less than a tenth of the ships they had used when setting out on their invasion.

Just two days later, far to the south, William and his fleet set off from St Valery and, at dawn on 28 September, arrived at Pevensey Bay. He immediately built fortifications before setting off for Hastings – about ten miles to the east – where he established a secure base.

It was probably on 1 October that a messenger arrived in the north with the news that King Harold now had to face a second invasion.

He was back in London within five days. He probably sped ahead with his *housecarls*, and once more set about raising yet another *fyrd*. He was by now testing to the limits the Anglo-Saxon system of mobilization.

By the evening of Friday, 13 October, Harold had arrived at a ridge some seven miles north of Hastings. The two armies were probably equal in number, but the Normans were fresh, fit and well trained – indeed, many were professional soldiers – unlike the English, who were ordinary citizens responding to an emergency.

At nine o'clock on the morning of 14 October, the first arrows were fired.

The English were positioned on the hill-top ridge, where they provided an excellent and closely packed target for William's army, which was deployed with the archers in front, then his spear-carrying infantry and finally his cavalry in three battalions – Bretons, Normans and French – to the rear.

William tried to break down the Anglo-Saxon wall of shields, and at first relied on his archers, firing uphill. They had little effect. Then he sent in his spear force. This, too, achieved little save a ferocious volley of spears and stones.

Finally, William sent in his cavalry against Harold's shield wall.

The Norman horsemen retreated in the face of a savage

axe attack – the two-handed battle-axe was a fearsome weapon capable of cutting down man and horse alike. At one stage the invaders believed that their leader had been hit – forcing William to remove his helmet to show his face and prove he was still alive.

The English surged briefly downhill against the retreating Normans, losing their strong defensive advantages of position and shield wall. William then demonstrated his tactical skills, ordering false retreats – aimed at luring the English into danger.

Late that afternoon, Harold was hit by an arrow, and eventually the leaderless English were beaten.

William marched on. He was crowned in London on Christmas Day, 1066.

Just who were these two men who led their armies to battle on that early autumn day nearly a thousand years ago? And what can we learn about them that might help us to understand their motives and the relative strengths of their armies?

William

William was nearly 40, tall, red-haired and stockily built.

He was born in Falaise in 1027 or 1028, not far from where the River Dives begins its short course to the English Channel in the north. He was the illegitimate son of Robert, Duke of Normandy, and Herleva, a merchant's daughter.

The Duchy of Normandy had been settled by marauding Vikings early in the tenth century, but by the time of William's birth it had become a stable, populous and cultivated community. Its ports were busy, its farmland productive. Normandy enjoyed close links with England and with Scandinavia, all three societies enjoying common trading links and a common heritage.

His father Robert persuaded his barons to accept William

as heir, just before he unexpectedly died on his way back from a pilgrimage to Jerusalem.

For the young boy – known to many as William the Bastard – it can have been no easy task to hold on to his accession through the years of struggle which resulted from such a sudden elevation at so young an age. His tutor and at least three of his guardians were murdered in the next few years. This tense struggle must have played a part in giving him a single-minded strength of purpose which was to serve him well. By the time he was 20, William had seen his first battle, taking to the field with the army of King Henry I of France; and, according to military historian Matthew Bennett, by the time he was 30, 'William was proving himself the pre-eminent warrior in northern France.'[2]

William was personally brave but brutally ruthless. Bennett recounts how he ordered that the captured defenders of a fort be mutilated by cutting off their hands and feet. 'Although this seems harsh', writes Bennett, 'according to the rules of war at the time, their lives were at his mercy for refusing an offer of surrender.' It also served a practical use in those brutal times: other towns began to surrender to William rather more readily.

William commanded loyalty not just because of his personal qualities of leadership, but because he was able to offer both success and rewards.

Although a powerful warlord, William – like most leaders of the times – avoided battles if he could: indeed, his first set-piece battle in command was to be at Hastings itself. His training had been necessarily hard in an era when a single mistake in battle could mean, at best, the loss of a dukedom and, at worst, the loss of his life. Sieges and campaigns which laid waste to the countryside were the preferred options of the mediaeval prince. Seeking battle was a high-risk strategy.

Harold

What of the man who lost – Harold of Wessex?

Harold was King Cnut's nephew. He was to be the last Anglo-Saxon king of England.

Harold was about 45. He was said to be 5 feet 10 inches tall, although one Norwegian saga describes him as 'a little man who sat proudly in his stirrups.' He was said to be handsome and to wear his hair long in the Saxon style. If William sometimes behaved like a stereotypical Viking, Harold perhaps looked like one.

We know that Harold led triumphant military expeditions against the Welsh, including a daring assault in midwinter 1062, and a naval attack on Wales from Bristol the following year which led – briefly – to Welsh subjugation to the English crown.

We know that, like William, Harold was personally strong and brave – not least in his efforts on behalf of the Normans during his time as a hostage in Normandy. We know that he was a master tactician – as he was to prove by his assault on Harald Hardrada at the battle of Stamford Bridge – and that, again like William, he was able to command personal loyalty.

But this is the stuff of history, and this information the result of the work of historians: it is based on documents. What can battlefield detectives usefully add about these two singular leaders?

The Management of Men

The director of the MBA Communications course at Cranfield University is a former engineer-turned-management strategy adviser called Stephen Carver. He lectures in project management, and researches the personality profiles of high-performing managers.

His lectures to the budding leaders of high-powered enterprises use the warrior leaders of 1066 as examples of classic management styles. He has made a special study of the Battle of Hastings in terms of project management – and, of course, in terms of the personality profiles of the high-performing kings involved. As a battlefield detective, he is able to bring a fresh insight to the course of the campaigns of 1066.

In Stephen Carver's world, a very simple model of how managers or leaders operate in a company is a spectrum that goes from pure operations management through line management to pure project management.

- *Pure operations managers* are, Carver says, 'people who just make instant decisions: they love "here – now – today". They are completely service-orientated. If you want a mental picture, think of dealers in a big bank, sitting at their desks with all these screens going off – they're making instant decisions as to what to do. The information hits them, and they make the decision.'

   Harold Hardrada of Norway was a pure operations manager: the kind of man, Carver says, who would 'just do it. He probably woke up one morning and said, "Let's invade England."'

- *Line managers* are 'a kind of middle management. They're loved by their staff, they've been there for many years, they're deeply respected. They can do a bit of project management but they're not particularly brilliant at it.'

   King Harold was a typical line manager. He was consultative, he wanted to take his people with him, he was a nice guy: a charming man. Women loved him. He liked people.

- At the far end of the spectrum, there are *project managers*. Carver: 'They love to plan. Some people might call them control freaks. They let things burn today because they've planned what's going to happen next week, next month and next year. They live in the future; they love planning.'

William was 'a classic project manager: the sort of man who would know what he was having for breakfast in two weeks' time. His predecessors were called things like "the Good." He was called "William the Bastard."'

When Stephen Carver first visited the battlefield, he realized that he 'knew nothing about Hastings apart from what I had learned as a schoolkid. I realized actually nothing has changed in management for the last thousand years. Those who cannot remember the past are condemned to repeat it.' What Carver decided to do was to study 'the hostile take-over of a company called England'.

He has a refreshing view of history – Edward the Confessor, he believes, was just a 'fluffy chairman'. He would have 'taken a lot of business lunches.' Edward was 'useless – he was a useless king and he was the son of a useless king – it ran in the family. He was heavily into the church. He wanted to build churches and abbeys – and Westminster Abbey, of course, was originally built by Edward the Confessor – that's why he later became a national saint. He left the running of the country to other people; he had no interest in management at all. The English people loved him because he left other people to manage the country quite professionally. But they were going to take over, because he didn't have any children. By 1065 he was dying.'

Battlefield Detectives asked Carver to analyze the management styles of the contenders for the throne of 11th-century England using modern management theory, and – in his terminology – to work out where they were coming from.

Harold, he says, was ' tall, moustachioed, dashing: women

loved him. He loved hunting, he was a good leader of men, he was a good soldier – much loved. He was very much a line manager – he'd been effectively running England for many years anyway. Harold ran the army. He was a classic line manager and he was a very good king. People loved him. They followed him because they loved him: he was there for the long term.'

Carver puts Harold's succession to the throne into a business context, and hints at the kinds of controls exerted on line managers: 'On the same day as the funeral there was a great gathering in London and they wondered, "Well, who's going to be king?"

'It was pretty obvious that the only guy who was up for the job was Harold. Now, he didn't elect himself – he had to go to a council of elders called the Witan. They were the board of directors, the main shareholders in England at the time – literally: they were the shareholders in terms of land – and they said, "Yep, we like you; we like your style; your dad ran England fairly well for us as managing director: OK – you can take over as king now that Eddy has gone. But, hey – you still have to report to us, because it's a very consultative type of arrangement! Yes, you be managing director – king, if you want to call it that – but you'll have to come back to us for some of the executive decisions."'

William of Normandy, however, was different. 'His father died when he was seven, leaving William as the sole heir to Normandy. How much chance would a seven-year-old kid have of actually hanging on to Normandy – a fairly violent place in those days?'

William survived, according to Carver, 'because he understood planning. He had no power, he couldn't go out and kill people with swords – yet. So everything was about planning.'

William 'had had his bodyguards murdered in front of

him, his friends murdered in front of him. He was the assassination target of many, many plots, and as a result he became quite paranoid. He was a very, very intelligent guy. His IQ was high, his EQ – his emotional quotient – was, like, zero. He became a machine because he had to, to survive. His motto in many ways was, "What you don't know can't hurt you, but what you do know can be managed."'

Stephen Carver sees William's support for 'The Truce of God', which permitted private wars between his barons except between sunset on Wednesdays and dawn on Mondays – and not at all during holy periods – as pure William: 'the ultimate control freak. Everything that happened in Normandy was clickity, clickity, clickity-click. You did it his way.'

The management consultant believes that when Harold was being held hostage in Normandy in 1064 he had had no choice but to accept William's invitation to go campaigning together, and that William had wanted to observe Harold in action: 'William was doing this to find out what made Harold tick. What sort of soldier was he: was he a go-for-it type, or was he a planner like himself?' William was learning about Harold in order to have a better chance of defeating him in the event of war.

With an illustration from the Bayeux Tapestry, Stephen Carver points out that Harold would have been a hero to William's men: 'This scene from the Bayeux Tapestry shows Harold – moustachioed, good-looking – pulling men out of quicksand. It was a river that had very quickly flooded.

'Now, he went in and got William's guys out – carried them out on his shoulders. William wouldn't have done that. William would have said, "We're two knights down! What's the plan? I've got a reserve, I've got a plan for that." But Harold risked his own life to go in and save his enemy – William's own troops. That was the sort of guy he was, and as a result the troops loved him. William never got love from his troops; he got respect, but never love. Harold got love.'

But neither love nor respect would, by themselves, decide the course of campaigns, let alone win the battles. Throughout that long summer of 1066, William and Harold were certainly preparing for battle in quite different ways.

Logistics

William, ever careful to prepare the ground, had persuaded Pope Alexander to back his cause. With the high moral ground secure, and with any possible rivals to his position in Normandy dealt with, he proceeded with the practicalities of securing the throne of England.

He held formal councils to coerce his vassals to join him in the enterprise. Those who were immune to his charm were nevertheless attracted by the idea of the booty such an enterprise might provide: William promised land and wealth in England.

Harold, meanwhile, began to gather what the *Anglo-Saxon Chronicle* called 'the largest army and the largest navy yet seen in England'. He was probably distracted by the necessity of holding other claimants, such as Tostig, at bay.

The Duke of Normandy, however, was not distracted. He was single-minded.

A central part of any general's responsibility is the way he feeds his troops, and the more one can learn about such provisioning the better one can understand the campaign of 1066. An army, after all, marches on its stomach.

Colonel Paul Budd is the commanding officer of the Royal Logistic Corps Training Centre at Aldershot. The Corps (motto: 'We Sustain') handles all the vital supply and logistics problems of the army, from baking to fuel. The Corps believes it provides 'the power to the punch'.

'Logistics is crucial,' explained Colonel Budd, 'because if you haven't got the right men, the right equipment and the right supplies in the right place and at the right time, then the commander can't prosecute his campaign. And the speed of his advance – and of his withdrawal – will largely be dictated by the logistic requirement.'

Colonel Budd can turn a modern military mind to the logistical problems of a mediaeval campaign. Many of the priorities of today's military would have been the same in 1066. The availability of food and clean water would have been essential. Armies, in whichever century, need food for obvious physical reasons: 'You have to give a soldier enough food in terms of kilo-calories to be able to sustain him in what could be a very intense period of combat.' But there is also a psychological need, 'particularly in what might be the lull before the battle, or between phases of the battle, where food is a very important comfort blanket to the soldier in terms of his mental preparation.'

Battlefield Detectives asked Colonel Budd to compare William and Harold's preparations. 'As William was going to invade across the Channel he would have had to have taken a far more centralist view of his logistic planning; he, after all, had to provide all the ships to get the initial thrust of logistics across the Channel.'

Harold, as we know, held his army in reserve for many weeks throughout the summer. His army was based on the traditional Anglo-Saxon *fyrd* system, where men were obliged to serve on the basis of the land they held. The *fyrd* was probably supplied from the surplus produced by the men left behind in their shires, and – when on campaign – towns would be expected to supply the army with provisions. Under the system, small groups of men were responsible for feeding themselves. Colonel Budd: 'Harold would have been able to take a far more pragmatic approach to his support and therefore he would have been able to have a far more flexible logistic organization, and be able to respond and change his forces more easily.'

Paul Budd believes that both Harold and William would have relied on local help: 'I suspect that both forces had taken all the logistic calculations they needed in terms of keeping their force there on the ground. I suspect there was a lot of self-help, a lot of localized assistance to the troops. Once the campaign started there would have been a lot of local foraging, and that would have been equally available to both sides.'

Colonel Budd knows what the daily calorific requirement would have been for Harold's army. The armies would have had to rely on produce such as barley and oats, rye bread, and vegetables such as onions, parsnips and turnips – but the ordinary soldier would probably not have had access to meat, and the mainstay would have been bread. Using his military software, Paul Budd worked out that each man would have needed 2,500 calories per day, and with the kind of ingredients they had, the food required would have weighed about four pounds per man per day, plus about five pints of water each, which would equate to about 32,000 pounds in weight of food each day. Colonel Budd's team conducted tests and found that 'if we accept that Harold's forces were largely cooking for themselves in small groups, what we've tried to demonstrate is that using very simple technology and some of the basic principles of cooking, you can take those raw ingredients and you can produce a sustaining meal.'

How long would the opposing forces have been able to hold out? Colonel Budd: 'When you're going on the offensive as William is, you have to be positive and on the front foot. When you're on the defensive as Harold is, you're very much waiting for the other person to engage you – and you probably come across as being far more reactive than pro-active. During the build-up to the invasion, when Harold's troops were sitting on the south coast, there would have been long sedentary periods and time to sit and reflect.'

Colonel Budd believes that you can measure the quality of a commander by his ability to understand and control his logistics.

Harold's *fyrd* was flexible and cheap, but not easy to control. William's camp was expensive, hard to maintain, but left him in complete command.

As time moved on without a resolution, Harold would have begun to come under pressure. In the language of military logistics, the 'logistics tail' is crucial – the amount of effort and the size of the resource you need to supply your force. Colonel Budd: 'July was probably the leanest month of the year. Last year's food would have been almost exhausted, the new season's harvest would not have been available – it's probably the most difficult month to supply. Harold would probably have had to have gone further in order to find resources to bring them forward – so his logistic tail would probably have been at its most extensive during the months of July, going into early August. The priority for all the villagers would have been in terms of getting the harvest in – there would have been a great deal of psychological pressure on his soldiers to return home and join in the harvest. From William's perspective, August was the time when all the grain stores were going to start filling up in England – and once he arrived there he would have probably been able to count on being able to obtain stores locally.'

William's camp had been carefully chosen. Bernard Bachrach, Professor of History at the University of Minnesota, notes the care William took to retain both the control of his troops and the support of the local civilians: 'The Dives area was a well-populated area, and soldiers' encounters with the natives, and especially the activities of foreign mercenaries, were not likely to engender good will. The planted fields in the late summer of 1066, with crops very near to harvest, and the meadows and uncultivated lands where their herds of sheep and cattle grazed, would likely suffer if William's army were not strictly disciplined. Indeed, William of Poitiers emphasizes that the crops, fields and herds were unmolested.'[3]

Bachrach argues that William provided all supplies at his own expense with 'a highly centralized process by which the duke's agents obtained a wide variety of purchases': he thinks it likely there was 'a massive granary' and 'a centralized system of collection, storage and distribution of supplies.' Working from old documents and with information from modern hydrographic specialists and geologists, Bachrach argues that the camp was probably a 280-acre site with good water, that it needed to be big enough to support 14,000 men and as many as 3,000 horses. He calculates that William needed '28 tons of unmilled wheat grain and 14,000 gallons of clean, fresh water per day at a ration of four pounds of grain and one gallon of water per man.'

Bachrach lists the need for between 14 and 20 tons of grain per day for the horses, who also needed up to 60 tons of hay and between 20,000 and 30,000 gallons of water. He reminds us that the horses, soon to be transported in small ships, were crucial to William's plans, and that 'the Norman horses at Hastings, which made repeated uphill charges under very stressful conditions throughout a battle that lasted for at least ten hours, clearly had been well fed and were well conditioned'. It had been preceded by a seven-mile ride, and ended, for some, only after they had carried some 250 pounds of rider and equipment in hot pursuit of Harold's retreating army.

He even extrapolates a requirement for 420 tons of firewood a month and a system for the removal of 5,000 cart-loads of horse manure.

Management strategist Stephen Carver sums up the planning and the logistics of that summer:

'William makes preparations – and I mean preparations. He was not the sort of guy to say, "Right, I'm going to go and invade England": he said, "Right – what's the plan about the plan to back up the plan to actually invade England?"

'This guy insisted that complete logistical back-up be provided. He worked out how many horses he was going to need – 3,000 horses. How are you going to get those across the English Channel at night in open boats; how are you going to get the soldiers across? He was very concerned about his soldiers, not because he loved them, but because he wanted them fighting fit.'

Meanwhile, says Carver, across the water Harold 'waited, because he knew that William was going to come over that summer. The *fyrd* were called up and they just waited on the south coast of England. Now the thing is, they had to get the harvest in at the end of the year, so they wanted William to come over as soon as possible.

'But no! William was not going to come over as soon as possible because he had not finalized detail 76 on his plan!

'There he was, chopping down trees, building boats and making sure that everybody had a plan, and a plan to back up the plan. Harold waited and waited and waited.

'William didn't come. In September the *fyrd* finally said, "Look, we have to go back and gather in the harvest." So Harold let them go.'

Harold disbanded his defences on the south coast on 8 September. *The Anglo-Saxon Chronicle* records that 'the provisions of the people were gone, and they therefore had to leave to go home.' The land army dispersed, and the fleet sailed back towards London, though they seem to have encountered storms. The *Chronicle* records that 'many perished before they came thither.'

Four days after Harold gave up, on 12 September, William's expeditionary force sailed from Dives. Had William, in fact, been waiting for Harold to give up – and if so, how had he known?

Could spies learn much from each other's camps? Colonel Budd: 'Logistic supplies are very difficult to hide because they tend to be bulky and always vulnerable to the enemy in terms of visibility. That can either work to your advantage or to your disadvantage. You can actually use logistics in order to give the wrong message to the opponent.'

The voyage to England was to be no easy matter – but was it to be the smooth passage recorded in detail in the Bayeux Tapestry?

The Tapestry

Much of what we know about the Battle of Hastings is based on the record provided by the Bayeux Tapestry. But as a tool for discovering what actually happened, and for working out whether William or Harold was the better general, it appears to be seriously flawed. Is it merely triumphalist Norman propaganda?

Jan Messent thinks not.

Jan Messent is an embroiderer and an author who has spent years studying Anglo-Saxon techniques and styles. She knows the Tapestry intimately and believes she can identify who made it and where it was made. She likes to think of it as 'a documentary picture which is long and narrow and was meant to hang at eye level around the walls of a great hall.' She believes that the Bayeux Tapestry was made by English women. 'There was a tradition of Anglo-Saxon embroidery which went back hundreds of years before the Bayeux

Tapestry was made: in fact, it probably preceded the coming of Christianity. It was made on linen, which was woven by the women themselves, and using threads which were spun and dyed by the women. It's a tradition that Anglo-Saxon women had – to make a record of the deeds of their brave menfolk.'

Who were these women who recorded the detail of their own defeat? They were women whose husbands had been killed at Hastings, 'they were noblewomen who would have been dispossessed, turned out of their houses – their husbands either killed or sent to war – who would have gone to nunneries for safety and taken refuge there with the nuns. That wasn't unusual. When women retired, they usually sought some accommodation in the nunneries – it was a kind of insurance policy. It was the obvious place for them to go, and they were the ones who actually did the embroidery.'

There are certain things which can only be read correctly with an expert embroiderer's eye. Jan Messent believes that most inaccuracies are to do with design and the limitation of colours – four – which were available. Jan can read the embroidery as easily as most people can tell handwriting apart. It was in the nunneries, she believes, that the work would have been undertaken – in sections. 'When you begin to take the tapestry apart along its joins – and there are seven joins in it – you begin to realize that each of the sections was done in a different venue. To an embroidery teacher, this is very obvious – every group has a different way of doing things – and if you give the same directions to each group, they'll all work in slightly different ways.

The Bayeux Tapestry is believed to have been commissioned by Odo, Bishop of Bayeux, so how can we be sure the views expressed weren't the Norman version of the truth? 'Although Odo was not known to be a sensitive man,

I think he would have had the good sense to see that if he put anything in which was blatantly anti-English, the English embroiderers would have downed tools and said, "No way." They had a limit and he had a limit. I don't think that they would have seen it as anything but a fair representation of how brave their own menfolk were, and how well they fought.'

'It sounds rather strange that Anglo-Saxon women would be making a Norman hanging for a Norman man, giving a Norman version of the events – but it wasn't all that strange. On the one hand, it would have been very traumatic for them. On the other hand, it might have acted as a kind of therapy for them to depict these events.'

Jan Messent insists that there is little within the tapestry which reflects badly on the English. The tapestry does, on the other hand, show the Normans burning and looting a manor-house, which can have brought them no credit. And English valour is shown as being equally courageous. The English are represented as men of honour. 'In fact,' says Messent, 'there is no Norman account that condemns them as being cowards, in any sense at all.'

In an age when few people were able to read, the surest way to explain what was happening was by the actions and the sign-language of the figures on the Tapestry. What many would regard as the over-emphatic posturing was, in Anglo-Saxon times a necessary cue to recognizing commands and intentions. But in that case, why is there any writing at all? 'I think Odo would have seen this as something to last for all time. And probably that's the reason that he wanted lettering in it – so there were no misunderstandings, no forgettings.'

The embroidery, then, didn't merely represent a Norman victory: it would have been in the tradition of such work, Jan Messent believes, depicting any noble battle, 'as a tribute to all of those who took part in it – not only the Normans themselves.'

But the Tapestry is sometimes economical with the truth.

The Voyage

We know that William set sail on 12 September. The Tapestry depicts a seamless voyage to England. But that was not the case.

His ships did indeed sail from Dives. But they did not then cross the Channel. They skirted Falaise before arriving at St Valery-sur-Somme, some 160 miles to the north-east. Several ships foundered – perhaps forced by the tides on to cliffs, or possibly as a result of the same storm which appears to have battered Harold's ships on their return to London.

Chronicles claim many died and the recovered bodies were buried by night, possibly so that the morale of the troops was not undermined. It had taken two days to reach St Valery but, once there, they were at least much closer to their target, and clear of the difficult conditions near the Seine. The English coastline was only 60 miles away.

And then – again – they had to wait.

They had to wait for a favourable wind to take them north across the Channel. William even prayed to the town's patron saint and paraded holy relics through the town as he did so. Historical sources mention that the fleet was delayed and, with autumn setting in, the likelihood of favourable weather was decreasing every day.

Gerald and Christine Grainge are sailors and mediaeval scholars who have made a special study of the Norman invasion fleet. They use meteorologys, sailing knowledge and a close reading of original sources in their work.

First, they looked at the situation in Dives-sur-Mer, William's original starting point.

'Strategically speaking Dives is the obvious place for the Norman invasion fleet to be assembled. It had to be within Normandy. Dives has excellent communications with the hinterland and with William's power-base at Caen. Ships and water transport can be used to bring everything together,' says Gerald Grainge, and Christine adds, 'It's about 90 sea miles – quite a long crossing, but quite a straightforward crossing: a crossing that Vikings had been used to making in the ninth century.'

A boat of the time – as shown on the Bayeux Tapestry – was quite manoeuvrable, but a fleet of some 700 ships would have been very difficult to co-ordinate. 'One has to bear in mind the sort of ships that were available to the Normans for the conquest. The Bayeux Tapestry indicates that we're looking at Scandinavian Viking-type double-ended ships with a single square sail.'

Sailing across from France is much the same today as it would have been then. The same weather patterns which affect the English Channel today affected it in 1066, but William's ships weren't really able to sail against the wind: 'To get to England you would need a favourable wind, which could be from the south, from the south-west or the south-east. But to understand that question better, you need to consider the sort of weather conditions that apply in the English Channel in a typical English summer. The weather in the English Channel is dominated by the Atlantic lows – these are low-pressure systems which follow each other in sequence from the Atlantic across north-west Europe. The wind sequence in the lows is very significant.'

But is it really possible for us to tell what the weather was like? Christine Grainge believes it is. 'Most of the sources say it was a terrible summer, and the winds he wanted – the southerly winds – just didn't come. I mean, we all know about terrible summers in England, and 1066 was just a terrible summer. And he had to wait a long time, with his fleet assembled, and it must have been quite difficult for him to hold his ships and his men together in those circumstances.'

She discovered that one near-contemporary source, *The Carmen* – the so-called 'Song of Hastings' – records that 'for a long time foul weather and ceaseless rain prevented you from leading the fleet across the Channel, while you awaited the favour of the winds.' To Gerald, this sounds like 'a typical description of a rotten summer, and a rotten summer is caused by depression after depression, Atlantic low after Atlantic low sweeping across the Channel.'

To get across the Channel, the Normans wanted winds to push the fleet north-east, but the danger of that was that they would be pushed against the coast of France – against the lee shore. 'A lee shore is a shore against which the prevailing wind is blowing. A lee shore is a dangerous place to be because it's a ship-breaker. If any ship, modern or ancient, is driven on to a lee shore it can't get off, and the waves lifting and dropping the ship, on the sand or on rock, will break it up.' In fact, it may well have been a lee shore which was responsible for wrecking Harold when he visited Normandy in 1064.

Eventually, as we know, William was able to leave Dives – but his decision to go when he did represented a huge gamble.

The fleet was forced to turn downwind, running for shelter in what was the only open harbour in the Somme estuary. William of Poitiers, writing in about 1072, says that William concealed the loss of those who had drowned by burying them in secret.

And he did indeed find himself pushed by the weather into St Valery. At this point it must have looked to William as if both his gambles – which led him first to wait until Harold had stood down his army, and then to leave Dives when he did – might bring failure. But in the meantime he was stuck.

'William would have needed a high tide in order to leave St Valery. There are two reasons for this: the first is that the high tide, as it began to flow out, would carry his ships more effectively out of the estuary, but more importantly his ships were most likely aground, and he would need the high tide to float them off in this shallow harbour.' *The Carmen* states 'God drove the clouds from the sky and the winds from the sea, dispelled the cold and rid the heavens of the rain. The earth grew warm, pervaded by great heat, and the sun shone with unwonted brilliance'. It was probably a classic Indian summer, a period of fine and settled weather associated with an area of high pressure.

Using modern databanks concerning the phases of the moon, the Grainges have worked out that on 28 September 1066, a high tide occurred at 3.15 pm. That night the moon set at about 10 pm. Lanterns – as recorded in the Bayeux Tapestry – would have been needed.

A single night's sailing brought the vast invasion force ashore at Pevensey.

The Grainges' discoveries can be summarized thus: William was not making a single-ship passage across the Channel, he was with a fleet of something in the order of 700 ships. He sailed from Dives in the middle of September in marginal conditions, with the intention of reaching England, but was forced downwind to the Somme estuary. The fleet suffered losses, which were probably significant. Only William's strength of character and the change in the weather by the end of September saved the invasion plans: had the change in the weather not happened, the fleet would have been disbanded for the winter.

Who can say what might have happened – or might not have happened – if the weather had not changed?

England, 1066

William's luck had held – and by an extraordinary coincidence, his adversary Harold was now at the far end of the country, engaged in a life-or-death struggle against another invader, Harald Hardrada.

Stephen Carver tells the story with his usual flair: 'Suddenly, out of absolutely nowhere, came a guy called Harold Hardrada: the Thunderbolt from the North.' Harald had also arrived to claim the throne of England. Stephen Carver doesn't see this 'pure operations manager' in a particularly gentle light. 'Harold Hardrada – Europe's pre-eminent warrior, King of Sweden, King of Norway, a killing machine – the greatest warrior Europe had ever seen. On 25 September, Hardrada was celebrating the capturing of the north of England. He didn't think that King Harold was going to be coming for a week, possibly two weeks. But 25 September is when Hardhead's luck finally ran out. Who arrived? Harold. It was unbelievable – he'd taken an army of 6,000 men in full combat gear up the North Road and in four days actually arrived. Those men could not have been driven up that road by Harold just telling them what to do. He must have been a natural leader.

'On 25 September at Stamford Bridge, there was Harold Hardrada, basically having a picnic – no body armour, most of the swords and weaponry had been left a few miles away at Riccall – and he was gathering in hostages, having a few beers with the lads and saying what a great army they'd wiped out up north, and how they wouldn't see Harold for weeks. Then suddenly, over the hill came the southern English army. You can imagine Harold Hardrada saying, "Bugger!"'

Down on the south coast, William knew nothing of this. He'd made it to England by the skin of his teeth: now he set to work building a base.

William had landed at Pevensey. The immediate area was

secured to his satisfaction, and soon he was in Hastings. Hastings doesn't appear to be on the obvious route to London. Why would he want to go there?

The Landscape

Paul Hill, an archaeologist with a particular interest in land-scapes, grew up near the battlefield. Together with geographic information specialist Dominic Fontana and sedimentologist Simon Jennings, he undertook a detailed investigation of the landscape for *Battlefield Detectives*.

And they made some astonishing discoveries.

There are no contemporary maps for the area, but using GIS technology the team was able to integrate data from documentary, scientific and topographic evidence to produce detailed and ground-breaking evidence showing the landscape of the area in the 11th century. They were able to add – or subtract – roads, tracks, forests, water, pollen data, aerial photography and geological information until they were able to produce views in two and three dimensions from any perspective. This provided a view of the landscape as it was in 1066.

It is known that the coastline has changed since 1066, and that Pevensey was probably at the side of a long-lost lagoon when William landed. But how extensive was this area, and how would it affect William's campaign?

Simon Jennings has investigated nearby Coombe Haven, analyzing sediment and fossil pollen content, which has enabled him to reconstruct the environmental history. He was able to establish that from roughly 2,400 years ago until about the 15th century the area was a tidal inlet, and that much of the land around Pevensey was marshland. Simon explained: 'The pollen can tell us the vegetation which is growing, and we can recognize from the pollen records that it is a very wet area – saltmarsh, freshwater marsh and reed swamp. There is no way you could cross that on foot: you could only get in there by boat. It was a completely different form of shoreline.'

The landscape has changed over the centuries – there has been a large accumulation of shingle in the last thousand years. It clearly would have been difficult, if not impossible, for the Norman army to have marched from Pevensey to Hastings, and there must be a strong case for the idea that many of the ships moved eastwards, carrying the troops and horses on board.

Paul Hill argues, 'It is difficult to see how they can march around the entire lagoon area to Hastings. We know something was going on at Pevensey – that William probably did garrison the fortress there – but perhaps it could be that the fleet then moved on. It would certainly make more sense to bring the fleet round by sea carrying the major part of the army – round to Coombe Haven – rather than trying to march inland.'

Simon agreed that it would only have taken two hours or so to reach Coombe Haven by ship – and that if they had originally approached the Pevensey shore in the morning with the tide rising, as the Grainges have shown was probable, the rise to high tide two hours later would make Coombe Haven an ideal landing site.

Paul Hill: 'The general picture is that this shoreline over the last thousand years has undergone enormous changes. When we are reconstructing the thousand-year-old geography of this area, it is the shoreline that is the thing that has really changed – when we look at the modern coastline, it is very misleading.'

If we've discovered new evidence about the site of William's arrival in England, what can the GIS work tell us about the battle itself? The new map the team created included the possible landing areas, as well as much of the neighbouring coastline and the battlefield itself.

It wasn't just the coastline near Pevensey that had altered. It became clear as more information was fed into their computers that Hastings itself had been practically surrounded by water. Paul Hill was amazed at the transformation of the landscape shown by the GIS results. 'What we have got now is that the Hastings area itself is almost becoming a self-contained area of land, like a peninsula.'

With marsh or water on three sides, Hastings was only connected with the rest of England by a narrow tongue of land.

This meant that William was in a dangerous position. If Harold could get down to Hastings quickly enough – and he would certainly want to get there, from a very personal point of view, as William had landed close to Harold's own manors and estates, his heartland – then William would be practically cut off. But if there was only one way out of Hastings, there was also only one way in.

Hastings was very secure from attack. The new maps suggest the route that Harold would have taken to the battle, and the route William would have followed.

Harold did get down there – as we have discovered – with astonishing haste. Against the advice of many he marched south, at speed, from London.

But the Battle of Hastings was not actually at Hastings, it was at Battle Ridge, on a hill seven miles to the north. By stripping the information in their GIS map down to their 1066 imagery, it becomes clear that the ridge is a good position – it's where the roads meet. Harold's army would be able to stand with the forest at its back. It looks as if he would have the advantage: he would have been blocking William's escape.

Paul Hill believes the landscape – and in particular the narrow isthmus attaching Hastings to the rest of England – was crucial: 'I think that neck of land must in some way play a key part in the overall strategic campaign in the minds of the two generals. William has got to get out, but he can't get out too soon. If he gets out of that neck too soon, he'll over-extend his supply lines – and we know what happened at Stamford Bridge.

'Both commanders, I think, probably thought that all their Christmases had come at once. Surely, if you're Harold, you think, "Right; I've made it all the way down from London to this crossroads, just south of the Wealden Forest, I'm getting reinforcements: we'll camp the night here, and what I want to do next is get inside the neck of this peninsula and trap William in it."'

Until the morning of the battle, Harold was probably confident that he was doing the right thing. What about William?

'With William, what is interesting is that he stays where he is. He must think, "This is my golden chance; I have to have a quick decision. I don't want him coming all the way to Hastings and bottling me up. I'm going to catch Harold at his forming-up point. When he wakes up in the morning, I'll be at the bottom of the ridge waiting for him."'

On the morning of the battle the impetus, which for so long had been with Harold, had switched to William.

'We don't know what was going through William's mind, but it may be that this is what he had always wanted; that he wanted Harold to come this far south so quickly and to trap him up against the woods – that's exactly what he did in the end. It might be that William had had to ride his luck a bit. I think a good general capitalizes on luck and takes his chance at the right moment.'

It was to be the longest battle of its times – eight or nine hours without a result. What tipped the balance?

We can see from the Bayeux Tapestry that when rumour swept though the Norman ranks that their Duke had fallen, William was forced to push back his helmet to show his face – to show that he was alive – and to rally his troops. It was a dangerous thing to do, but a necessary one.

It seems that in terms of such an evenly fought battle there was only one thing which really mattered: Harold died first. So William won.

Was the future of England – and English – all down to one random arrow fired high into the sky a thousand years ago?

The Blinding of Harold

David Bernstein is one of the few people to have been allowed to examine the Bayeux Tapestry from both the front and the back. He is particularly interested in the death of Harold. He believes that the figure that is Harold is duplicated in the Tapestry's 'death scene': that there is not one, but two images of Harold dying.

The inscription above the figures is ambiguous. One of the men has an arrow in his face, and the second man depicted has fallen while a Norman on horseback slashes at his thigh.

The second man has no arrow in his face. But what Bernstein found was very revealing – a detail which, until then, had gone unnoticed. In his paper 'The Blinding of Harold', Bernstein writes: 'I refer to several small holes in the linen ground... The question that needs to be asked is, "Why are there stitch marks in a line leading to the fallen figure's forehead at this critical moment in the narrative?"'[4]

The only sensible solution is that there used to be an arrow in this figure's forehead too. So was Harold alive when he fell down, only to be finished off by the sword? There is, in fact, an account, in *Carmen*, which suggests he was chopped in the thigh. And David Bernstein thinks there's more to the Bayeux Tapestry's depiction of Harold with an arrow in his eye than merely a record of the manner of his death.

Blinding was often used in mediaeval art to illustrate a punishment from God. Perhaps, Bernstein argues, this is intended to show that Harold has been punished for breaking his oath of loyalty to William: perhaps it is the Norman way of showing that God was on William's side.

Stephen Carver has a table which he uses to rate people in management.

'So who won in the end? If we do some management theory and we look at some of the attributes in terms of setting objectives, defining the scope of the project, planning resource allocation, technical skill, scenario-planning, stakeholder management, patience and team maintenance, then: Hardrada 27 per cent, Harold 60 per cent – not bad – but the winner at the battle of Hastings had to be William, the control freak, at 80 per cent.'

William had acquired a country which hated him and rebelled against his rule.

He and Harold were well matched as opponents. Both had good luck, and bad. But on the day of the battle, victory at Hastings came down to the fact that Harold was killed first; and, deprived of their leader, the Anglo-Saxons lost.

For Paul Hill, 'William woke up that morning and he knew that he had all the mobility and all the capability. And Harold lined his ridge as best he could with his strong troops. But the day was a Norman day.'

William was victorious. And the future of western Europe was set on a new course.

Agincourt – 1415

Introduction

The flat fields of northern France, between Calais and Paris, reveal little about the momentous events which took place there nearly six hundred years ago.

Driving along the narrow D928 road towards today's tiny village of Azincourt, there seem to be few clues that here was fought one of the most famous battles in English history. It was a battle in which a small and seemingly demoralized army overcame a confident and far more powerful foe. It was a battle which culminated in the deaths of almost all the leaders on one side, and what can only be described as the cold-blooded massacre of hundreds of disarmed French prisoners.

An exhausted English army, led by a young king – he was only 28 – had marched for days in an attempt to extricate itself from France and from a campaign which had started to go badly wrong. Tired and hungry, weakened by illness, they were far from home, soaking wet and – one can surely presume – miserable.

They were facing a confident and well-armed force which outnumbered them by at least three to one.

Then, on the evening of 24 October 1415, the English discovered that their enemy, which had been keeping pace with them for days, had deployed for battle across their path, blocking their route to safety and home.

Yet by the next afternoon they had overcome the French, and destroyed their army. The English had slaughtered the French knights in a terrible mêlée at the heart of the battle, and then executed most of their prisoners, in complete contravention of the laws of chivalry.

Within three weeks King Henry V had returned to London, fêted and honoured, a leader who had triumphed against all odds by – it was said – the will of God. He had led his men to victory in a battle which would resonate through the years and, according to William Shakespeare, until 'the ending of the world'.

The battle has an enduring place in English history. Do the English remember it because of their traditional virtue – or vice – of admiration for the underdog? Or do they recall it because the battle was such an extraordinary and over-whelming triumph?

Certainly it has entered England's cultural memory in a strikingly persistent manner. Shakespeare's play, *Henry V,* sets the tone: written in 1599, it enjoyed immediate success with its portrayal of the ideal king conquering all in an epic story. In a later age, the field of Agincourt became known to an even wider world with Laurence Olivier's wartime epic and Kenneth Branagh's exhilarating 1989 film.

If one looks across those sombre, flat fields lined with electricity pylons towards the old red-roofed farm buildings and the insignificant woodlands and scattered copses of this bleak northern landscape, with little but the crowing of farmyard cocks and the rare sound of a passing car, it is hard to imagine the battle. In this quiet landscape it isn't easy to imagine the turmoil and shouting, the simultaneous release of thousands of arrows from the longbows of the English, the shrieks of dying men and terrified horses, the noise of axe against steel armour, the crunch of bone. It is difficult to conjure up the terror of knights literally immobile on the ground who themselves, moments before, had regarded themselves as lords of chivalry and masters of all they surveyed.

Images of knights in shining steel and banners unfurled have entered the collective memory. But how much is myth and how much is truth? Could Henry have been such a perfect leader? Were the French dead really piled in heaps higher than a man? Did the longbow really turn the tide? Did the armoured King Henry need a crane to mount his horse? And was it at Agincourt that that peculiarly English gesture of contempt, the V-sign, originated?

The battlefield detectives hope to find out.

There have been no excavations at Agincourt since the 19th century. Any bones which do exist may be buried in pits nearby. There are a few rare artefacts – bits of tiling, an arrowhead or two, a single spur. So can it really be possible, nearly 600 years after the event, for our battlefield detectives to learn anything at all about this unprepossessing foreign field?

In fact, some of the answers to what happened lie precisely here, at Agincourt, by the side of the D928 – in the very soil underfoot. More answers lie in the even less likely fields of metallurgy, maths, police work and theoretical physics.

And extraordinarily, after all this time, there still are secrets to be uncovered in the archives.

Combining scientific investigation with unusually reliable documentation – four separate eyewitness accounts exist, two of them French and two English – our battlefield detectives can indeed shed new light on how and why the English won the day.

The Road to War

England and France had been enemies for centuries. Ever since William of Normandy had crossed the Channel, defeating Harold near Hastings in 1066, relationships had been uneasy. William, as Duke of Normandy, was a vassal of the French king, and being crowned King of England did not change that relationship.

By the beginning of the 13th century, Normandy had been conquered and reclaimed by the French, although the English retained Aquitaine and Gascony in the south and Calais in the north. Yet still the French insisted that every new English king should perform homage. When the English King Edward III decided to lay claim to the throne of France himself in 1337, a century and more of conflict began, now known as the Hundred Years' War.

Edward himself won a famous battle at Crécy in August 1346, but more often the wars of the era involved campaigns called *chevauchées*, seasonal raids in which the armies would ravage enemy territory – burning crops and villages, looting and despoiling as they went. It served to belittle the French crown, denied the enemy provisions and provided the army with easy pickings. Gradually this policy failed as the French found ways to counter it – they started to get their retaliation in first by destroying the land before the English got to it – and the French started to mount their own raids on England.

By 1415 the young King Henry V, who had succeeded to the throne two years earlier, had decided to invade France in a rather more serious way.

The Protagonists

Professor of History at the University of Reading, Anne Curry has for years been fascinated by the battle which has rung down through the centuries as a triumph of the

English spirit. She is probably the leading authority in the field, and writes in an engagingly fresh, honest and approachable way. Henry, she writes, was 'the golden boy of 15th-century history – strong, decisive, athletic, energetic, pious and, above all, successful.' He was 'renowned for justice and he was praised for ruling firmly but without oppression or partiality. All kings were feared, but Henry was admired and appreciated by his people as a whole, by his friends who knew him intimately, and even by his enemies.'[1]

Henry had been schooled young in the ways of the warrior king. He took part in a campaign against the Scots in 1400, and by 1402 he was fighting against the Welsh and their allies. He fought at the Battle of Shrewsbury, aged only 15, and was to learn about the power of the Welsh longbow when he was hit in the face by an arrow. His next battle was to be at Agincourt.

Practised in the reality of war and battle, Henry, when he succeeded his father in 1413, soon proved himself a man able to command loyalty from nobles and commoners alike. He appointed able men to help him achieve his ambitions. He was to prove a brave leader.

'In contrast to the English', writes military historian Matthew Bennett in *Agincourt 1415*, 'the French were in a mess. Their king, Charles VI, was subject to fits of insanity to which he had been victim for 20 years. Despite his undoubted bravery and moments of sanity, he was unfit to command. His son, the Dauphin Louis, was an unhealthy and unmilitary lad of 19 with no experience of war.'[2] He adds that King Charles's insane belief that he was made out of glass was a particularly unsatisfactory delusion for a soldier.

If Charles was not to command his own army, who was? The country was riven by opposing factions scrabbling for influence under a weak king. Eventually three leaders – all of them young and inexperienced dukes – were appointed, along with two more experienced royal officials both with a military background; Charles, Constable of the Royal Household, and Boucicault, Marshal of France.

Five lesser, joint leaders against one decisive foreign king was not an ideal solution. The two professionals were not able to command. As Matthew Bennett says: 'When the day of the battle came, they were overruled by the arrogant young dukes, Princes of the Blood, over whom career soldiers such as they could claim no authority... On the fateful day itself, if one were to ask who commanded the French army, the answer must be: no one.' [3]

These, then, were the leaders of the two forces who were to meet on that autumn day. What of the armies?

The Men-at-Arms

Mediaeval armies at this time were essentially made up of men-at-arms and archers, give or take crossbowmen, the rare gunner or two and thousands of varlets, grooms and hangers-on. A man-at-arms was the fully-suited, armour-clad warrior of the Middle Ages.

Men-at-arms held higher rank than the archers. Some were esquires, but many were of higher rank – they were knights. Literally, they were the knights in shining armour of our story books. All were trained cavalrymen and by the time of Agincourt, all would have worn a coat of riveted plates, often with external breastplates covering steel hoops under-neath. The entire body was protected with a complex arrangement of hinged and riveted armour from the tips of their toes to the tops of their heads. Helmets – which were always the last item to be put on before battle – were attached to chainmail neck defences or even plated neck-guards. The weakest point in a suit of armour tended to be the visor. Because suits of armour became hot very quickly, men-at-arms only closed their visors at the last possible moment. Christopher Gravett, Senior Curator at the Tower Armouries, writes: 'The greatest drawback was the lack of ventilation. The body's heat could not escape easily and the wearer soon got hot, especially when the helmet was in place, since much of the heat is lost from the head.'[4]

Suits of armour were not as heavy as is sometimes supposed. Estimates of their weight range from 45 to 75 pounds, spread evenly over the body. This is not much heavier than a modern marine's battle-pack. Men in armour could indeed pick themselves up if they fell over, and the idea of being lifted on to a horse by crane originated only in Laurence Olivier's *Henry V.*

Men-at-arms used lances, but more often relied on the sword, made of the finest steel they could afford. It was usually three feet or so long, double-edged, with a heavy pommel (a weight below the grip to balance the blade), and worn in a scabbard. They would also carry a dagger and sometimes a mace or a war hammer.

A man-at-arms – both esquire and knight – could expect to receive about one shilling [5p] a day, although the very highest ranking of them might expect more.

The Archers

English archers occupied a less elevated status than men-at-arms, but they were trained, skilled and relatively wealthy men. On campaigns, archers were paid 6d [2.5p] a day: this meant that they earned as much in a month as a skilled artisan could earn in a year. Most archers rode to battle on horseback, but would dismount to fight. Apart from simple helmets, archers rarely wore armour other than chain-mail shirts and skirts.

Historian Anne Curry confirms the esteem in which archers were held: 'they'd proved themselves in the 14th-century campaigns of the Hundred Years War, and in the recent campaigns against the rebels under Owen Glendower in Wales. The beauty of the archers was that you could recruit larger numbers of them. They cost less in larger numbers, but of course archers are only any good in large numbers. They are effectively the mass artillery of the Middle Ages, and they needed to be in large numbers to have the effect of massed firepower.'

To be skilled at archery, practice was essential. It's been said that archery training was compulsory for many adult men, and that Edward III had even banned football and other diversions in case they interfered with archery practice.

The archer's main weapon was, of course, the bow. Usually it was as long as its owner was tall and made out of yew, elm or ash. Bows were kept unstrung until they were needed, and it is said that archers kept their strings dry under their hats, whence – it is claimed – came the expression, 'Keep it under your hat'. The pull, or force, required to draw a bow ranged from 80 to as much as 150 pounds.

The range of the longbow is a matter of some dispute: it is said they could kill at 200 yards, but according to Martin Bennett, 'real execution was probably not achieved over 50 yards.' Archers were also armed with daggers or knives, and usually had a long-shafted wooden hammer and perhaps an axe or woodcutting tool.

At Agincourt the English archers carried something else which was to prove crucial – sharp wooden stakes which they were to plant in the soft ground, facing the enemy.

The Campaign

The course of the campaign and battle can be told quite simply. Unusually for a mediaeval battle, there exists authoritative documentary evidence and solid eyewitness testimony: ideal for the battlefield detective.

Henry set sail for France on 11 August. As always, different sources give different estimates of numbers, but there were probably more than 10,000 fighting men in his army, made up of roughly 8,000 archers and 2,500 men-at-arms. Matthew Bennett calculates that since each man-at-arms required two, three or four horses, and since at least half the archers were mounted, they must have taken some 10,000 horses with them, and presumably many more men to look after the horses and the troops themselves. They arrived off Harfleur in Normandy, with an enormous fleet which must have numbered at least 300 ships – one source even claims there were 1,500.

The English immediately laid siege to Harfleur, but the town held out for five weeks before surrendering on 23 September.

Henry had secured a foothold, but with winter on the way he no longer had the time to mount a campaign. Not only that, but the English were now suffering the most dreaded fate faced by every army until the mid-20th century – disease.

Dysentery – or 'the flux' – spread through the English army, killing some 2,000 men.

There's a suggestion in the histories as to the cause of the illness: bad seafood, which carried away a disproportionately large number of the higher-status soldiers, the men-at-arms. Anne Curry: 'The archers perhaps had a simpler diet – a more grain-based diet – and therefore didn't suffer as badly. There are various other possibilities. Certainly life at court wasn't all that healthy. Throughout the centuries courts have suffered diseases of this kind. Perhaps these young men, the men-at-arms, were in close contact with each other, and transmitting the disease quite easily from one to the other.'

An eyewitness, a priest with Henry's army, wrote: 'Because the dysentery, which had carried off far more of our men, both nobles and others, than had the sword, so direly affected and disabled many of the remainder that they could not journey on with him any further, he caused them to be separated from those who were fit and well, and gave them leave to return to England.'[5] In fact, those sent back probably numbered another 2,000 men. The 10,000 troops were now down to about 6,000.

This lengthy stalemate had created a problem for Henry. The siege had lasted five weeks. He was running out of men, supplies and time: he couldn't carry out campaigns towards Bordeaux or Paris in the winter. But Henry was determined not to lose face. If he had sailed back the way he had arrived having merely set foot in France, and with only Harfleur to his name, his reputation would have suffered. In order to prove his valour and to show the flag on French soil, he set off on a long march northward across Normandy towards Calais, then an English possession, and thence home.

He set out some eight weeks after he had arrived, on 8 October. With only one week's supplies, the plan was nearly his undoing. The River Somme lay between his army and safety in Calais. A river in mediaeval Europe represented a far more difficult barrier than it would today. The chronicler priest wrote: 'All at once, we were told by our scouts and mounted patrol that the bridges and causeways had been broken.' Not only that, but 'a great part of the French army was on the opposite bank to obstruct our passage.'[6] Eventually, the English found a ford, and Henry personally supervised its crossing.

With a French army of possibly 20,000–30,000 men keeping pace with him (the number of them was 'terrifying', wrote the priest) the English had travelled more than 200 miles by the evening of 24 October.

Anne Curry points out that the journey wasn't really a march. The English had horses with them – including the horses of those who had been invalided home – which probably accounted for the speed of their journey.

They camped by the small village of Maisoncelles, near a castle called Azincourt. They were so close to the French army that Henry and his bone-weary troops could hear their enemy talking to each other, calling for servants and chatting to friends. It was said that the French were so confident of victory and the chance of taking hostages the next morning that 'that night they cast dice for our king and his nobles.'[7]

Both sides, of course, would have hoped for riches. Anne Curry explains that it would have been 'like winning the National Lottery: you could take one very important French prisoner and live off that ransom for the rest of your life. But the chances of it were as slim as winning the National Lottery!'

On 25 October, battle was joined. The result was not to be the foregone conclusion the French had assumed.

At first light the English men-at-arms and archers took up their positions on the recently planted fields, and by eight in the morning both sides were ready for battle. But for a long time nothing happened. The historian John Keegan says the stand-off lasted four hours; Matthew Bennett thinks two.

The French, who were blocking the English army's route home, knew that they had nothing to lose by waiting: either the English would attack or they would surrender, and if they attacked they would surely die in the face of such overwhelming odds. Henry's only option was to close with the enemy. He ordered a very cautious advance. Matthew Bennett: 'Great care was taken to keep his men-at-arms and archers alike in formation, and to do it slowly so that they were not exhausted by moving over the sodden ground. When they came to within bowshot of the enemy, perhaps a furlong (220 yards) away, the English took up their positions. In the centre stood the 900 men-at-arms'.[8]

The English archers – probably to either side of their force of men-at-arms – planted their sharpened stakes firmly in the earth, their points towards the enemy. The French were drawn up ahead of them in three 'battles', or battalions.

The archers let fly volley after volley of arrows, and the French were stung into action. Some crossbowmen probably responded first, but then the French cavalry, led by knights and nobles eager for glory and the easy pickings they expected to get by capturing the English leaders, charged forward. Matthew Bennett thinks it doubtful they could have got up much speed on the recently ploughed, rain-soaked ground.

Wounded – or worse – by the arrows, the knights and their horses (which were far more difficult to protect) stumbled into the sharpened stakes. Men were thrown off and down on to the mud. They turned about and headed back to their own lines, only to collide with the second wave of the French assault – the dismounted men-at-arms, also in full armour, who were now advancing.

There was total disarray and panic, though many of the French men-at-arms pressed on. But, says Bennett, they were already near exhaustion: 'The ground they were crossing, unlike that traversed by the English earlier in the day, was a morass. It had been broken up by the horses of their army, which had been exercised by the pages and varlets throughout the cold night; it had been further churned up by the cavalry charge and its returning horses; now thousands of heavily-armoured men, perhaps eight to ten ranks deep, ploughed it still further.'[9] The French – unlike the English archers who now descended on them with axes and mallets – were so tightly packed together they may not have been able to even draw their swords.

The English chronicler priest was terrified: 'I, who am now writing this and then was sitting on a horse among the baggage at the rear of the battle, and the other priests present did humble our souls before God'. Perhaps from this position he could not see the mêlée itself, but certainly he would have quickly heard the details: 'The battle raged at its fiercest, and our archers notched their sharp-pointed arrows and loosed them into the enemy's flanks, keeping up the fight without pause. And when their arrows were all used up, seizing axes, stakes and swords and spearheads that were lying about, they struck down, hacked and stabbed the enemy.'[10]

Amid this mayhem, French knights tried to surrender – a perfectly honourable action in mediaeval warfare, when high-ranking prisoners could expect to be looked after until ransoms were negotiated. But the men they were fighting were not fellow knights: they were lowly archers, and the rules of chivalry were not – probably could not be – applied in the chaos. The French were routed. Their leaders were killed, and the third battalion, presumably looking on with horror, melted away if they could.

Could so much death have been avoided? Anne Curry thinks it must have been almost impossible for anyone to have offered themselves for ransom. 'Perhaps you've had your sword knocked out of your hand – you're not able to fight any more, and therefore you are a prisoner of the person you've been fighting against. But how do you indicate that? How do they manage to get you off the battlefield? Did you just lie down? Did they have a page near at hand to escort you to the rear?'

A few hundred French prisoners were taken to the rear of the battlefield. But King Henry, perhaps fearful that the day might yet be lost, ordered their execution. John Keegan refers to this episode as an 'outright atrocity', and the English eyewitness Le Fevre described it as 'a most pitiable matter'. It seems that the English men-at-arms refused to take part, but a company of archers dispatched the prisoners, stabbing them to death through the visors of their helmets.

Anne Curry: 'The killing of the prisoners would suggest that perhaps they were in a defined area, but I doubt if it had been possible to move them very far away from the battle and that, of course, I think, is the key to understanding Henry's order to kill the prisoners. These people are still around. They are still a threat if the French had attacked, and that was what Henry was worried about. There was another group of French looking as though they were going to come against him. I think he couldn't take the risk of these men, within his ranks, who could at any moment attack... so these people had to be killed.'

The battle was over. The actual fighting had probably lasted less than an hour. Some 6,000 French lay dead – 2,000 of whom were knights and men-at-arms, princes or dukes. Both the Constable and the Marshal of France were killed.

The next day Henry resumed his march to Calais.

So what exactly had happened? How had a force of a few thousand tired and hungry men defeated a confident army many times their size?

New research points to new theories.

- Was the English army driven purely by its loyalty to Henry?
- Was the English longbow as crucial as we've been led to believe?
- How can geology help us to understand the loss of French men-at-arms?
- Did the French really have no sensible plan to attack the English?

- Can theoretical physics and mathematics help solve the riddles of Agincourt?

Detective Work

Tim Sutherland and Simon Richardson work together. Tim is a postgraduate archaeologist at Bradford University: he's a specialist in geophysical surveys and together with Simon, a professional metal *detectorist*, has played a leading role in new understandings of battlefields. In particular, they made major discoveries at the site of the Battle of Towton, a critical conflict in the Wars of the Roses. Each battlefield, they believe, has a unique signature which can be detected with magnetometers and sophisticated metal detectors. At Towton Simon Richardson has logged more than 730 artefacts, all registered and plotted on maps.

Richardson uses a state-of-the-art detector, and has been recovering objects and information for more than 20 years. His detection equipment is programmable and can be set, using a 'relic program', to find specific artefacts – buttons, musketballs, arrowheads will all have different 'signatures'. The position in which artefacts are found can determine the direction and scope of the fighting. It can also detect slight changes in the composition of soil which can provide the location of grave-pits on battlefields.

But Simon and Tim know there's a lot to be learned from the terrain of the battlefield itself. At first sight, the site seems to be a classic mediaeval battlefield. The French appeared to hold a strong position on an open plain near to a road, which would have meant supplies could reach them easily. It seemed all the French had to do was cover the road – and wait. But a closer look at relief maps of Agincourt shows subtle differences in height – not apparent at first glance, but crystal-clear when only contours are shown. And as we'll see from another battlefield detective, physicist Keith Still, those French positions may not have been as strong as first appearances suggested.

Tim and Simon conducted a survey of the battlefield in August 2002. Arrowheads, which usually provide a major indicator of mediaeval battles, are hard to locate. Their metal content diminishes over the centuries and, once ploughed up, they disintegrate quickly.

Tim's geophysical survey seemed to show, for the very first time, physical evidence of French casualties. Working near the 19th-century memorial to the dead, Tim reports that 'when we downloaded the data there appeared to be several subsurface anomalies – and some of them looked as if they could be very large pits.' Work remains to be completed, but it seems probable that these would be French grave-pits.

Simon's *Battlefield Detectives* work at first produced unexpected and disappointing results. On his first sweep of the site, his very first signal produced a silver coin – a denarius of the Roman emperor Vespasian. Working for ten hours a day over five days, Richardson found some sixty artefacts, covering every period up to the Second World War, with the surprising exception of the mediaeval world. Then, on his very last day, near Henry's supposed camp at Maisoncelle, Richardson discovered what seems to be one of the few surviving objects from the battle itself – a short, narrow 'bodkin' arrowhead. 'One arrowhead doesn't make a battle,' he explained, 'but it's a step in the right direction.'

Though Anne Curry is probably the leading authority on the battle whose legend has rung down through the centuries as a triumph of the English spirit – and her approachable writing style brings the participants vividly to life – she is frank about the limitations of historic inquiry. 'We may never fathom out the man himself,' she writes of Henry. 'We can scarcely understand those living and close to us today, so what chance with a monarch who lived over five hundred years ago?'[11]

Yet through her detective work we can actually get a sharp sense of the times. In her academic career Anne Curry has conducted an exhaustive trawl through the archives of the time: and a prodigious archive it is.

The shelves of the Public Records Office (PRO) hold more than a hundred miles of documents which stretch unbroken from the 11th century. These are not limited to major documents of state such as the *Magna Carta* or the *Domesday Book* – they include the minutiae of official life too, from laundry lists to telegrams, lists of British subjects born at sea or receipts for old rope at dockyards. And from those little details, we can learn a lot. The records offices and libraries of England contain a meticulous record of equipment, people and payments for the battle.

Deep in the shelves of the PRO, Anne Curry came across a white leather bag, prosaically labelled PRO E101/47/20. The contents of this bag were to provide critical clues to understanding that savage day in 1415. 'It's one of the most fascinating sources that we have for the Battle of Agincourt', she explained. The bag contains the financial accounts of a knight called Sir Thomas Erpingham who 'must be one of the most famous and intriguing people at the Battle of Agincourt, and one of the oldest.'

Sir Thomas is thought to have been in command of at least some of the archers at Agincourt. He's referred to many times in the literature: the French witness Monstrelet refers to 'a knight grey with age' who gave the signal for battle to commence: 'Thomas exhorted them all on behalf of the King of England to fight bravely against the French in order to guarantee their own survival. Then, riding with an escort in front of the army after he had set up its formation, he threw high into the air a baton which he held in his hand, shouting, "Nescieque" [Strike now!]. Then he dismounted to join the king and the others on foot. At the throwing of the baton, all the English suddenly made a great cry which was a cause of great amazement to the French.'

But what's interesting about the bag's contents is not that they tell us whether Sir Thomas was in command, but what they tell us about the campaign. 'They show us just how sophisticated the administration of the army was at this point in time', says Curry. 'It shows us really how careful they were to record presences.'

By the 15th century the feudal arrangements for raising armies had given way to a system of contracts. Rather than granting lands in return for soldiers, lords and nobles were offered money to provide the king with a specified number of troops. The agreements, or indentures, could be very detailed, and the specifications would be written out twice on a single document which would then be torn in two, often with a deliberately ragged tear. The Crown would keep one half, and the indentee would keep the other. If there was to be any dispute, the documents could be matched together: it was an insurance against fraud.

The contract outlined the details of service, the rates of pay, the rules governing conduct and any financial gains from war – from which the crown would extract a percentage. Anne Curry fills in the details: 'This indenture was sealed on 29 April 1415, well before the campaign began, but it was a contract with the crown – in fact, it's an indenture made between the King and Sir Thomas Erpingham, which says that he is retained to serve the King with a retinue for a certain length of time, during his – the King's – campaigns overseas. Sir Thomas has to bring along two knights, 17 esquires – or men-at-arms, probably – and 60 archers. All of his company was mounted, and that was quite a common thing for the Agincourt campaign. It goes on to tell you about the sharing-out of the gains of war – for instance, if they capture anybody very important like the Dauphin, or the King, or a leading commander, they've got to pass him over to the crown – they can't just ransom him themselves.'

For Anne Curry, the fact that records like this are kept opens a window on the 15th century. Sir Thomas had in fact died some years after the battle, but before his final accounts could be reconciled. His executors were required to present all the evidence to the Exchequer for a final settlement of his estate.

The white leather bag she found at the PRO contained a copy of the contract, and an account of his pay and that of his men. It named every man in his retinue and details what happened to each and every person in his company. Even though the men of the army were being provided by individuals, it was almost certainly a royal army: there was central control of wages and conditions.

Sir Thomas was to be paid four shillings a day, his knights a shilling and men-at-arms forty marks. If the army went to French-controlled France as opposed to English-controlled Gascony, they were to be paid more.

Professor Curry believes that her discoveries demonstrated that the 15th century's 'age of chivalry' has also to be seen as an age when battles were a way of earning a living.

Erpingham's company got back from the campaign on 16 November. The details are telling: 'Seventeen men-at-arms are listed. The marginal note tells us that two of them, Thomas Geney and John Calthorpe, had been knighted at the landing at the Chef de Caux. Both had become ill at Harfleur, and had died shortly after being sent home. Only one fatality was noted as occurring at the battle: an archer, Stephen Gerneyng.'[12]

One-eighth of the wages was paid when the contract was

drawn up, and another eighth when the company was lined up for muster. Guarantees were made for the following quarter, but for the rest redemption was due nineteen months later.

The accounts in the bag show that Sir Thomas had been given jewels as a guarantee of payment. Anne Curry discovered that King Henry 'was actually pawning his crown jewels. He gave jewels to the men who indented to serve in his army – he set up a system whereby he would redeem them slightly over a year after the campaign, and in the meantime, presumably, they toddled off to the pawnbroker or the London goldsmiths, deposited these objects and got money, which they then paid to their troops.'

Financially, the stakes were high for the king: he had to win so that he could pay his soldiers back. And the stakes were high for the soldiers as well – they weren't paid everything up-front.

These accounts reveal an enormous amount of information. Working from the contents of the Erpingham bag, Anne Curry thinks it's possible to get closer to the real number of those present at Agincourt on the English side. She calculates that there must have been about 1,500 men-at-arms and 5,500 archers. The records show that 'Henry had a superabundance of archers at the battle compared with men-at-arms. We know that his line of men-at-arms was actually quite small, that they were only standing in lines three deep. The archers are on the flanks – of course, there's been quite a dispute about that – but I think the ratio of men-at-arms to archers very much affected the way Henry fought the battle, and it would make sense really to have the men-at-arms in the middle, and then the archers curving round on the flanks.'

Although Anne Curry is sure that a major factor for organizing the army like this was related to cost, she points to other advantages: archers were useful at sieges and in aggressive land campaigns, providing they were mounted, which most of them were by 1415. They were effective in pitched battles, good at softening up the enemy and had the flexibility to go in for the kill as circumstances allowed, and they needed less training. But the fact that they used cheaper equipment and cost half as much as a man-at-arms in pay must have been the overriding factor. 'So if Henry wanted to take a sizeable but not-too-expensive army in 1415 – which we can be certain he did – recruiting archers to form over three-quarters of his army was a sensible move.'[13]

It seems then, that the English king had a strong financial incentive in using archers, and that the English archers had a strong financial incentive in securing victory.

That Gesture

But is there any documentation about the V-sign? Anne Curry seems the most likely detective to unravel the popular legend that the infamous, and peculiarly English, gesture is in some way related to the alleged practice of captured archers having their string-pulling fingers cut off. 'Well, there is an early account where Henry gives a battle speech to his men and says that if they're captured they'll be mutilated, and it's often thought that this is where it starts from,' she says. A French chronicle of the 1440s quotes another speech by Henry in which he reportedly tells the archers that if they're captured they'll have the three fingers they use for pulling the bow string cut off. 'From that, in later centuries, came the idea that after the battle the English put up two fingers to the French in order to show they hadn't lost any limbs: in other words, they'd been victorious in the battle rather than been defeated. But there's nothing in contemporary sources about the V- sign;

there's just this threat to mutilate. I suspect it's a 19th-century story.'

Arrows and Armour

We know that the archers at Agincourt were armed with longbows. The idea that the French knights were killed by a veritable storm of arrows seems ingrained in the English psyche. Was this why the French lost?

David Sim is an archaeologist and engineer at the University of Reading; he's also a blacksmith with a particular interest in arrows – especially arrowhead design – and bows. 'The object of an arrowhead,' he says, 'is to kill people. There are really only two places where you can get an instant kill: the heart and the throat. The rest of the time, whoever gets hit by the arrow is going to die slowly. So the object of an arrowhead is that you have a large amount of cutting head on it – so that when it penetrates, it cuts through large quantities of blood vessels in order to produce massive haemorrhaging – because if you can't kill your opponent instantly, what you want him to do is to lose large quantities of blood, very quickly, so that he becomes disabled'.

The question is, were they capable of piercing plate armour?

The suit of armour epitomizes the Middle Ages. In the 15th century, an arms race was taking place: the armour was becoming more sophisticated, and the fittings were becoming more complex in order to cope with the energy of bows.

The bow was an effective piece of machinery. When pulled back, it became subject to two forces – the outside of the bow is stretched, the inside is compressed. If it is capable of great tension and also survives great compression, it produces great power which is transmitted to the arrowhead.

Providing the archer has the strength to make full use of his particular bow, and thus puts as much energy as possible into the arrow, it is a remarkably potent weapon.

The longbow, in particular, was a highly effective killing machine. It took much less time to load than the crossbow, and this high rate of fire could create a 'machine-gun' effect which was lethal and psychologically intimidating.

Alan Williams is an archaeo-metallurgist, a specialist in mediaeval armour and, like David Sim, based at Reading. He points out that steel was a very expensive material – it cost five or six times as much as iron, but steel armour was worth the price. 'This might sound like a second-hand car dealer guaranteeing the mileage on the car – since it was the salesman who was making the claim – but nevertheless the claim had to be fairly believable for anybody to buy, and the experiments that we've been doing at Reading University confirm that armour of this sort was proof against the crossbow.'

And the longbow? David Sim says many of the stories about its potency are myths. 'There are limitations to what any projectile will do under any set of circumstances, and arrows are no different. It was said that an English longbow could put an arrow through a four-inch oak door. Well, I've conducted tests myself, and it's simply not possible.

'There are also myths about it penetrating armour. It could penetrate thin armour, but it wouldn't go through breastplates', says Sim. 'If one takes a bodkin arrow, for example – if you have a piece of quite low-quality steel, or even low-quality iron, if it's more than a millimetre thick – then one of these arrows will not penetrate.' Sim does, however, agree that arrowheads can penetrate some kinds of armour – for example, chainmail.

In laboratory conditions, battlefield detectives including David Sim and Tony Atkins, Professor of Mechanical

Engineering at Reading – a man who lists among his interests 'why things break' – replicated the effect of an arrow hitting armour. The process of steel production wasn't really understood until the 19th century and much of the armour of the 15th century would have been made of a steel more like iron than we normally see today.

To test the advantages that steel gave over iron, *Battlefield Detectives* undertook a series of tests using mathematical modelling and high-impact ballistic apparatus. Iron was softer, but even so, none of the arrow substitutes managed to penetrate it. And penetration was even more unlikely if the projectile was aimed at anything other than 90 degrees. This is critical, because very few arrows would strike at 90 degrees. Firing at a distance, an archer would have to aim up into the air, making the path of the arrow's descent towards the target a curve: a straight line parallel to the ground could only be achieved at very short range. And in the tests, whenever an arrow struck a steel plate – even the narrow-pointed bodkin arrow, with its small frontal area – it just bounced off.

At 90 degrees, using the allegedly armour-busting bodkin arrow against a modern mild steel plate – a harder steel than would have been achieved in the Middle Ages – the arrow just failed to penetrate, though the steel showed signs of fracturing. At 45 degrees the denting was smaller. At 70 degrees, the projectile ricocheted. Using the sort of impure metals we would expect mediaeval steelmakers to have produced, the arrows made very little impression on their targets. Was there something wrong in our experiment?

'What you need to do is get a large number of arrows in the air at the same time', says Sim. 'The archers could easily fire twelve rounds a minute. The best use of archery is in large quantities. All archers like to think that they're capable of knocking an apple off somebody's head: but in reality, when one looks at the size of the target at any distance, you can see that using archery as sniping is not really the best use. If you have a tightly-packed body of men and you fire a lot of arrows at them, you're going to cause an awful lot of injuries and deaths.'

But how – if the arrows can't penetrate plate armour? According to Sim, there were two reasons: firstly, because there were a lot of unarmoured men at Agincourt, but secondly, because an archer will aim at the largest part of the target – the horse. Horses were very expensive and very difficult to protect with plate armour. 'If the wound isn't bad enough for the horse to collapse,' says Sim, 'then the pain is going to cause it to sheer, scream – it's going to lose control – and if you have a number of horses losing control, then the knock-on effect of that is absolutely enormous.'

Alan Williams agrees that the horse was the cavalry's weak point when facing archers. 'If you were a knight, protected from arrows, riding a horse which wasn't, then the arrows might injure your horse and force you to dismount – so you could no longer ride into battle but you had to walk. What the longbow did, which was still extremely important, was to force the knight in plate armour to dismount. And having got him on the ground, he lost a lot of his effectiveness.'

Dr Williams's research into armour throughout Europe disclosed the extraordinary fact that the calves of knights on the Continent, measured from their surviving suits of armour, were much thinner than those of modern men, 'because they took very little exercise that involved using their legs.' English knights were accustomed to dismounting and fighting on foot 'because that was their job: they were paid to do that. In France and Germany – throughout Europe – the aristocracy would spend most of their lives in the saddle, so much that they took very little exercise at all.'

There is, thinks Dr Williams, another problem too. 'French knights who weren't in the habit of fighting on foot would not only have felt humiliated by being asked to fight alongside the infantry, but wouldn't have been accustomed to it, and would have found a long walk uphill to face the English difficult physically, as well as being demoralizing.'

So just how vulnerable were the French men-at-arms? And how did the lightly-clad archers survive when they charged into the plate-clad warriors?

The answer may lie in the soil.

The Battlefield

The English priest who chronicled the events of that day recorded his impressions of the critical life-and-death struggle itself: 'So great was the undisciplined violence and the pressure of the mass of men behind that the living fell on top of the dead, and others falling on top of the living were killed as well, with the result that...such a great heap grew of the slain and of those lying crushed in between that our men climbed up those heaps, which had risen above a man's height, and butchered their enemies down below with swords, axes and other weapons.'[14]

Both our battlefield detective historians caution against accepting any contemporary account at face value, and Matthew Bennett adds: 'Some chronicles speak of piles of dead as high as a man. While there were doubtless many bodies strewn around, some dead, some unconscious, some merely trapped, such a thing was a physical impossibility; but it captures the feeling of a massacre.'[15]

We can't be sure if it was raining at Agincourt, but we do know from several witnesses that the land had been recently planted, and that the soil was wet.

We also know, now, that by the time the French men-at-arms made their initial charge, the ground underfoot had become churned into mud.

Imagine the scene: knights encased in armour, on terrified and injured horses, came swirling at speed back from the English lines towards the tightly-packed and plodding men-at-arms. Some horses were riderless. As this mass of confused compatriots and animals hurtled into them, and as the English archers rushed headlong after them with axes and hammers raised, what might have been the result?

It seems impossible not to imagine that many men fell over. In the mud.

We know it to be a fallacy that the armour worn by men-at-arms made them too heavy to get up, but it must have been difficult for men in shiny steel to regain their feet in a field of mud – especially when you consider that mediaeval shoes had no heels. *Battlefield Detectives* decided to test just what would happen.

Andrew Palmer, Professor of Petroleum Engineering at Cambridge University, is one of the world's most eminent specialists in soil structures. An understanding of the way soil, sand and mud works is essential for his research in the Department of Engineering. He agreed to test the soil from the battlefield of Agincourt. Did it have some special property which our historians may not have known?

'When you look at Agincourt soil when it's dry, it doesn't look particularly unusual,' he explained. 'However, we did a few tests and, actually, when you add water to it you get pretty interesting results. Some soils are more affected by being waterlogged than others – so, for example, in sand or silt water goes straight through. In clay it runs off, but in this particular soil it gets absorbed and quickly becomes very sticky.'

Professor Palmer applied the same techniques he uses in oil pipeline research to discover information about men falling over on a battlefield in northern France nearly 600 years ago. With a sophisticated piece of equipment – a soil-testing Instron machine – he measured the forces which slow movement in different types of mud.

The Agincourt soil seemed normal when dry, but when wet it developed characteristics which would have made walking particularly difficult. 'It would have been like walking with 15 bags of sugar on your legs', he says. 'It isn't the weight of the armour that's the crucial factor at Agincourt. Actually what is important is suction – to do with how readily soil sticks to different materials.'

Andrew Palmer tested the effect of different materials in contact with Agincourt soil. Put simply, he discovered that it was harder to move in armour on the Agincourt soil not because it was heavier, but because of the interaction between smooth plate armour and the soil.

In other words, a fallen man-at-arms wearing plate armour would have been in danger of sticking to the soil because of suction.

Cambridge archaeologist John Carman has argued that the fault lay rather with what he calls 'the landscape of macho men'.

'At each of the three great victories of the Hundred Years' War against France – Crécy (1346), Poitiers (1356) and Agincourt (1415) – apparently flat space was sought to fight on, neatly bounded by woods or obviously wet ground, an ideal theatre for the head-on clash of armoured horsemen and foot soldiers. In all three, the French mounted men-at-arms, encased in heavy armour, recklessly charged home, foundered in mud and confusion, and died not only under accurate fire from longbows, but also of drowning, heat-stroke, dehydration and exhaustion. They never learned – charging home was how war was done.'[16]

Was it that simple? Were the French merely incredibly stupid?

A recent discovery at the British Museum shows that the

French in fact did have a plan. Matthew Bennett reports: 'It's on a much damaged document, just a small scrap really. Written in French, probably at the command of the French leader of their advanced guard. And it shows that the French had a way in which they could have defeated the English. The intention was to dismount the main body of the French men-at-arms, flank them with missile men – that's archers and crossbowmen – in order to counter the English archers – but to keep in reserve two flanking forces of cavalry. The idea was to send them into the English archers at a crucial moment, to combat the English on equal terms.' But there was a problem: 'It had been designed by an experienced military man. But it was put into operation by a mass of rival noblemen who either didn't understand it or weren't capable of organizing it.'

Our detectives have made discoveries which shed new light on the Battle of Agincourt. Why was it that such a small army could so easily topple a large one?

A Crowd Disaster

Could the second wave of the French attack have been disorientated by the returning horse charge? John Keegan, one of Britain's foremost military historians, has little doubt about what occurred when the advancing French force collided with the returning charge. 'We can get a clear idea, curiously, from a cinema newsreel of the Grosvenor Square demonstration against the Vietnam War in 1968. There, a frightened police horse, fleeing the demonstrators, charged a line of constables on foot. Those directly in its path, barging sideways and backwards to open a gap and seizing their neighbour, set up a curious and violent ripple which ran along the ranks on each side, reaching policemen some good distance away, who, tightly packed, clutched at each other for support, and stumbled clumsily backwards and then forwards to keep balance.'[17]

Could then, the effect of the returning horses not merely have caused a disorientating effect – might it have sent scores of men tumbling into the mud?

Keith Still, our final Agincourt detective, thinks it was even more inevitable than that. The French would have died, he argues, even without a single weapon being used.

Dr Still, a mathematician, is a solidly built and fast-talking Scot. In fact, he's a perfect detective. Some years ago, frightened while stuck in a heaving crowd waiting to get into a rock concert at Wembley, he became intrigued by the pattern of movement made by those around him who were able to move. It seemed odd to him: he was in the middle of a bottleneck, but people were flowing past him and through the turnstiles. Suddenly he realized that people moved fastest nearest the walls, and because they were moving, he wasn't. The next day he dug out all the scientific literature on crowd flow.

Some time later, lying in bed, he noticed a cobweb dangling from the ceiling. As air moved along the cobweb in complex waves, he realized that the motion of the cobweb's shadow seemed simpler than that of the web. Maybe, he thought, the movements of crowds were somehow 'shadows' of some other aspect of reality. He realized that people stuck in a crowd look at empty space and move into that.

His research was to point to extraordinary and paradoxical ways to speed up crowd pattern flows. He discovered that a central barrier in front of a fire door can increase the flow by up to 75 per cent; that a one-foot increase in the width of a door can double the flow rate through it; that widening a corridor can slow down the evacuation of a building; that in an emergency people try to leave by the door they came in through, even if there's a clearly labelled emergency exit closer.

Keith Still became one of the world's foremost crowd experts. He found that up to a certain density, crowd behaviour is the result of an individual's psychology, but that once the number of people reaches a certain level – two per square metre – movement is governed by dynamics: it is dictated by geometry rather than by emotion.

For *Battlefield Detectives*, Dr Still looked at the maps and plans and read the accounts of the Battle of Agincourt.

He noticed straight away that the terrain effectively squeezed the opposing forces between woods on either side of the battlefield. He developed complex computer models of movement. His models show that the French had the worst possible set of variables, and that lining up in ranks would have created more problems – any kind of delay causes density high-spots.

The English, on the other hand, were in a far safer configuration. If their use of space became a problem, they had more flexibility available. In his model, almost all the high-risk, high-density areas are on the French side. The French commanders should not have allowed so many people to move forward into this terrain at once.

Because of the shape of the terrain, for every metre the French moved forward, they lost a significant amount of freedom – and this density increased exponentially. When the horses charged back at the ponderous ranks of French moving forward, they fell over and lost all freedom of movement. They suffocated and drowned in the mud.

The battlefield, he says, has the recipe for a crowd disaster written all over it.

But there are, of course, many theories about what happened that day, which might all have contributed to the eventual outcome.

The English won because they were better led, because they were a professional army, with a financial incentive and a simple command structure. They were led by an inspirational and inventive leader.

The French lost because they were thrown together, they were disorganized and had a divided command. If they had any plan other than beating the English, they weren't able to adapt it to the conditions they found themselves in. But they also lost because they weren't expecting to fight on foot, and in a type of mud which meant they had little chance of a clean fight. The landscape of France killed the French.

Perhaps we should allow our detective, Anne Curry, the battle's leading authority, to have the last say: 'Despite the vast quantity of writing on Agincourt, or perhaps because of it, it is impossible to know what really happened. This is because of the nature of the event itself. No one could have a full knowledge or understanding of a battle even if they were there at the time.' And, she concludes: 'The desire to "know Agincourt" is destined to continue.'[18]

The Spanish Armada – 1588

Introduction

Some time during the night of Friday, 29 July 1588, a lookout on an English ship, scouting warily through the squally showers off the Cornish coast, spotted a sail on the horizon.

Before long it must have become clear that there were many more sails. The moment the English had been expecting for months had finally arrived: a vast fleet of ships, one of the largest in all history, was approaching.

The English vessel, probably a small pinnace called *The Golden Hind*, turned tail and raced back to port with the news. The first beacons in England's recently upgraded early warning system were lit, and as signals flickered from hilltop to hilltop, messages sped up the coast towards Plymouth.

There, the main English fleet had itself recently arrived after an abortive attempt to mount a pre-emptive strike at the Spanish port of Corunna – the weather had been against them. Weary, irritated and low on supplies, the English Lord Admiral, Charles Howard, and his navy were about to confront the first attempted invasion of England for more than 500 years. But could they stop it?

One week later the Spanish fleet of some 130 ships, with nearly 2,500 guns and 30,000 men aboard, had sailed almost unmolested up the English Channel and lay anchored off the French coast at Calais, in accordance with the plan carefully prepared by King Philip of Spain. To have got this far would have been a magnificent achievement at any time in history. To have achieved it in the 16th century was almost miraculous. Meanwhile, an additional 30,000 men waited ashore. Veterans of the Spanish army in Flanders, they were supposed to embark on transports for the short crossing to the English coast. These were the finest troops in Europe – hard-bitten veterans, proven in battle and already expert in combined operations and amphibious landings. They were, wrote the treasurer of the English Navy, 'the greatest and strongest combination that was ever gathered in Christendom.'

England was in as great a peril as it has ever been, before or since. It was practically defenceless, and Queen Elizabeth's coffers were nearly empty. Her fleet was said to be running out of ammunition. Her army had been hastily improvised and was poorly armed and barely trained.

If the Spanish had crossed those last few miles, England would have been unable to resist, and within a matter of weeks – or even days – London would have been captured and Queen Elizabeth forced to surrender.

Yet within a matter of hours, the great Invincible Armada had scattered and been forced to run for home with their great galleons and huge Mediterranean transport hulks on the 'northabout' route – which would take them all the way round the coasts of England, Scotland and Ireland. It would be months before Spain counted the cost. They had lost, in appalling circumstances, some sixty ships, and many thousands of men.

England could breathe again, not to face another such threat for more than 350 years.

The English have always revelled in this victory, especially that version of history which tells how that salty sea-dog Sir

Francis Drake had 'singed the King of Spain's beard' when he raided Cadiz with fireships; how the lively little English ships had run rings around vast Spanish galleons which had been unable to respond against targets sailing so low in the water; and how the most powerful naval force in history had been outsmarted and destroyed.

Historian Felipe Fernandez-Armesto, had the misfortune to go to an English boys' school in the 1950s. More than 30 years later, he could still vividly recall history classes which demonstrated a 'loathsome chauvinism' and a pride bolstered by an uneasy mix of fact and fiction. The English version of this history has, he believes, 'a disproportionate part in defining English self-awareness. Two elements of the English self-image – sang-froid, and a preference for the underdog's role – are linked in almost every English mind with the myths of the Armada: the supposedly plucky little ships worsting the Spanish giants, like David and Goliath: and the probably apocryphal game of bowls played on Plymouth Hoe.'[1]

But if the English are mistaken to have venerated this tale of English heroism in the face of the most magnificent fleet ever to have sailed, and if they are wrong to celebrate the triumph of Good Queen Bess and her gallant sailors, then what exactly did happen?

It is incontrovertible that the Spanish lost half their fleet, while the English lost not a single ship. Something extraordinary must have happened.

New research into the Armada has cast a different light on those events of 1588. For years, generations of historians had pored over the details. By the 1960s, there hardly seemed much point in further research. Colin Martin, who, with Geoffrey Parker, was to re-cast the history and is, more than anyone else, the leading detective in this trail of clues – commented that when he started research, 'extensive documentation from both sides had been examined, and the story of the Armada seemed to be a historical reality unlikely to be greatly added to or questioned by further evidence. Then the wrecks were found.'[2]

The wrecks were those of a fleet which had come to grief on its terrible journey around the British Isles. This too, was part of the English legend, a story usually laced with mysterious, black-haired, dark-eyed Irish or Scots supposedly descended from Spanish survivors. But the wrecks themselves had been lost – still wrapped in the mystery of their sudden watery end – and no modern search had ever been undertaken.

And then in 1967, off the coast of Antrim in Northern Ireland – close to the Giant's Causeway – a Belgian archaeological diver, Robert Sténuit, discovered the remains of a long-lost Neapolitan galleas, the *Girona*. It was to mark the beginning of a new and completely different history of the Spanish Armada.

Not only did research on that wreck – and on the other Armada wrecks which were soon located – revolutionize our understanding of the past, but the archaeological discoveries themselves encouraged new and revealing research among the written archives. It is in this combination of scientific and archival research that we can begin to see that the English were not, after all, clear-cut victors. They simply got away with it. The result was, if anything, a draw.

The Campaign

In the summer of 1588 England was in turmoil: a poor country on the fringes of Europe, she had incurred the anger of the greatest empire in the world. Retribution was on its way.

After years of provocation, King Philip II of Spain

launched what he called 'The Enterprise of England'. The English, ruled by his former sister-in-law Elizabeth – he had been married to her half-sister Mary – had become the allies of the Protestant Dutch provinces which were in rebellion against his rule in the Spanish Netherlands. Elizabeth had agreed to support the rebels with both troops and funds – a decision which King Philip regarded as an act of war. She also gave permission for English priva-teers – armed vessels, privately-owned, which the Spanish regarded as nothing less than piratical – to attack Spanish ships, destroy Spanish possessions in the Americas and even raid Spanish ports. Philip was determined to crush this state-sponsored terrorism.

Over and above these issues, the king was a deeply devout Catholic, and in Catholic Europe, England was increasingly being regarded as a rogue state. Philip believed it was his duty to rid Europe of dangerous 'heretics' such as Elizabeth and her government, and he decided that nothing else would do but a complete and rapid conquest: it was to be, in effect, a new Crusade.

His two chief military advisers, the Marquis of Santa Cruz and the Duke of Parma – in command of Spanish forces in the Netherlands – suggested different strategies. Santa Cruz proposed a full-scale invasion from Spain: he planned first a feint, a mock invasion of Ireland to lure English forces across the Irish seas, and then the main objective – a real invasion of southern England. Plans were already under way when King Philip received Parma's suggestion – a lightning attack from the Netherlands with a force of 30,000 men, who would march at speed to London and catch the now unprotected English off their guard. Philip decided that both were excel-lent ideas, and decided to go ahead with – both.

But the English were becoming so volatile – Sir Francis Drake even raided Cadiz – that the king then adapted his plans, deciding to aim directly at this impertinent enemy, ruling out the diversionary raid on Ireland. He decided that a vast Armada should sail for England, carrying its own invasion force, pausing only to meet the Duke of Parma's troops off the Spanish Netherlands, and escort this additional army across the Channel. He set in motion a huge logistical undertaking the like of which was not to be seen again until the Allied invasion of Europe in 1944. The king himself took direct and personal control of almost every aspect of planning, overlooking only one detail of the invasion – but one which would be devastating to the eventual outcome: how could the Armada and the Duke's army keep in touch with each other to arrange their rendezvous?

The Armada, with its enormous force of soldiers, eventually set sail from Lisbon under the command of the Duke of Medina Sidonia on 28 May 1588. Pausing at Corunna to recover from storms in the Bay of Biscay, the Armada sailed on with favourable winds towards the English Channel, where it adopted a gigantic crescent-shaped formation and serenely sailed on towards the rendezvous off the Flanders shore, where Parma's additional 30,000 men would be waiting. Medina Sidonia sent messages ahead in fast boats, trying to alert the Duke of Parma to his progress.

- On 31 July the English fleet slipped out of Plymouth and managed to cross in front of the Armada, then manoeuvred so they were to windward – upwind of the Spanish. This gave them an immediate tactical advantage – they could choose to move with the wind towards the Spanish, or reduce sail and hold back from contact – whereas all that the Spanish could do was keep going forward. The English gunners loosed off some 300 rounds at long range before withdrawing.
- On 2 August a change of wind off Portland Bill seems to have given the Spanish a brief advantage, but the tide

prevented the Spanish from engaging the English closely.

- On 3 and 4 August the winds dropped and occasional skirmishes took place.
- Finally, on 6 August, the Armada reached its preliminary destination, and anchored off Calais.

But the Spanish army was not ready, and Parma announced that it would be six days before he could embark. This was the devastating detail Philip II had overlooked, and one which had been troubling Medina Sidonia for some time: his fast messenger ships to Parma, warning him of his impending arrival, had not arrived in time.

In truth, it wasn't a detail: Parma could hardly put 30,000 men and supplies in frail barges awaiting a navy which might take months to arrive. And when Medina Sidonia did arrive off Calais, the Spanish admiral could not take his Armada any closer to the Flanders shore for fear of being stranded in shallow waters. Could Parma's army row several miles out to sea to meet the Armada? It would seem an unlikely plan at the best of times – 'These vessels cannot run the gauntlet of warships; they cannot even withstand large waves,' Parma had warned the king – and these were the worst of times to chance the transfer: Dutch rebels controlled the shallow waters of the Netherlands' coast. No deep-water port was available.

For Medina Sidonia, the question now was not how and when he was supposed to join up with Parma, but rather what he was supposed to do next. The English fleet hovered nearby.

The next night the English sent fireships – small vessels packed with explosives and tinder – into the Armada's midst. 'Now this is a terrifying prospect,' says leading historian Mark Corby; 'blazing ships coming down on top of you. The Spaniards' immediate reaction is to cut their cables and run – no time to crank up the anchor. Medina Sidonia is aware that he may well be attacked by fireships and has taken some precautions – but effectively it's difficult to communicate with the fleet. Most people assume the worst, and virtually the entire fleet cut their cables; you don't sit there and wait for it actually to arrive. By the following morning the entire Spanish fleet has cut its moorings and has been blown towards the coast in total disarray.'

So the Spanish cut their anchors to escape, and the fleet dispersed in haste, suddenly at the mercy of the elements.

At dawn on 8 August the English warily attacked, and the nine-hour running battle of Gravelines was joined between the fleets. The Armada regrouped and remained more or less intact, but in the evening a strong north-westerly sprang up, and for a few hours it looked as if the entire fleet might be driven on to the Flanders sandbanks and end the campaign in ignominy. Then – miraculously, according to the Spaniards – the wind turned and freshened from the south-west. The Armada was able to move safely further out to sea. But they were now to windward off the Flanders coast. They were unable to return towards Calais, or indeed to the English Channel itself.

Medina Sidonia, at a council of war held on his flagship, decided to take the only course open to him – to abandon his plans – and sail north towards Scotland, then west out into the Atlantic and, when once well clear of Ireland, south towards Spain. The English followed as far as the Humber until, low on ammunition, they gave up the chase.

The great Armada, with many of its ships now damaged or lost, had hardly any hope of staying together. The weather worsened as they fought their way round Scotland, and grew worse still as they turned south. Huge storms lashed Ireland that September. At least one-third of Medina

Sidonia's ships were lost on those wild Atlantic coasts. Probably half the Spanish force taking part in the extraordinary venture had died.

The Duke of Medina Sidonia arrived back at Santander on the coast of northern Spain on 21 September, his vast flagship held together by three great ropes wrapped around the hull to prevent her seams from splitting open. A hundred and eighty of his own crew were dead and most of the survivors ill with dysentery or typhus.

His navigation had led him to a port several hundred miles east of his intended landfall. 'I am unable to describe to your majesty the misfortunes and miseries that have befallen us,' he wrote to his king. The 'Enterprise of England' was over.

- What had gone wrong? How could this astonishing fleet, armed with the most modern weapons and under the most experienced commanders, have come to grief like this?
- Were the Spanish really unable to bring their guns to bear on the English? If not, why not: and if they could, why was not one of the English ships sunk? And why were a mere handful of the Armada's vessels actually sunk by accurate English cannon fire? Did either side really run out of ammunition?
- How important was the design of the English ships to their victory?
- Was it inevitable that the Spanish fleet would succumb in that late summer weather off Ireland and Scotland? And why were the ships so close to those dangerous waters at all?

Battlefield detectives are able to answer all these questions.

The Weather of 1588

More than 400 years on, is there any way we can possibly know what the actual weather was like from day to day in the summer of 1588?

Ken Douglas, an accountant from Ulster and a self-taught meteorologist, believed – against the odds – that it was possible to do just that.

He had become interested in the Armada in 1968 after Robert Sténuit had located the *Girona* practically on his doorstep. He read all he could find about the campaign, and noticed that almost every account mentioned the weather. History suddenly came alive. Ken Douglas, like all the best detectives, is a meticulous man, and he started to make notes whenever the weather was mentioned in a history or a document. 'Everybody said there were storms and gales and fogs and squalls – but nobody had actually tried to put it together,' he explained. He spent months assembling data from English accounts and getting friends to translate Spanish sources, which included the detailed journal kept by the purser aboard the *San Juan Bautista*, Marcos de Aramburu. He then drew up simple maps and took them to his local meteorological office.

But was it possible for anyone to know whether this amateur sleuth's weather records were accurate?

Remarkably, it was. Douglas's hand-written notebooks eventually reached Hubert Lamb, of the Climatic Research Unit at the University of East Anglia. Professor Lamb, who was working on a thousand-year history of the British climate, recognized an exciting body of research, and by an extraordinary chance he could compare Ken Douglas's detective work with the daily observations made in 1588 by the Danish astronomer Tycho Brahe on the tiny island of Ven. He was able to show that the analysis was reliable at least 72 per cent of the time, and the team at East Anglia was able to draw up synoptic weather maps for the period from July to October 1588.

But what does this really mean? What reliance can be placed on the clues left behind by a 16th-century astronomer?

Dr Steve Hall is an oceanographer and runs the Science Missions unit at the Southampton Oceanography Centre. He describes Tycho Brahe as an extraordinary individual who, like many of those early scientists, had a broad range of talents and interests. Like Ken Douglas, Brahe was a meticulous man who made regular, accurate observations. 'Finding observations made by Tycho at the time of the Armada gives a scientist very high confidence that what they're seeing is an accurate representation of what was seen,' says Steve Hall. 'You could pick up patterns and accuracies that simply wouldn't have been recorded by anybody before him.'

What about the figure of 72 per cent reliability? Steve Hall: 'In the 20th century, 70 per cent was good enough to give the go-ahead for the D-Day landings.'

So the new weather charts drawn up by Ken Douglas and the East Anglia team, together with Tycho Brahe's observations and the surviving Spanish logs, were able to establish, among much else, that:

- The battle off Plymouth was fought in brisk sea conditions.
  Medina Sidonia's journal: 'The wind and sea rose considerably.'

  Tycho Brahe: 'Wind north-east, light. Cloudy. Afternoon rain which lasted all day and through the night.'

- The English fleet had the advantage of what winds there were almost all the time the Armada sailed up the Channel – except for 2 August, when a land wind with an easterly component gave the Armada a brief advantage until about 10 am.

Medina Sidonia's journal: '[The day] broke fine, the enemy's fleet being to leeward.'

Zuñiga's log: 'A land breeze sprang up.'

- For the week of 8 to 13 August, constant south-westerly winds prevented the Armada from returning to the Channel.

  Medina Sidonia's journal: 'The wind from the south-south-west kept increasing in violence.'

  Tycho Brahe: 'Afternoon clear with west wind. At night, strong storm.'

- From 21 August to 3 September the Armada, which had now passed between the Orkneys and Fair Isle and moved out into the Atlantic, was held in high northern latitudes by south and south-west winds.

  Aramburu's log: 'When night fell the wind began to drop and passed through south-west to the south.'

  Tycho Brahe: 'Westerly breeze. Variable cloud, sometimes raining.'

- On 3 September, the wind turned to the north of west for the first time, and the Spanish ships were released from the northern latitudes. Medina Sidonia's fleet was at last able to turn towards the south, heading back towards the safety of Spain.

  From 12 September onwards, a vigorous cyclonic south-westerly sequence developed.

  Aramburu's log: 'The wind began to freshen and the sea to rise.'

- The great gale of 21 September, which sank at least 17 and probably more ships on the coasts of Ireland, had probably originated as a tropical storm.

  Aramburu's log: [at anchor in Blasket Sound] 'It began to blow from the west with the most terrible fury. At midday the *Santa Maria de la Rosa* came in... he fired a piece as if asking for help. All her sails hung in pieces except for the foremast mainsail. She managed to come to a stop with one anchor, which was all she had... she began to swing on her anchor and dragged down the Sound. She struck a submerged rock in the south entrance and went down right away with everyone aboard. Not a soul was saved.'

Captain Cueller, at Streedagh Strand, off Sligo: 'Such a thing was never seen for, within the space of an hour, all three ships were broken in pieces.'

Tycho Brahe: 'Southerly storm. Cloudy, sometimes raining. At night, slashing rain, south-west wind.'

Battlefield Detectives has also had access to Steve Hall's OCCAM computer model, developed on one of the world's most powerful supercomputers. It's capable of picking out the most extraordinary detail of the world's oceans across time and space. Steve has fed in information relevant to the Armada's passage up the English Channel. Using it, we discovered that if Sir Francis Drake really did announce that he'd finish his game of bowls on Plymouth Hoe before turning to deal with the Armada's arrival, he had good cause. Steve Hall explains: 'We've been able to plot exactly what the tides were doing on 29 July back in 1588, and we can see that if Drake had been wanting to finish his game of bowls, there wasn't really anything he could do until 8.30 or 9pm.' His ships would have been pinned into the Tamar estuary. There was no way he could have moved out into the Channel before nightfall.

It seems as if another piece of English propaganda has been exposed!

Dr Hall's computer model analysed more about the conditions facing the invader's fleet.

On 2 August, when a brief change of wind seemed to give the Spanish the advantage, the model shows the variable tidal flows, eddies and currents near Chesil Beach. Local sailors would have known about these and been able to manoeuvre round the sandbanks. The Spanish would not: 'They would have been quite unable to get in and tangle in close,' says Hall.

Five days later, the computer model for 7 August: 'The Spanish have made it as far as the area we'd now call Calais – didn't have a decent harbour at that time. We've got some very strong tides; it's three knots, a full moon. That's as fast as the ships would have been able to travel: they're pinned into the harbour.' At this point, the English fireships drifted in on the strong tide. The Spanish tried to escape, but Steve Hall points out the obvious problem: 'The tide changes and would have carried any of their ships that did get out back into the direction of the waiting English fleet. The only chance they'd have had would have been to get some sailors out in a boat to physically row the ships out to sea, and on a dark evening that just wouldn't have been possible. It would have been very confusing, they'd have lost formation and very quickly the fleet would have broken up into individual ships.'

The Wreckage

Dr Colin Martin, a marine archaeologist at the University of St Andrews, has been investigating in the cold waters of northern Europe for years. It is challenging work, full of surprises but also fraught with danger: the sea is no ordinary field of war. The clues here are even harder to find than they are in battle-scarred landscapes, and as a battlefield detective Colin Martin first had to learn how to dive before he could begin to piece together the truth, and the evidence he needed to unravel the mysteries surrounding the Armada. He first undertook a stern apprenticeship in Blasket Sound, the exposed seaway off south-west Ireland.

What secrets do wrecks such as these hold which might help us understand what went so badly wrong?

'Until the 1970s, no one had really seen very much of the actuality of the Armada,' says Dr Martin. 'There were a lot of documents, but not the hardware – the ships, the guns, the accoutrements of the men who took part. The wrecks have changed all that. We've literally been able to go aboard some of the Spanish ships and see how they actually functioned. We're getting not just the ship herself, but everything she contained and the people who were on board. We're getting a snapshot of not just what life was like, but what the military objectives were, in terms of the equipment they had.

'By analyzing this and then going back to the documents, we've been able to get a much more detailed understanding of what the Armada was actually composed of, and this has a very real bearing of what it set out to do and what it actually achieved.

'The impact on the Armada has been dramatic, in an unexpected way. The archaeological finds pose new questions which have prompted people to go back into the archives, which hadn't really been studied for more than a hundred years, and that helped to reconstruct the Armada in quite extraordinary detail'.

These battlefield detectives argue that there is more to history than broad outlines, and that their work can enable us to follow each stage with greater certainty, and explain why events turned out as they did.

To piece together the truth, they needed to know about motives. Exactly what was the Armada for?

- Was it a fleet which had set out to destroy whatever naval power England possessed, and then support and transport an army from the Spanish Netherlands to England?
- Or had it set sail as an invasion fleet in its own right?

The answer began to emerge – literally – in the waters off Kinnagoe Bay in Donegal in 1971.

Colin Martin and his team were investigating the wreck of *La Trinidad Valencera*. This huge 1,100-ton, Venetian-built troop-carrier had been one of the very largest ships in the Armada and, under the command of Don Alonso de Luzón, she had played a distinguished part in the fighting. But with his ship battling her way out towards the North Atlantic, her sails damaged beyond repair and her pumps no longer coping with numerous leaks. Luzón decided to run for shelter. Approaching the Irish coast, the *Valencera* grounded on rocks. She split open and sank.

Four centuries later, Colin Martin discovered three enormous guns aboard the *Valencera*. Each one weighed two and a half tons, and would have been capable of hurling a solid iron shot weighing more than 40 pounds. It wasn't difficult to imagine the effect they would have against an enemy ship at close range: but the guns carried more telling clues than size alone. Each one carried the royal arms of King Philip, and by checking the detailed inventories of the fleet – which still survive in the archives – they could be identified as part of a 12-strong battery of similar pieces. The divers also found the dismantled components of gigantic field carriages. It became clear that the cannon weren't naval weapons at all.

'We were expecting to find a fighting ship,' explains Martin, 'but these they were siege-guns, intended solely for use on land, for knocking down the defences of castles or town walls. This brought a completely new complexion on the Armada. It wasn't a sailing battle fleet: it was an invasion task force. It was an army afloat that was going to deliver a shattering blow against Tudor England. We're looking at a battle before it happened – a battle that never happened.'

In the conventional archaeological world, investigators usually study the relics left behind *after* the fighting. 'With the Armada it's everything that was put together *before* the battle,' says Martin, 'but was sealed in the wrecks before the battle took place. We're in the unique position of being able to see a 16th-century army prepared for battle.'

So the Armada hadn't arrived off the coast of southern England merely to knock out the English navy and escort troops across the Channel. It had arrived with everything necessary to land, invade and destroy the enemy.

In that single time-capsule off the coast of Antrim, Martin's team discovered all the impedimenta of Renaissance warfare: a fourth huge Turkish cannon; rounds of heavy ammunition; a gun hoist; material for the construction of gun platforms and making defensive emplacements; stakes and axes, rollers and sledgehammers, wedges and handspikes, specialist tools for farriers and wheelwrights, tents, buckets, lanterns, carts, sandals, shovels – all the tools and materials with which to conduct sieges. In short, *La Trinidad Valencera* represented the attention to detail, the enormous complexity and the purpose of the great Enterprise.

The Planning

It was an extraordinary undertaking for the times. One hundred and thirty ships had been gathered from all over Europe – tall fighting ships, vast auxiliaries, fully-loaded supply vessels, even hospital ships. They had been loaded with weapons and the other materiel of war – there were guns which had been specially cast, there was ammunition and, of course, there was sufficient food and water for a long voyage.

And then there were thousands of men, who brought a special kind of problem. In that era, as naval historian Nicholas Rodgers explains: 'If you gathered any large number of men together in one place for any length of time, one thing was virtually sure: they will all fall sick and probably die. If you're going to gather an army together or a fleet together, you've got to gather them and use them quickly. They won't remain usable for long.'

Colin Martin agrees that the Spanish effectively had to run to stand still: 'To gather together such a large number of men was almost impossible. As soon as you got a large number of men you started losing them – and it's the same with the ships. Wooden ships with rope and canvas sails and rigging are constantly falling apart: they're degrading and rotting.'

The Armada had taken shape in the Escorial, King Philip's newly-built palace in Madrid, from which he insisted on controlling everything. Says Nicholas Rodgers: 'Spain didn't have central institutions. All the lines of communication met on his tiny desk in his tiny office in the Escorial, and he ran his empire of empires by the ceaseless exchange of correspondence. "The Bureaucrat King", they called him. A king who ran everything from an office was a very odd and unlikely figure of the time.' A master of detail, Philip received between 30 and 40 reports a day and seemed in danger of drowning in a sea of paper. He shut himself away in his office and directed operations with his pen, avoiding any form of confrontation – rarely meeting his advisers or even his commanders. He was personally involved in the smallest details of acquiring ships, finding men and drafting orders.

In modern terms, Philip was a hopeless delegator and his command and control systems were practically non-existent. Yet this didn't stop him trying to run, single-handedly, an empire which stretched round the world; an empire on which, it could be truly said – for the first time – that the sun never set. 'The problem was', says historian Mark Corby, 'this enormous empire was way beyond the ability of one small man, in a small study on the outskirts of Madrid, to control.' But this didn't stop him bombarding his commanders with instructions.

Once at sea, however, the Armada used a very simple and effective means of control. The ships had to adhere to a specific crescent-shaped formation, except for the most powerful ships commanded by the most noble officers – these were allowed to divert as needed to where the battle was hottest. The fleet could plod on under this self-regulating formation, and no further orders were needed beyond the initial starting signal as the whole ponderous machine moved off from Corunna.

But if the fleet which arrived off The Lizard in the late July of 1588 was actually an invasion fleet rather than a purely fighting navy, it still doesn't explain why they weren't able to do much more than fire a few ineffective shots at the English. Were the Spanish incompetent, were their armaments inadequate or were their tactics at fault? Some of the answers lie in the archives, and others lie under the waves.

Incompetence certainly seems an unlikely factor, although the image of an Armada as an efficient force manned by superior sailors is certainly at odds with the traditional English perception. As Nicholas Rodgers points out: 'You have to throw away the ideas which you could find in old history books which implied that the English were the wonderful seamen and the Spanish were incompetent. It really was the other way round.'

In 1588, Spain lay at the centre of an enormous empire and enjoyed colossal wealth – much of it from the silver mines of the New World. The Spanish had been trading across the Atlantic for nearly a hundred years. The Portuguese had been trading with the Far East for more than a hundred years. These people were not only the best, but almost the only experienced deep-sea sailors in the world. And they were well-trained. The English had nothing like the long experience the Spaniards had of organizing ocean convoys. The principal admirals of the Spanish fleet were tough and professional Basques, who had been commanding ships or fleets all their adult lives and were intimately familiar with the naval tactics of the age. Furthermore, Medina Sidonia proved a strong and eventually severe commander, to the extent that he had one of his captains, Don Cristobal de Ávila, hanged at the yard-arm for disobeying an order at the height of the campaign.

So if the Spanish were great seamen – and the evidence that they had few problems in moving 60,000 tons of shipping from Lisbon to the North Sea is clear – what could have gone wrong? Were their guns or their ammunition inadequate?

The Guns and their Ammunition

The archives show that Queen Elizabeth had spent half a million pounds on improving her defences – and that was more than the entire annual income of the State. Had the Spanish spent enough? The answer, again from the archives, is that they spent a very great deal of money indeed. Many of the heavy cannon – 2,500 guns in all – had been acquired from all over Europe, as had many of the ships themselves. New cannon were being specially cast for the fleet. In addition to this formidable firepower, almost all the Armada's 19,000 soldiers carried firearms, many so heavy that they had to be fired with their barrels supported by a forked rest. But was this enough, and was it, indeed, the right sort of firepower?

The most extraordinary statistic of the entire expedition is surely that the Armada was not able to sink a single English ship. Why did the largest task force the world had ever seen make so little impression on the enemy?

The Battle of Hastings

'Which figure is the king?' asks Professor David Bernstein. 'Is it the one who's pulling an arrow out of his head, or is it the one who is more obviously down and whose leg is being slashed by this knight? If the first figure is not Harold, where does that leave the famous story about Harold having been killed by an arrow to the eye?' Bernstein was the first to notice the small holes, just visible, pointing to the brow of the second man (inset), and concludes that the tapestry once showed an arrow in his brow, too.

He also points out that the Bayeux Tapestry was the first account which referred to Harold being killed like this and that the blinding of Harold was in fact a metaphor for the terrible punishment he deserved for breaking his oath to William. Bernstein believes that both men may represent Harold, but that his death as depicted here is an invention by the creators of the tapestry.

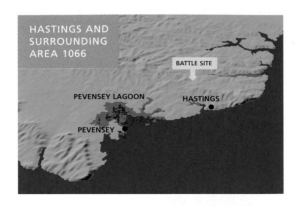

HASTINGS AND SURROUNDING AREA 1066

BATTLE SITE

PEVENSEY LAGOON

HASTINGS

PEVENSEY

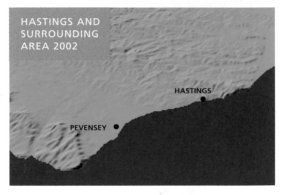

HASTINGS AND SURROUNDING AREA 2002

HASTINGS

PEVENSEY

Recent work by the University of Portsmouth shows just how much the coastline and landscape near Hastings has changed over the last thousand years. A lagoon would have made overland travel between Pevensey – where William landed – and Hastings very difficult. Hastings itself was almost surrounded by marsh in those days.

The Battle of Agincourt

Above: Historian Matthew Bennett with the recently discovered French plan
for the battle. It was never put into action.
Below: Simon Richardson, Britain's most experienced battlefield metal
detectorist – he records every find precisely.

Above: Battlefield archaeologist Tim Sutherland conducting a geophysical survey at the supposed site of the battle.
Below: Sir Thomas Erpingham's white leather bag, still held at the Public Records Office, contains his accounts and his contract to take part in the French campaign of 1415.

The Spanish Armada

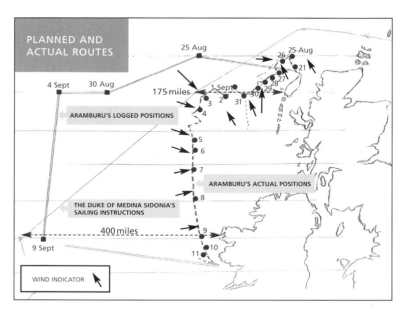

PLANNED AND ACTUAL ROUTES

25 Aug

25 Aug

4 Sept 30 Aug

175 miles

ARAMBURU'S LOGGED POSITIONS

26

21

27

28

29

1 Sept

30

31

2

3

4

5

6

7

ARAMBURU'S ACTUAL POSITIONS

8

THE DUKE OF MEDINA SIDONIA'S
SAILING INSTRUCTIONS

400 miles

9

9 Sept

10

11

WIND INDICATOR

Above: Amateur meteorologist Ken Douglas's map, showing his meticulous plotting of the disastrous route taken by Marcos de Aramburu aboard the San Juan Bautista. Douglas believes that the Spanish quite simply failed to take account of the Gulf Stream, and that many of the ships which did survive only did so by a whisker. *Battlefield Detectives* used particle-tracking software to confirm his theories.

Right: From this tiny office in the Escorial Palace near Madrid, King Philip II of Spain ruled his enormous empire single-handedly.

Top: The replica cast bronze culverin used by *Battlefield Detectives*.

Left: Marine archaeologist Colin Martin's work with Spanish cannon balls and Spanish gunners' rules (seen here at the Ulster Museum) clearly demonstrated inaccuracies in both the rules and the cannon balls themselves.

Waterloo

Top: The *Battlefield Detectives* series re-enacted many battles: a field in Shropshire served for Waterloo.
Above: Major Gordon Corrigan, author and battlefield guide, surveys the scene of the battle.

Top: Many paintings of the battlefield tried to capture the literal fog of war. Here, Marshal Ney is seen in the midst of the action.

Left and Below: Two detectives at work: Surveyors Daniel Schnurr and James Kavanagh working with the latest GPS technology, which mapped the battlefield to centimetre accuracy. The artificial Lion Mound dominates the battlefield.

Colin Martin and Geoffrey Parker knew that the Spanish, like the English, complained they had not enough ammunition – a senior military officer with the Armada claimed, 'There was great scarcity of cannonballs.' But the archaeological discoveries were to throw doubt on this complaint.

The bronze foundries in Lisbon were producing new cannon as fast as they could. Naval historian Nicholas Rodgers believes the Spanish were very concerned that they were about to be outgunned: 'The Captain General of artillery had spent the previous two years in a desperate scramble to collect heavy guns from anywhere – ransacking fortresses through the Spanish Empire and trying to buy guns publicly, privately or secretly, trying to get gunners from anywhere he could, trying to cast guns, trying to set up gun foundries and so on.' The archaeology, was to cast new light on the subject.

Colin Martin has been diving on 12 of the Spanish wrecks for more than 20 years, and the evidence he has uncovered contradicts the Spanish claims that they were short of ammunition. 'We now know that's completely untrue. On the Spanish wrecks we found enormous quantities of unspent ammunition. This was a great surprise, because all the history books said there was no ammunition left. But the wrecks showed that this was manifestly untrue.'

On the wreck of the *San Lorenzo,* archaeologists found no fewer than 2,650 unused cannonballs – yet this was in a ship which had been involved in every one of the sea battles in which the Armada was engaged. And the extremely detailed inventory of ammunition returned by those ships which did return to Spain shows that the vice-flagship *San Francisco* came home with no fewer than 8,489 rounds of the 8,731 with which she had been issued.

It seems, then, that the archaeologists had established that the Spanish had a lot of ammunition but fired very little of it. But why? As so often in detective work, part of the answer lay in a tiny and at first insignificant-looking clue.

Deep under the seas off Northern Ireland, divers working on *La Trinidad Valencera* found a gunner's rule. The wooden rule was a simple device which enabled a Spanish gunner to determine the weight of shot appropriate to a given bore, and thus ensure that the correct size of cannonball would be used in the appropriate gun. But the calibrations on the gunner's rule and its associated matching wooden rings were, Martin found, so full of inconsistencies as to have rendered it virtually useless.

And this wasn't an isolated error: recently, he located a second rule – a bronze one – which had been found earlier in the remains of the *San Juan de Sicilia*. It, too, showed that the gunners would be unable to predict correctly the size of cannonball needed.

But why would any ship's guns have loaded the wrong sizes in the first place? The answer lies in the diversity of Europe at the time: there were no 'right' sizes.

The Armada was made up of elements drawn from all over the Spanish Empire, and there were many different sets of weights and measures. There was no consistency and no standardization. These were flaws that were to prove fatal in the heat of battle when it came to finding the right shot to fit the right cannon.

Colin Martin explains: 'There was no common standard of gun size. The apparently simple business of matching the cannonballs to the cannon aboard a particular ship caused logistical problems of enormous proportions. It's difficult for 21st-century minds to comprehend; but it was very different from the perspective of a 16th-century mind.'

So it turns out that the docksides of Spain were awash with ammunition of differing sizes, and cannon to match – or rather mismatch. Before the fleet ever set sail, ships were loaded with shot which was too small or too big for their cannon. This could result in an exploding barrel, which would be fatal – not to the enemy, but to the crews firing the guns.

There was another fatal weakness discovered by the archaeologists – in the wreck of *El Gran Grifón*, which came to grief off Fair Isle, and which had been allocated new bronze cannon cast by the Lisbon foundries just before she sailed. The bore of one gun retrieved from the sea is so off-centre that it could never have been fired safely: if it had been, it would have blown up. Another piece, located in the wreck of the *Juliana*, obviously did just that: a huge hole close to its muzzle shows that it must have exploded as it was being fired, probably evidence of poor workmanship or sub-standard materials at the hard-pressed foundries.

Even if the Spanish guns and artillery-pieces had been in perfect working order, would they have been able to use them to much effect? Colin Martin thinks not: and his views have more to do with Spanish gun-carriages and tactics than with the guns themselves.

'It seems that the Spanish were not well prepared to work their guns, reload them and fire them over and over again during a sea battle,' he says, 'and the reason for this is very simple: they weren't anticipating that sort of sea battle at all.'

The Spanish wanted to close with the enemy and engage them as rapidly as possible, so that they could use their short-range weaponry – the muskets, small arms and incendiary devices they carried – followed up with rapid boarding by armed men.

Tactically, they intended to use their cannon in one single salvo at the moment they closed with an enemy ship, partly to cause damage to ships and men, and partly to spread confusion and fear among the enemy at the pivotal moment of boarding, while the assault went in. The Spanish pre-loaded their guns ready for action long before battle was joined.

Investigations among the wreckage and within the archives shows that the Spanish would have been hard-pressed to fire their cannon very often, even if they had wanted to.

Their major problem was that many of the cannon were just too large and cumbersome to be used at sea. Excavation of the *Trinidad Valencera* revealed a massive sea-carriage – the base and wheels on which the gun would sit – which, together with the gun itself, made an overall length of 19 feet. But the deck of the Spanish ship was only 36 feet wide. To manoeuvre the gun so it could be reloaded would have been difficult enough in a calm sea in the absence of the enemy: to do the same in battle would have been almost impossible.

These guns could only be reloaded through the muzzle, which would either involve manhandling it entirely inboard or, alternatively, the gunner climbing out along the barrel, over the sea, and clinging on while undertaking the complex business of reloading through the muzzle.

The English guns had no such shortcomings. In a 1988 experiment conducted by the Royal Navy with replica cannon, it took far longer to load and fire a Spanish gun inboard than to do the same with the English equivalent.

The English guns 'were mounted on specially designed short gun trucks that made it possible to reload at sea much faster,' says Colin Martin. 'As a consequence, we know that the English managed to fire three shots to every one from the Armada'.

The sturdy little four-wheeled English gun truck, he believes, was England's secret weapon in 1588. But were the failings of the Spanish gun trucks known to the English?

Early in the small-scale battles up the Channel, Sir Francis Drake, disobeying orders, had left the main fleet and boarded the heavily-armed squadron flagship *Rosario*, which was lying crippled and isolated following two separate collisions with others in her fleet.

With his ship no longer able to defend herself, the *Rosario's* commander, Don Pedro de Valdés, was forced to surrender to Drake, who was afterwards strongly suspected of pursuing personal gain – the *Rosario* was carrying 50,000 ducats, and it is not at all clear that this reached Elizabeth's government. But Drake must surely have inspected his prize with great care, and he could hardly have failed to realize that the Spanish were incapable of firing their cannon quickly or effectively. He would surely have realized, too, that the English tactics of long-range gunnery had had little effect. Assuming he reported this to his own admiral, perhaps he could take some credit for the later tactics of fireships, and even for the improved gunnery in the final battle off Gravelines.

But if the Spanish weren't able to sink a single English ship, the English weren't much more efficient. Only a handful of Spanish ships were sunk during the entire campaign as a result of gunfire.

Naval historian Nicholas Rodgers is scathing about the English guns: 'As to why the guns were relatively ineffective,' he asks, 'perhaps the question ought to be put the other way round – why did the English think that they would be any different? Most were not much bigger than nine-pounders, firing at a range of maybe 200 yards to 400 yards! Why did they think that they were actually going to sink substantial ships?'

Rodgers believes that a captain of Nelson's day would have laughed at the idea that these guns could do any serious damage. The effective range was just too short.

He thinks there may also have been another problem. The English fleet had recently adopted a new and more effective type of gunpowder which probably meant that they were firing iron shot at high velocity – it would have left the gun at a higher speed than had been known before. The effect of this was perhaps not what the English would have expected. 'If you fire small-calibre iron shot with good powder at the side of a wooden ship, it'll go straight through one side and straight out of the other side, making a small, round, neat hole in each side. Bad news, of course, if you're likely to be standing in the way, but from the point of view of structural damage to the ship it's actually not that serious – it's very easy to plug a hole like that above the waterline.'

Documentary and archaeological evidence, as well as modern military testing, support this view. Martin and Parker point out that, in the most serious battle of the campaign, off Gravelines, the *San Martin* received no fewer than 107 direct hits on the hull, masts and sails by cannon-shot. The *San Juans'* commander estimated that more than 1,000 rounds were fired against his ship. The *San Mateo* was described as 'a thing of pity to see, riddled with shot like a sieve'. The *San Juan de Sicilia*, the *Santa María de la Rosa*, the *Santa Ana* – all were holed. More than 1,000 crewmen of Armada ships were estimated to have been killed; but divers, using oakum and lead patches, saved all but one single ship.

What were the English doing wrong? Is it simply a fact that in the late 16th century, the guns weren't effective enough, nor used efficiently enough, to influence the outcome of the battle? Or was part of the problem for the English that they were using the wrong kind of ammunition?

The English were proud of their iron industry and the cheapness of the cannon shot that it produced. But could the money have been better spent? Iron shot was perceived as the high technology of the 16th-century weapons industry. But would it, in fact, have been better to have stuck to the old-fashioned but more expensive stone cannonball?

Nicholas Rodger: 'It's always the way when you go to war with new weapons. Every generation has its new superweapon – they think it's going to work wonderfully. They've all done trials – your missile always shoots down the enemy plane on trials – but when it comes to real war, somehow things are different.' Were the new weapons more successful? He doesn't think so: 'small charges, with big stone shot flying slowly, had a kind of smashing effect which was actually much more destructive. Later generations learned to imitate that, with heavier guns firing iron shot, and by reducing the charges quite considerably and firing at much closer range. But this is something the English didn't yet know.'

Nicholas Hall, Keeper of the Royal Armouries Museum of Artillery, told *Battlefield Detectives* that by the time of the Armada, 'naval gunnery had settled on the big, muzzle-loading, single-piece gun as the weapon of choice. They would have been expensive, they required a high degree of technological skill to cast, but what they seemed to have been able to do was to fire a heavy cast-iron projectile to a reasonable range. I think it would easily penetrate any wooden warship's side – it might even go out through the other side.'

Hall feels the result would have been far more serious than Nicholas Rodger believes. 'The effect of that would be to cause massive casualties on any crew on that ship, because large pieces of timber – rather euphemistically known as splinters – would be flying around in a devastating way.'

To check the range and effectiveness of bronze culverins – the medium-sized cannon – *Battlefield Detectives* arranged with Nicholas Hall and Alex Hildred of the Mary Rose Trust to test-fire a replica cast-bronze culverin at the Ministry of Defence range near Shoeburyness.

One thing the tests showed conclusively was that the bronze culverin was a long-range, accurate gun: tests showed that the cannonball could – and did – travel a very long way indeed. Nicholas Hall found that 'if you get the roll of the ship right, you should get some accurate shooting. The ball will travel up to a mile and more; you would certainly worry enemy ships at really quite a considerable range.'

Were our contemporary cannon-firing skills as accurate as those of the English seamen of the 16th century? Well, perhaps: the cameras and radar systems showed that although the Shoeburyness testers never hit the small target, they were close enough to have hit the hypothetical ship on which the target was placed. 'I think that at a hundred yards, with the gun in good order, you could hit probably more or less where you wanted to – you could be certain you would hit somewhere on the main body of the ship.'

In fact, the tests proved one other thing – that casting bronze cannon is, as expected, an imprecise science. During the tests, the replica cannon's muzzle became so weakened that the planned programme was not completed. Alex Hildred felt that one more firing might have been one too many.

The tests did show the enormous range of the English guns. Alex Hildred reckons that the English fleet had something like 150 long-range culverins to a mere 21 among the Spanish ships. The English, she says, 'really knew where their strength lay, which I believe was in long-range warfare, and in using the ship as a fighting platform to keep the enemy away and stop it from boarding.'

Nicholas Hall agrees: 'The Spanish, as I see it, were perhaps trying to fight a land battle on ships, which is a rather mediaeval style of naval warfare. The English, knowing that they have good guns, must have thought it worthwhile to keep at a good distance – try a bit of gunfire. It didn't necessarily matter if a lot of the shots missed: they were showing that they were there.'

We should not underestimate, from our 21st-century perspective, the fact that a wooden warship has an inherent buoyancy by virtue of being wooden.

So the Armada's inability to get close enough to grapple with the English, Dr Hildred believes, was 'intensely frustrating for the Spanish. You have to look at them as being the aggressive force – they are coming to invade England – and they can't get close enough to the ships because the English won't let them.'

So the Spanish were unable to beat the English simply because they couldn't reach them.

Was the inefficiency of their cannon the only reason why the Spanish could not sink the English ships? Detective work into other aspects of the campaign reveals some surprising answers.

The Ships

We know that the now-discredited English version of history claims that huge Spanish ships were unable to bring their guns to bear on the small and agile English vessels. Were there other aspects of the two sailing fleets which led to the eventual defeat of the Armada?

Many of the Spanish ships were large, but most of these were not fighting ships; they were transport ships like *La Trinidad Valencera*. Martin and Parker describe the reports of the colossal size of the Armada's vessels as 'the first and most persistent legend.'[3] Documentary records show that all the 13 English ships over 500 tons were heavily-armed royal galleons, and that the largest of these, Martin Frobisher's 1,100-ton *Triumph*, was bigger than any comparable ship in the Spanish fleet. Further, Martin and Parker say, 'once the size of the Spanish ships has been reduced to realistic proportions, another of the legends can be demol ished. Their guns, some claimed, were mounted so high on their towering sides that the balls flew harmlessly over the low English vessels, whose every shot, in return, told upon their huge adversaries. This ludicrous view, rejected by serious historians since the late 19th century, now has few devotees.'[4]

However, although the size of the fighting ships was not dissimilar, there was a difference in design. Elizabethan ships were lower in the water, leaner and possibly more capable of quick manoeuvring. It is clear that ship design in England was evolving.

Jonathan Adams, Director of the Centre for Maritime Archaeology at Southampton University, has worked on the history of ship design and uses high-resolution equipment in his research. Taking the *Mary Rose* – built some 70 years before the Armada – as his starting-point, he is able to trace the development of warship design. Then, as now, it was a highly secret business. Elizabethan shipwrights such as Matthew Baker designed their ships on paper, using complex and sophisticated techniques to shape the hull in an attempt to predict how they were going to perform when afloat. Ship design was a secretive art, and shipwrights would pass on their secrets to their sons.

The *Mary Rose* represents the first time that the ship is built from the keel up,' says Dr Adams, who points out that ships had now begun to be designed for war, and were less likely to be expected to serve as merchant ships in time of peace. Soon after the *Mary Rose* had been built, 'in a very, very short time,' emphasizes Adams, 'we see the hull form and the construction changing. The rig – the thing that powers the ship along – has changed as well. It seems to be simplified as three masts… the sail starts working more effectively as an aerofoil, so it transmits more power per square foot, and this allows the ship to be used in ways that are much more inventive. If you sailed some of the faster, newer galleons of Elizabeth's reign alongside the *Mary Rose*, she would be left standing.

'The ships of the Armada campaign – even if it is barely a generation later – represent almost a revolution,' says Adams. Their revolutionary design was perhaps most evident at the first contact between the English and the Spanish fleets. 'As Medina Sidonia and the Spanish fleet were sailing up the Channel, they could see elements of the English fleet coming out to meet them – but because of the direction of the wind they were initially quite comfortable in thinking that the English fleet would be unable to get into threatening positions.' But the Spanish stopped feeling comfortable when they found that 'to their horror, the English ships were sailing much closer to the wind than the Spanish had thought possible.' Essentially, the English design meant that their ships could sail more directly against the direction of the wind than ships had been able to before.

Jonathan Adams's research shows other changes in English ship design. Ships in the time of Henry VIII's *Mary Rose* had high and substantial castle structures at both the stern and the bows. 'They were designed to provide shelter and a base for a large number of men,' says Adams, 'and the castles – as the name implies – would have been heavily armed.' But by the time of the Armada, these castles had been reduced in size – ships now carried two- or three-ton cannon on their decks – and the more compact English ships consequently became much more seaworthy in high winds.

Was design innovation a decisive issue? Was this the reason why the English weren't beaten by the Armada: that English ships were technologically superior? There was another reason. It was to do with tactics.

Colin Martin and Geoffrey Parker unearthed a letter in the archives which they believe may have been written by Martin de Bertendona, commander of one of the Armada squadrons – a letter which was sent to a papal agent in May 1588, before the Armada sailed.

'Unless God helps us by a miracle,' he wrote, 'the English, who have faster and handier ships than ours, and many more long-range guns, and who know their advantage as well as we do, will never close with us at all, but stand aloof and knock us to pieces with their culverins, without our being able to do them any serious hurt.' [5]

Although we don't know how common this view was, we do know that the author of this letter was right – this was exactly what happened. The Spanish had always planned to close with the English ships and board them, using their sea-going soldiers to conquer the English. The English, however, as we have seen, had no intention of getting close, preferring instead to fire at the Armada from a distance. Even at the battle off Gravelines, in the closest fighting of the campaign, the English were wary, and backed away when they sensed danger, ignoring the taunts of cowardice recorded by a survivor from a Spanish ship: 'The enemy thereupon retired, whilst our men shouted to them to return the fight.'

Even in that very first minor engagement off Plymouth, the English tactics surprised the Spanish. The accepted formula for battle envisaged that ships approached the enemy in a single line, firing from the prow. Yet the English passed in a ragged line, bringing broadsides to bear on the Armada. Martin and Parker believe that these were the first such attacks in European naval warfare, although Nicholas Rodgers describes the tactic as being more like a figure-of-eight approach. Whatever the precise tactic – and naval libraries bulge with the contested accounts of naval battles as recent as World War II, let alone the 16th century – we do know that the Spanish were unable to respond effectively.

Our battlefield detectives have offered convincing explanations for much of what occurred in that summer of 1588; but what of the eventual outcome? If archaeological investigation and the resulting historical research has shed new light on strategies and tactics, ship design and weaponry problems, it still does not explain the tragedy which was to befall the Armada. When Medina Sidonia decided to abandon any further attempt at a rendezvous with the army still waiting in Flanders, and sail 'northabout' around the British Isles, his tactics were sound and not exceptional: he was setting out on a voyage that many had successfully undertaken before.

But it was to turn out to be a disaster. As we have seen, the weather, which had favoured the English at almost every crucial turn of the Armada campaign, would tear the so-called 'invincible' fleet apart.

Jonathan Adams believes that local knowledge – or rather the lack of it – played a part in the loss of so many ships. Navigation, he says, quite often relied on pilotage – derived from weather conditions, clouds, the behaviour of the sea itself, birds, fish, floating weed and so on. 'All these things would give the experienced navigator very strong clues as to where they were.'

Additionally, he adds, the Spanish suffered severely from a major problem – they had, quite literally, 'no port in the storm'.

Few of the ships themselves had actually been sunk, but they had all been weakened by the campaign. Medina Sidonia did the best he could. He instilled discipline harshly. He gave orders for the fleet to stay together, reduced rations and ordered all animals to be thrown overboard to conserve drinking water. Yet one after another, the ships sailed into a nightmare.

Throughout the campaign, every twist and turn in the battle had been subject to the vagaries of wind, tide and currents.

We know that the violent storms of August and, especially, September 1588 destroyed much of the Armada's fleet and killed thousands. But why were the ships so close to the Irish coast in the first place? If they had obeyed Medina Sidonia's instructions, surely they would have been far enough away from those rocky coasts? Or could they really have been swept hundreds of miles to their end?

Oceanography

Ken Douglas, the amateur weather expert, has other ideas which, until now, he has kept to himself.

Marcos de Aramburu's log had been the first clue. Aramburu held the position of purser aboard the 750-ton galleon *San Juan Bautista*. At midday on 9 September, while still stuck in the high latitude of 54 degrees north, he had recorded his position as being 100 leagues – 368 miles – to the west of Ireland.

On 10 September he noted light winds as he sailed southeast. Yet on the morning of 11 September he was on the Irish coast. This didn't make sense to Ken Douglas. With light winds, it would have been impossible to travel 368 miles in such a time.

His second clue was the fate of the Duke of Medina Sidonia himself, who arrived back in Spain on 21 September. The Duke thought he had arrived at Corunna – but he was actually in Santander, some 275 miles to the east. Was his navigation faulty too?

Ken Douglas is convinced that the ships of the Armada were never as far out into the Atlantic as they thought they were, or as the maps have placed them ever since.

He believes that, quite simply, they failed to take account of the Gulf Stream. They thought they were making headway westwards, but they didn't realize that the effects of the current pushing against them meant that they were losing about 25 miles a day – and so they didn't deduct that figure from their logs. He reckons that error would have placed them between 250 and 300 miles further east than they thought.

So they were all out of position; but was it the Gulf Stream, rather than the weather alone, which brought about the final destruction of so many ships and lives? Did Medina Sidonia himself survive through sheer luck?

Ken Douglas believes the Spanish admiral must have missed Ireland 'by a whisker. The ships which turned up on the Irish coast were stragglers.'

They had been unable to keep up with the others because they couldn't tack against the wind, or because they had suffered damage in storms or battle. 'When they turned south on 3 September,' he explained, 'these ships were lined up to descend on Ireland. They arrived singly, or in small groups, at scattered locations, between 12 and 17 September.'

Can it really be possible that Ken Douglas's amateur detective work has solved a puzzle that has resisted a solution for more than 400 years? Ocean scientist Steve Hall gives his view: 'Unless you are working in the marine field, it's easy to overlook quite how strong these currents are and how they could carry a vessel some considerable distance over a period of days. A lot of historians or archaeologists might never have worked at sea, or not quite appreciate just how powerful these natural features can be. It's no great surprise that people haven't taken into account the currents in the past, particularly because you'll very rarely get an oceanographer and a historian talking together about the same subject.'

As a final check, *Battlefield Detectives* commissioned Dr Roger Proctor of the Proudman Oceanographic Laboratory to model the effect of the Gulf Stream on computer simulations of a Spanish Armada ship. Proctor used a particle-tracking program called *Eurospill*, originally developed for tracking oil spills. The results were astonishing.

Factoring in all the information from Ken Douglas, his

records and East Anglia's climatic research maps, together with information about the ships themselves and the navigation techniques of the Spanish mariners, it was possible to see what had happened.

It was almost impossible, given the weather conditions and the Gulf Stream, for the fleet to be making headway out into the Atlantic. As the team watched the computer-simulated ship struggling against the conditions, it was clear that Ken Douglas's theory was correct. Two hundred years before the marine chronometer had been developed, the navigators would have had no idea that they were failing to clear Ireland. When they did turn south, they were on course for disaster. Dr Hall believes that one can now look back several hundred years and demonstrate that a ship could 'have been displaced several hundred kilometres to the east of where a navigator may otherwise have thought its location to be.'

Those who died were the victims of a colossal error of navigation – and of a natural phenomenon which they may never even have known existed.

The cost of the Armada had been enormous for Spain, in terms of human life, in wealth and in prestige. She was never again to pose a serious threat to England. It had been a fatally flawed plan.

Marine Archaeology

Marine archaeology is a relatively recent development in the study of the past, but one which opens up new and exciting fields of research. It involves the same basic principles of observation, discovery and recording that are the basis of all archaeology, but with the special conditions and dangers of working under water: it is challenging work, involving meticulous research in an alien and often forbidding environment.

The strictest safeguards have to be employed, and although

recently, technology which has been developed by the undersea offshore oil and gas industry has made it possible to do 'remote' archaeology, there's no escaping the fact that most marine archaeologists have to learn how to dive.

Working beneath the sea has a long history. Less than a century after the Armada, in 1663, Dutch salvors obtained the right to work on the wreck of the *Vasa*, a Swedish warship which had foundered on its maiden voyage in 1628. They located and raised 53 cannon with the aid of a primitive diving bell. By the end of the 18th century, the first very cumbersome diving suit had been developed.

However it was not until 1943, when a young French naval officer, Jacques-Yves Cousteau, developed SCUBA – self-contained underwater breathing apparatus – that it became possible to work independently of the surface with the aqualung. By 1948, Cousteau was exploring a Roman-era shipwreck off Mahdia in Tunisia.

New standards in marine archaeology were developed in 1960, when the American archaeologist George Bass investigated a Bronze Age wreck at Cape Gelidonya off the Turkish coast. Before then, archaeologists had been content to stay on the surface while divers went below to explore. But George Bass learned to dive – he held the view that the essential difference between marine and land-based archaeology was the lack of time an underwater archaeologist had when working on a site at any great depth, but he saw no reason why those 20 minutes of work should not be carried out to the same standards.

In 1965 work started on the excavation of the *Mary Rose*, Henry VIII's great warship which sank in the Solent in 1545. It was to be one of the largest marine archaeological projects ever undertaken, involving some 24,000 dives on the seabed, spaced over 11 years and culminating in the raising of the hull in 1982.

But the discovery of physical treasure and the raising of hulls is not the purpose of marine archaeology; rather, it is learning about the past. Sites are discovered, sometimes as a result of historical research, which are then surveyed, photographed and mapped. Only exceptionally are wrecks then excavated and their contents removed.

Colin Martin points out that ships are normally only excavated if they are under some kind of threat, such as a shift in the environmental balance. He writes of the sort of discoveries that can be made: 'Parts of the hull tell the marine archaeologist how the ship was designed and built. Toolmarks reveal woodworking techniques used by the shipwrights. Fragments of rigging and rope – sometimes even pieces of sails – help to show how the ship was operated by its crew. Other finds throw light on activities such as navigation, medical care, everyday crafts, food storage, cooking and domestic routines. If the ship was a merchant vessel parts of its cargo may have survived, perhaps revealing where it came from. Warships contain evidence of the weapons they carried. Above all, items of clothing and personal possessions bring us into immediate contact with people who lived and died long ago.'[6]

If finds are ever removed from wrecks, new methods of conservation are utilized. Metal objects such as cannon have to treated by electrolysis to reverse corrosion. Organic materials must have the water they contain replaced by a more durable substance so that they can retain their shape when they dry out. Large ship hulls which have been excavated – such as the *Mary Rose* and the *Vasa* – have to be bathed continuously in water spray for several years.

The Archaeological Diving Unit of the University of St Andrews, with which Colin Martin has done much of his research, is at the cutting edge of British marine archaeology. Among the techniques its personnel have developed for their work are remote sensing methods which include Acoustic Ground Discrimination, a modification of echo-sounding systems. Specialist processing of the echo provides not only an index of seabed roughness but also a measure of hardness – useful wreck location factors. Additionally, they use bathymetric plotting and magnetic surveying – which can locate ships buried under sediment by detecting the tiny changes in magnetic fields caused by iron objects such as ballast or guns – and sidescan sonar, which is particularly useful in examining upstanding wrecks.

Marine archaeologists don't jump into the water as soon as they hear of a wreck – indeed, the pioneer George Bass claims that 'the hardest but the most interesting part of an excavation is the 20 years of library research, and the writing of the final report that follows the diving.' [7]

British waters contain very many thousands of wrecks – over seven thousand in the 20th century alone – but they are very dangerous environments. Even swimming near wrecks calls for special awareness, and all wreck exploration is strictly governed by the Protection of Wrecks Act 1973.

Waterloo – 1815

Introduction

A little less than a hundred miles to the east of Agincourt lies another great field of conflict.

Here, just as at Agincourt, the battle was waged between exhausted armies who stumbled through the mud to their own particular date with destiny: 18 June 1815.

But it is the site of a battle on a far greater scale.

The Battle of Waterloo was the culmination of nearly 30 years of war in Europe. On a single Sunday afternoon, 11 miles south of Brussels, on one small patch of ground measuring about three square miles, some 200,000 men were to meet and 50,000 were to die or lie wounded on the field. An empire had fallen.

Nobody who took part would have been able to see the entire battle. Most of them would only occasionally have been able to see their enemy at all, and would have had very little idea of their own contribution to the overall battle.

It was the bloodiest of battles: men and horses alike were cut down with the sword and blown apart by shot. Some were burned alive, some were torn in two, and hundreds lost their limbs to the shattering fusillade of shot which filled the very skies for hours on end. Men were impaled by lancers, decapitated by cannonballs and bayoneted by fusiliers. They were even killed by fragments of their comrades' shattered skulls hurtling through the air. Throughout the day – and the battle only lasted from about noon until sundown – a terrible noise filled the valley. It was an uproar the like of which had never been heard before and would not be heard again in this, the very cockpit of Europe, for nearly a hundred years: the constant boom of the volleys of some 400 cannon, the thundering of hooves, the screams of the wounded, the beat of the drum, the explosion of shells. Men shouted in a cacophony of languages as English and French and Prussians and Belgians and Germans wheeled and marched and charged and fled. Trumpets blared, sword clashed against sword – and against shot and against bone. Horses shrieked. It wasn't merely metaphorically deafening – by the end of the day, many men were literally deaf.

It was almost impossible for most of the participants to see what was going on: it wasn't the fog of war, it was the dense, eye-stinging stench and smoke of war. Hundreds of cannon and thousands of muskets produced thick clouds of dark acrid smoke which engulfed large areas of the battlefield. 'We were almost choked by it – and simply fired blindly into it,' reported one officer.

And on the heights of a ridge, a man sat calmly astride his chestnut horse, ignoring the mayhem around him and the lead flying by, as he directed his forces hither and thither across the rolling countryside to engage the enemy – an enemy commanded by one of the greatest generals in history. For this was not just a battle between armies, but a battle of minds: the minds of the Duke of Wellington and the Emperor Napoleon.

By nightfall the field of Waterloo was filled with the chilling sounds of thousands of wounded men and horses. Alongside this just-living nightmare lay the exhausted victors, bone-weary, hungry and thirsty. For the wounded, the terror of that long night was compounded by the fear that they might at any moment be killed by the hundreds of booty-hunters picking their way slowly through the carnage.

The battle was done. But the questions remain.

The Battle of Waterloo has probably produced more books, more paintings, more learned journals and more armchair generals than any conflict in history. The fate of Europe had hung in the balance on that one summer's day. Napoleon had been poised to seize victory, a mere hundred days after escaping from claustrophobic exile. Yet he lost.

Is it possible for our battlefield detectives to discover anything remotely new from the evidence of Waterloo?

- They looked first at the long-changed landscape of the battlefield itself.
- They unearthed naval log-books for clues about the weather.
- They recreated the conditions under which artillery was used.
- They analyzed both the cutting edge of 1815 surgery and what we now know about the effects of warfare on the mind.

They tried to discover not so much why Wellington, on his chestnut horse, won the battle, but rather why Napoleon, the greatest general since the days of Julius Caesar, should have lost.

The Campaign
It had all begun on the tiny island of Elba, off the coast of Tuscany. Napoleon had been banished there after he had been persuaded to abdicate in April 1814.

The greatest empire seen in Europe since the days of imperial Rome had imploded and a new king, yet another Louis –

the eighteenth – was returned to the throne of France. The great powers of Europe met in congress at Vienna to decide the fate of nations. As they argued among themselves, it became clear to an increasingly frustrated Napoleon that he had but one chance left – and on 26 February 1815 he escaped from his island exile and sailed for France.

Within only three weeks, the new King Louis had fled, Napoleon had re-installed himself in Paris and the great powers, electrified by this extraordinary turn of events, had pledged to form an army of 600,000 men to bring about his downfall.

The Duke of Wellington himself was in Vienna, where he was representing Britain at the conference of the victorious nations. But with Napoleon now on the loose once more, Wellington immediately abandoned his diplomatic office for military command. Fresh from his victorious campaigns in the Peninsular Wars against Napoleon, the man who was to be called 'the Iron Duke' was an obvious choice.

Europe was united, but Napoleon was in a hurry – and as the armies of Russia and Austria could not be mobilized overnight, Wellington found himself in command of a Dutch–Belgian and British force which he evidently considered to be a rag-tag collection of misfits. 'I have got', he wrote, 'an infamous army, very weak and ill-equipped, and a very inexperienced staff.'[1] But his armies were not alone. Wellington would be fighting alongside the Prussians commanded by the veteran Marshal Blücher.

Blücher was 72. Revered by his troops, he was very much a soldier's soldier. His army – and his sense of honour – were to prove vital to the campaign. The historian David Chandler describes him as 'a blustering, tempestuous corporal of hussars. A stronger contrast with the egocentric dynamism and brilliance of Napoleon, or the cool and disdainful British Milord, would be hard to find.'[2]

For *Battlefield Detectives*, the historian and battlefield guide Gordon Corrigan emphasizes the reasons for Napoleon's haste: 'There's a huge Russian army on the way. There's a huge Austrian army on the way. What he's got to do is defeat the British before they can link up with the Prussians and before the huge mass armies of the Russians and the Austrians descend upon him – because once they descend upon Paris, Napoleon's had it.'

So Napoleon knew that in order to win he would have to fight his enemies one by one, and that in the first instance he would have to defeat either Wellington or Blücher before his two opponents had a chance to unite. It would be necessary to keep the Allies apart, but a swift defeat would force each army back along their supply lines in opposite directions.

The Build-up

The Allied armies – the British, Dutch and Belgians, together with the Prussians – were dispersed in an arc south of Brussels. Napoleon's immediate plan was simple: he was going to punch his way through the British, Dutch and Belgian army with a massive frontal attack, and continue on to Brussels.

A few months before, Wellington had been inspecting the frontier defences of the Low Countries and had noted what he described as 'advantageous positions' near a little village called Waterloo. His plan was simple: he was going to stand on the ridge there, hiding his troops until the last possible moment, beat off any attacks and wait for the Prussians to join him.

But before they reached that stage, other engagements had to be fought.

On 15 June 1815 Napoleon, at the head of his Armée du

Nord, engaged with the Prussians, who – surprised – pulled back across the River Sambre. Napoleon ordered Marshal Ney, who had been summoned from Paris with no notice, to engage the Prussian rearguard immediately. Ney pushed the Prussians north-east towards Ligny before making camp for the night.

Wellington – who famously heard the news of Napoleon's approach while attending the Duchess of Richmond's ball in Brussels – arrived at the crossroads of Quatre Bras at 10 am on 16 June to discover Ney's force enjoying a leisurely meal in the distance. Wellington and Blücher, briefly together, climbed up a windmill – and through their telescopes saw, far off, Napoleon with his staff.

That day the French and British fought an inconclusive engagement at Quatre Bras, while a separate battle between the French and the Prussians took place at nearby Ligny, forcing the Prussians to retreat further. However, they didn't head east, back towards Germany, but north: surprisingly, the French commanders received no orders to follow them.

Napoleon was keeping himself distant from the battle, and from his commanders. The next day he toured the battlefield of Ligny, but it wasn't until towards midday that he finally ordered Marshal Grouchy to pursue the Prussians. Grouchy's force of 33,000 men constituted about a third of Napoleon's army. They were to play no significant part in what was to follow.

Meanwhile, Wellington withdrew his forces towards Waterloo. At 2.30 pm Napoleon arrived at Quatre Bras, only to discover that the British had left, with the exception of their rearguard, and that Marshal Ney and his men were still eating lunch.

As the great forces of Europe wheeled and manoeuvred in this lethal game, the weather broke. It poured with rain. Very quickly, the narrow country roads became churned into mud.

The heavy cannon, often axle-deep in the ruts, could be moved only with difficulty. As night fell, hundreds of thousands of men sheltered as best they could in the quagmire. If they were lucky, they had a blanket. Some opted to remain standing upright rather than lie on thé soaking ground.

The Battle

And so, on Sunday 18 June, the die was cast. The Prussians had regrouped. The British, with their Dutch allies, were formed up behind the ridge south of Waterloo as the French faced them three-quarters of a mile away across the valley. But nothing happened. For hours Napoleon delayed his attack, perhaps to wait for the ground to dry, but it was unusual behaviour for a man who once said that strategy was the art of making the best use of time and space: 'Space we can recover; but time, never.'[3]

Finally, at about midday, the French guns opened fire as Napoleon's brother Jérôme Bonaparte led a diversionary attack on the Chateau of Hougoumont, which lay between the two armies. Although the purpose of the attack was merely to divert the British, Jérôme spent most of the day committing more and more troops in a wasteful, futile and unnecessary attempt to capture the chateau.

Shortly after 1 pm, more than an hour after the battle had started, the first major attack was launched. A force of some 11,000 French infantrymen pushed in a huge column up the slope towards Wellington's army which was formed up behind the ridge, two abreast.

Gordon Corrigan describes what happened: 'The British gunners thought that all their Christmases had come at once. They fire maybe three or four rounds of shot, and probably one round of canister. The French infantry are marching blindly up the hill. Just as they get short of the top, they halt – perfectly correctly – and start to move into line again. That's what you do: you move in column, because it's easier to control, and then you deploy into line. And just at that moment, General Picton orders his men to stand up, orders them forward on to the top of the ridge and they fire two volleys – and it's shattering. It's fired from about thirty yards. The British cannot possibly miss, and the French start to go down. Those at the back start to panic. There's chaos. They're not in column and they're not in line. Commanders are all shouting at once. And at this moment, Wellington releases the British heavy cavalry…'

Now Napoleon found himself with very few infantry available – some were looking for Prussians, some were tied up in the wasteful battle at the château and his main force was scrambling to reorganize itself. He was determined to keep his remaining unused force – the legendary Imperial Guard – fresh for the final moment of triumph he still anticipated.

With time ticking away, Marshal Ney noticed the British redeploying, and – in what was to prove a crucial error – assumed they were retreating. He ordered a cavalry attack. What started as a charge by a single brigade soon multiplied, until a huge force of 5,000 – without any artillery support – was heading up the hill towards Wellington's armies.

The British were bemused: it was almost unknown for an unsupported cavalry force to attack infantry, and with good cause. The British lines were quickly formed into squares – the outermost troops knelt, planted their muskets in the ground with long bayonets fixed and faced the cavalry. Horses could rarely be persuaded to brave such a defence, and as the French impotently wheeled about the squares, the second and third rows of British troops took turns firing deadly volleys directly into them. The result was carnage – for the French.

By 4 pm, Napoleon had launched his one successful attack of the day, seizing the strategically useful farm buildings of La Haye Sainte. But to exploit this position he needed more troops – and he didn't have them. Meanwhile, the Prussians were nearing Waterloo from the east.

At 7 pm, in a last desperate throw, Napoleon launched his Imperial Guard at the Allies. He told his men that the Prussians, who had at last arrived and were now visible on his flanks, were in fact French reinforcements. Marshal Ney, rather than marching the Guard beside La Haye Sainte, led the column struggling into a hail of artillery. As a fusillade of fire rained down on them, and as they became increasingly aware that the so-called reinforcements were actually their Prussian enemies, the Imperial Guard – for the first time in its glorious history – retreated. The retreat turned to panic as Wellington waved his forces forward, and Blücher with his Prussians then turned the retreat into a rout.

Napoleon was defeated. The proclamations of victory addressed to the people of Belgium which he carried in his baggage fluttered into the muddy lanes near Waterloo. Louis XVIII came scuttling back, and Europe breathed a sigh of relief.

But why had Napoleon lost? Could it be that Wellington had not in fact outmanoeuvred his rival, but that Napoleon had merely been fatally unlucky – and that it was this bad luck which had lost him both the battle and the war?

The Landscape
The battlefield today seems miraculously unaffected by the urban sprawl of Brussels although, thanks to the modern motorway system, moving from location to location can sometimes feel as frustrating as it must have done nearly 200 years ago.

For *Battlefield Detectives*, Gordon Corrigan has no doubt why Wellington and his army had chosen this spot. 'The ridge is a brilliant defensive position. It commands the valley. There are loads of killing areas for the British infantry; loads of killing areas for the British artillery.' Wellington's famous 'backward-facing slope' sheltered and concealed his troops from attack. Corrigan: 'As Napoleon looks up here, he really cannot see very much. He can see the occasional flag, the occasional regimental colour. He can see the occasional officer on horseback, and he can of course see the Allied guns. So he knows Wellington's here – but he doesn't know exactly where his infantry are.'

Sheltering most of the Allied armies behind the ridge didn't merely render the men partly invisible: it also protected them from the deadliest arsenal Napoleon commanded, his cannon, especially the great bronze 12-pounders. These two dozen guns – the largest field guns in the world – were known as The Emperor's Beautiful Daughters. Gordon Corrigan points out: 'The 12-pounders can certainly hit anything on that forward slope, or on top of the ridge,' but to hit men behind the ridge, 'all they can really do is fire a few shots over the hill – on spec, as it were.'

There were eighty French guns, all told, and they were positioned as close as 700 yards to the British lines. But try as they might, it was almost impossible for the French to hit those troops sheltering behind the ridge: the shot would either plough into the ground just short of the natural defence, or sail harmlessly overhead.

The Duke of Wellington was notoriously unwilling to outline his plans before a battle. Elizabeth Longford, in her biography of the Duke, writes of an exchange between Wellington and Lord Uxbridge, the officer who would have taken over had the Duke fallen in battle. Uxbridge, the evening before, 'wished to know before he went to bed something of the great man's strategy. The Duke listened to him in formidable silence. At the end of the recital he briefly asked: "Who will attack the first tomorrow; I or Bonaparte?" "Bonaparte."

"Well, Bonaparte has not given me any idea of his projects: and as my plans will depend upon his, how can you expect me to tell you what mine are?" Then he got up, put his hand on the general's shoulder and said encouragingly:

"There is one thing certain, Uxbridge; that is, that whatever happens, you and I will do our duty."'[4]

If he wouldn't tell anyone about his tactics before the battle, Wellington was also unhappy to analyze them after the event. As John Keegan points out in *The Face of Battle*, 'The Duke of Wellington strongly disapproved of all attempts to turn the Battle of Waterloo either into literature or history. His own account of it in his official dispatch was almost dismissive and he advised a correspondent who had requested his help in writing a narrative to "leave the battle of Waterloo as it is… The history of the battle", he explained, "is not unlike the history of a ball! Some individuals may recollect all the little events of which the great result is the battle lost or won; but no individual can recollect the order in which, or the exact moment at which, they occurred, which makes all the difference as to their value or importance."' [5]

So if we cannot learn from the Duke himself about the advantages of the ridge, what does the landscape itself tell our detectives?

At first sight – not very much. The shape of the battlefield is clearly crucial but, contrary to appearances, it's not the place it was. Today it is dominated by an artificial hill called the Lion Mound. Built soon after the battle as a memorial to the Dutch and Belgian troops who fell at Waterloo, the construction of this 120-metre-high earthwork involved removing thousands of tons of earth from the very ridge which had played so vital a part in the battle itself. Wellington was furious when he found out what had happened.

Now, for the first time, using the most up-to-date surveying techniques and computer applications, our battle-field detectives were able to recreate a picture of what the landscape of Waterloo was really like. Using the latest geophysical techniques a team including Paul Hill, land-scape archaeologist, together with James Kavanagh, Head of Geomatics at the Royal Institute of Chartered Surveyors, investigated. Kavanagh explained: 'Geomatics is basically the measurement, analysis and presentation of all spatial information related to the natural and the built environ-ment.' Geomatics includes traditional mapping, global positioning systems, digital terrain models, imagery, satellite imagery and photography. One of the beauties of geomatic technology is that it can work on many levels, from a global one to that of the actual terrain of a battlefield. 'You'll be able to form a model of what the terrain looks like in reality,' explained Kavanagh, 'so what you're looking at is what the people who are on the battlefield would have seen at that time – or any time – whereas if you're looking at a normal map it's very difficult.'

James Kavanagh has a special interest in the evidence from Waterloo: his Irish great-great-great-grandfather fought there – on the French side. Moved by his visit to the battle-field, he wondered what it must have been like in June 1815. 'The landscape would have felt different on the day; it would have been a human landscape with so many thousands of people here dying – we're standing on a mass graveyard. The landscape lives and breathes. It feels quite a sad place.'

By identifying the origin of the soil used to construct the mound, it became possible to recreate digitally the original structure of the ridge.

Paul Hill is interested in this part of the battlefield because it has changed so much, and because he is sure 'that the slope here was a critical factor... and we need to work out the volume of all of the material here and get it back from that mound and stick it back on the landscape.'

What were our detectives able to learn by turning the landscape clock back?

'We've been able to estimate how the battlefield looked in 1815, by taking the earth that's in the mound and putting it actually on the battlefield,' said surveyor Daniel Schnurr. The team's geomatic techniques demonstrated that 287,500 cubic metres had been removed to form the monument, and showed that the now reduced ridge actually used to give a much more commanding view of the entire area. Schnurr, who had surveyed the site with Kavanagh, found that the slope which the French had to climb now proved to be a hundred metres longer than the landscape suggests today.

So for the first time in nearly 200 years we could see the battlefield as it actually was. We could see clearly the well-protected defensive position of Wellington's troops, and compare it with the position of the French Armée du Nord which was, for the most part, deployed out in the open and would be forced to attack the British uphill.

As Duncan Anderson, Head of War Studies at the Royal Military College, Sandhurst, tells *Battlefield Detectives*, visitors to the battlefield today can find the terrain confusing because 'the ridge on which Wellington disposed his army is now very much lower. It's 20 to 30 feet lower than it was on 18 June 1815.' Without this new detective work, Anderson believes it's 'difficult to understand why it took the French so long to get over what appears to be a very inconsiderable obstacle.' The slope behind the ridge, where Wellington's men were concealed, was a brilliant defensive position: Wellington often used this reverse-slope ploy. Duncan

Anderson: 'He could see no good reason for having his men killed in large numbers on forward slopes: a forward slope position is almost the worst you can adopt. He could see no good reason for squandering the lives of his men.'

The French were to find it difficult to hit, or even to see, the British or their allies. Major Simon West of the Royal Artillery, an expert on Napoleonic artillery tactics, explained to *Battlefield Detectives* that roundshot was normally aimed to hit the ground in front of the enemy, from where it would skim or bounce with murderous effect through the ranks. But with the Allies positioned behind what we now know was a high ridge, that became impossible.

Major West experimented with another favoured projectile – the explosive shell. This was designed to be lobbed high so that it fell down and exploded – known to be devastating on dry or stony terrain. His experiments at the Ordnance Testing and Evaluation Centre on Salisbury Plain, on specially created sodden ground like that of the morning of 18 July 1815, showed that the explosives would be harmlessly absorbed by the mud and not even tear a paper screen he'd placed a few feet away.

The newly reconstructed landscape also makes it clear why Marshal Ney had assumed the British were retreating just before he launched his huge unsupported cavalry charge. From where he was positioned, down by La Haye Sainte, any British troops redeploying towards the north would seem to have disappeared. It would be natural to assume that they were fleeing, and the cavalry would merely have had to mop up the tattered remnants. Ney initially ordered a single brigade to move up towards the ridge, but somehow – perhaps it was the excitement of battle – some 5,000 French cavalry joined in the charge.

Historian Mike Robinson summarized the situation for *Battlefield Detectives*: 'The smoke is thick on the ground.

There are troops everywhere and Ney makes a fundamental military mistake: looking through that smoke, he sees the withdrawal of some of the Allied troops and mistakes it for a retreat. He then orders the French cavalry to charge. Having given the order, the general whom he'd directed to charge refused, saying, "I will take no orders other than from my corps commander." This sets Ney off – he explodes. Not only does he commit that brigade of cavalry: he commits the entire cavalry corps. So in the space of the next 30 to 40 minutes, thousands of French horsemen are committed to the battle on an area where, frankly, there is insufficient room for two regiments to charge. By losing his self-control, Ney has wasted Napoleon's entire cavalry reserve.'

The Weather

But if the particular landscape of the battle happened to obscure Wellington's manoeuvres at a vital moment, it can be argued that this was the Duke's intention. He, after all, had deliberately chosen this very ridge to stand and fight. Was there something else, perhaps, which he could not have foreseen, which might have made life more difficult for Marshal Ney?

There was. And it was something even Wellington couldn't have predicted.

As day dawned on that Sunday morning, the Prussians were near Wavre, some ten miles or so from Wellington. Napoleon already knew that the Prussian threat had not been eliminated – he'd received a dispatch from Grouchy in the early hours which said that the Prussians had divided into three columns, so he should not have ruled out the possibility of at least some Prussians linking up with Wellington's forces. This meant that the sooner

Napoleon attacked, the more the odds would be stacked in his favour; and the longer he delayed, the greater would be the chances of the Prussians coming to the aid of the Allies. But there was a problem.

Mike Robinson reminds us of what it must have been like for an infantryman the night before the battle: 'It's teeming down with rain, their clothes are saturated, they're exhausted – they're weighed down by pounds and pounds of mud. We often think of the finery of the uniforms: not so – they would have been caked from head to foot. They couldn't light fires. Their weapons weren't in any sort of shape to fire – a thoroughly, thoroughly miserable night was had by all.'

Few people today, and even fewer in 1815, could predict the weather. Exactly 400 years before, the English and the French had met in a field turned to mud at Agincourt, and now another two armies were to meet at a battle in which the tides would be turned by the unpredictable weather of northern Europe. There were to be two major factors: one of them obvious, one of them less so.

We know that the weather on the evening before battle was atrocious. Gordon Corrigan, investigating the position for *Battlefield Detectives*, describes the moment: 'Napoleon's army has struggled up into this position on the evening and the night of 17 June. It's a filthy night – it's pouring with rain, the men are up to their knees in mud. They struggle in through the night and take up their positions – and as the dawn breaks, it's still wet and miserable and muddy.'

It had indeed been a terrible night. A violent storm had erupted over the rolling countryside. Everyone was caked with mud – from Wellington's mule trains to Napoleon's Imperial Guard. General d'Erlon, who was to lead the first disastrous assault against the British, wrote that the earth was so soaking that his deployment of artillery was seriously affected, and his troops spent the night without shelter. More importantly, perhaps, he noted that their muskets were too damp to fire.

A young English officer serving with the King's German Legion – part of Wellington's polyglot 'infamous army' – kept a journal, which he was writing for – or to – a young girl called Eliza Brookes. His entry for 18 June began, 'Nothing could exceed the miserable state in which I found the army in the morning. The rain had poured down in torrents all night, and that so powerfully as to preclude all possibility of kindling a fire.'

David Howarth, in his masterly account of the battle, drawn from the personal recollections of those involved, opens his account, *Waterloo – A Near Run Thing*, with the sheer misery of that morning: 'It had rained all night. At dawn, in the fields of rye along the southern edge of the forest of Soignes, you could hear a murmur like the sea on a distant shore. This was the blended voices of 67,000 men, grumbling, yawning, shivering, stretching cramped limbs, joking as people do when they share discomfort, and arguing about what would happen next: not about what Napoleon or what the Duke would do, but about more pressing problems: where to find something dry to light a fire, where to look for the wagons with the gin rations and whether there was anything for breakfast.'[6] Historian John Keegan records the 'supperless and breakfastless' condition of many of the troops.

But supperless and breakfastless is often the way battles have to be fought, and Napoleon's men had experienced such privations before. Napoleon was also used to fighting his battles from a less protected position than his enemies. And he had a numerical superiority over Wellington as the two armies faced each other across the sodden fields.

So why did Napoleon delay? He knew that the Prussians had not been routed, and had not moved, as he'd expected, away from their allies. Was it because the French emperor had little respect for his opponent? 'He is a bad general,' he told his chief of staff that morning. 'The English are poor troops. This affair will be no more serious than breakfast.' But it cannot merely have been overconfidence which led him to delay his attack until nearly midday.

David Paget is an artillery expert and a student of the Napoleonic Wars. He believes the delay was caused by the weather, and we know from the historical record that Napoleon had indeed been advised by his staff to wait for the ground to dry out.

Paget has often wondered to what extent the heavy ground would have slowed down the French gunners. Would they have been able to run the big 12-pounders back into position after the considerable recoil caused every time they fired? At Waterloo, some guns had ended up a long way from their original positions. Were the French too exhausted to run them back properly after each shot?

Paget experimented for *Battlefield Detectives*, putting the problems which may have faced the French artillery to the test. Using an accurate replica of a Napoleonic 12-pounder cannon, and a troop of fit officer cadets, he first recreated the sort of sodden field that Waterloo had become, and then they tried to manoeuvre the gun. It soon became obvious that mud and guns made an exhausting combination.

Napoleon was an artilleryman by training, and a feature of his way of waging war was to concentrate overwhelming firepower. He invested a lot of time and energy in ensuring that the French artillery was among the best in Europe. But Mike Robinson agrees that the problems facing the French before the ground had dried out would have been immense, because 'such heavy pieces as Napoleon had were difficult to manoeuvre: they're incredibly heavy. They require enormous teams of horses and men, even in good conditions. The minute you encounter poor weather conditions, your ability to move that artillery is severely, severely restricted.'

If a fresh and fit squad of today's young soldiers found the task so difficult, what must it have been like for those of June 1815: men who had marched across France, who had faced nights in the open, culminating in a rain-sodden nightmare in which many would have been unable to rest, let alone sleep?

It had become obvious that the weather of the night of 17 June had rendered the cannon less manoeuvrable, and the men less efficient. Napoleon, then, appears to have been right to have delayed his assault, especially as he would have known that the weather would also have affected the Allies, and in particular the Prussians.

There is a way to check the weather on the battlefield. On 18 June 1815 there were Royal Navy ships in the harbour at Ostend, only 30 miles from Waterloo. Ostend was an important link in Wellington's supply and communication lines.

Every naval vessel completes a daily written record – a log. In the Royal Navy, each log records the weather every day – wherever the ships are in the world. And the Royal Navy preserves its logs.

Our battlefield detectives went to the Public Records Office at Kew to search the archives. Here geographer and climate specialist Dennis Wheeler investigated the weather records. There he found the written evidence of the time: 'It's the observations made by officers on deck: they'll observe wind direction, wind strength, fog, rain, all noted together – often with the state of the sea – so you do have a very detailed picture of how the weather each day evolved almost hour by hour. It's a bit like looking at a modern-day forecast but written in 18th- and 19th-century terms. So what we have here is a piece of detective work'.

Taking data from different sources, Wheeler plotted them together on a map – and it became obvious that it had not only rained throughout the night, but it was still raining at dawn. Then, some time between 8 am and 9 am, the rain ceased and the sun came out. Wheeler believes this would have made a huge difference to the French. Wellington was holding a defensive position and needed only stand and wait: Napoleon had to move. 'I strongly suspect that had the weather been dry, Napoleon would have launched his attack far earlier than he did,' he says.

But was it only the appalling conditions of the night before that was a crucial aspect of the weather at the battle of Waterloo? Many people who took part in the battle mentioned the dense smoke. An anonymous officer in Picton's Division wrote on the morning after the battle, 'The smoke still hung so thick about us that we could see nothing. I walked a little way to each flank, to endeavour to get a glimpse of what was going on, but was obliged to return to my post as wise as I went.' [7]

A hot afternoon following on from a very wet night would have left a lot of moisture in the air. This, combined with the enormous amount of smoke and gunpowder, would have led to a condition some meteorologists call 'the perfect haze', a form of pollution we're familiar with today.

Duncan Anderson studied Sir William Allen's Wellington panorama depicting the battle. He points out that the artist would have had to limit the amount of smoke in order to portray the scene at all. Nevertheless, 'if you take a look at the destruction of the Imperial Guard which is right in the centre of the painting, that's more or less what it would have looked like at the height of a battle. You can see dark shapes, grey shapes, coming out of this swirling mist.'

Anderson uses the painting as evidence of one of the little-known problems of this kind of warfare: 'Before the 1880s, commanders could actually see very little of the battlefield, because they didn't have smokeless powder, so after about half an hour the battle would be shrouded in something that looked like a fog. And, of course, in a battle like Waterloo where you have close on 200,000 people in an area of little more than three square miles – 200,000 men shooting black powder at each other – there is going to be an immense fog. Now it does clear occasionally, but it creates huge command and control problems. These are depicted reasonably accurately in this painting, though one of the difficulties of course is that if you're going to produce a panorama like this, you can't actually paint a fog: it just wouldn't have done! So it's about half-right.'

By mid-afternoon, it seems, Napoleon may have been unable to see into the valley, and Marshal Ney unable to see out. And it was at precisely this time that Ney would have needed the most direction from his Emperor – the time that he unleashed his foolhardy and pointless cavalry charge. The weather – and crucially, the polluted environment – affected the outcome.

In the final analysis, what mattered was the survival of armies, not whether they were cold or exhausted or wet. The British and their allies were in the more commanding position because the French had to move uphill to attack; because the British tactics in forming defensive squares and in their timing gave them superiority at crucial moments; and because of their ability to take advantage of the terrain by ducking below the incoming artillery.

Battlefield Medicine

We know that between 30,000 and 35,000 human beings died that day, and thousands more were terribly wounded. It is difficult, in an age of modern medicine, helicopter casualty evacuation and 'precision' bombing by pilotless drones, to realize just how different things were in the field in 1815.

There were no anaesthetics. There was little concept of hygiene. There were no disinfectants or sterilization. *Battlefield Detectives* decided to take a closer look at the medical techniques employed at Waterloo.

Both sides suffered terribly, but it has often been said that the French had one big advantage – a much more advanced system of battlefield medicine than any other contemporary army. In such a finely balanced conflict, why didn't this give them the edge?

Dominique Larrey, Napoleon's chief doctor, was the outstanding surgeon of the era. He took part in at least 25 campaigns, and revolutionized the treatment of the wounded. He treated his own troops and his enemy's troops without distinction. He tried to change the almost universal apathy which the authorities exhibited towards soldiers who had been wounded in war. Napoleon himself described Larrey as 'the most virtuous man I have ever known.' Indeed, when Larrey was captured at Waterloo and sentenced to death, he was freed and given safe passage by the Prussian Marshal Blücher because he had earlier saved Blücher's son.

Larrey developed the first purpose-built military ambulance – the *ambulance volante* or 'flying ambulance', a lightly built horsedrawn wagon which collected the wounded from the field and rushed them to surgery. He developed the concept of triage for prioritizing casualties. He investigated the advantages of fly larvae treatment for wounds, noting that maggots devour only dead tissue and not living.

Mick Crumplin is a retired surgeon who has conducted research into Napoleonic medical history for more than thirty years. He has enormous respect for Baron Larrey.

'The trouble with Larrey was that he was a very honest man,' he said. 'He would always treat lightly wounded generals after more severely wounded junior officers or NCOs, which didn't go down very well!' But Larrey had important friends. 'Napoleon had a lot of time for Larrey. He gave him a tremendous amount of support, particularly in difficult campaigns such as Russia when he had to bypass more senior officers and go straight over their heads to Napoleon.'

Technically, Mick Crumplin has no doubt about Larrey's skills as a surgeon – a man who personally performed 200 amputations in a 24-hour period at the Battle of Borodino: 'He was one of the most proficient manual operators in surgery in the Napoleonic wars.'

But it was for his advances in the concept of battlefield medicine that Larrey led the way. 'His greatest invention was a system of going into the front line rather than following behind the army, so that he could actually treat men where they were wounded – sometimes even fighting off enemy attacks on the wounded. He formed a unit of 340 men which could be split up, with these well-sprung ambulance vehicles which gave the wounded less pain when they were being carted across ruts and probably caused less death from the transportation of the seriously wounded patient.'

Wellington was not opposed to medical advances – his chief medical officer in the Peninsular Wars, Dr McGrigor, had in fact persuaded him of the value of prefabricated military hospitals – but he rejected McGrigor's suggestion of introducing the French system of ambulances.

In the British army, a surgeon ranked below the youngest ensign in the regiment. In theory, each battalion was allocated one regimental surgeon and two unqualified assistants. Mick Crumplin's research however, shows that the real figures were somewhat worse: 'The 28th Foot – 557 officers and men – had 253 casualties at Waterloo and Quatre Bras, and had one assistant surgeon.'[8]

For *Battlefield Detectives*, we used special effects to work out what happens when various forms of weaponry hit human flesh and bone.

There were three major types of injury:

- what our surgeon-detective describes as 'macerating or avulsing' wounds – flesh which had been pulped, or torn-off limbs. These were caused by cannonballs. 'A nine-pound ball was capable of killing a dozen or more in line. Fortunately the ground was wet on 18 June and this probably prevented many roundshot ricochet injuries.[9]
- injury caused by low-velocity lead musket or pistol balls, which fragmented inside the body or limbs on hitting bone.
- cutting or piercing wounds caused by the sword, lance or bayonet.

Mick Crumplin described some of the effects of our tests:

'The main cause of instantaneous death was dismemberment or decapitation. There would be no survival with roundshot or musket-ball at close range. The next group would be people who were hit from very close and who would bleed out very quickly on the field, or have – for instance – penetration of the chest cavity or the head, or a wound in the neck. The next group were men who were not dismembered beyond the loss of a limb, and who managed to have their bleeding controlled.

'The impact of a musket ball on a human body would very much depend on the range. If a ball was properly loaded, at 30 yards it would almost certainly pass right through the body, but many ball strikes were from beyond 100 yards – they might well enter the body and be deflected initially by clothing – deeper in the body, they would be deflected by bones. It would cause damage to the soft tissues, arteries, nerves and so forth.' This was an era when even a small musket-ball wound could quickly lead to infection and death.

'If the patient wasn't expiring, the wound would be explored with a finger – and the surgeon might place the man in the position in which he received the wound. Then he would explore it with a probe and try and extract the missile from the depth of the tissues – but beyond two or three inches it was getting to be quite difficult.'

Probably the biggest – and the most common – operation to be carried out near the field of battle would have been amputation. Amputation was the only real choice for survival – even a complex fracture would normally lead to death at the time. Up to 500 amputations took place at Waterloo. Mick Crumplin believes that the operation would be very quick: from fifteen seconds to a few minutes: 'It had to be a very speedy procedure because of patient pain and the need to press on with other cases.' With the dispassion you would expect of a professional surgeon Mick explained the technique, and demonstrated it – on a model – using his own collection of instruments from the period:

'The patient would be supported, and the tissues would be withdrawn from the bone which was cut down to and then sawn across. None of these instruments was sterilized, of course – just cleaned between cases. A quick sweep of the fat and skin was made with a large knife. The wound was then approached from the point of view of securing the arteries, which would bleed if they weren't sorted out. The way we'd do that would be to use a sharp hook – a tenaculum – which would pull the blood vessel out of the tissues just a little so that a ligature – a piece of silk or linen – could be thrown round the vessel and tied by hand by the surgeon. Then a few stitches using a half-curved needle would be inserted into the skin to draw the edges together, or adhesive tape would be used to do the same job, and a roll of bandage would complete the procedure. These were the modern tools of the time, carried by the surgeon in a hamper.'

There was no anaesthetic.

Was the perception of pain different in 1815? Certainly there were some extraordinary stories. In a medical journal, Mick Crumplin recounts the story of Sergeant Anthony Tuttemeier who, having had his left arm carried off by roundshot, 'rode upright into Brussels 15 miles and presented himself to Dr Bach at the Hospital of St Elizabeth. When put into bed he fainted and remained insensible for half an hour.' [10] Lord Uxbridge, who is famously – but probably erroneously – quoted as having remarked to Wellington, moments after being hit, 'By God, sir, I've lost my leg!' never once moved as it was sawn off, casually remarking that he thought the saw to be not very sharp.

Mick Crumplin believes that 'the large majority of patients, because they were in a shocked or septic condition, or because they were simply very brave men, who knew what to do and had seen others go through it, kept quiet. Afterwards they'd be revived with a cordial – usually a mixture of water or fruit juice and rum or brandy.'

Was French battlefield medicine better than the English? The fundamental differences all point to French superiority – the French had been taught to operate on the spot: 'If an operation was needed it was done straight away, preferably within 24 hours,' says Mick Crumplin. 'The outcome was known to be better. On the British side, we had no system of stretcher-bearers as the French did: we had no sprung vehicles – we used farm carts which were hard to procure and slow. They were more aggressive in immediate amputation – actually on the field in the front line. I would say probably there were fewer able surgeons present on the British side than on the French side.'

But battlefield medicine itself was hardly enough to turn the tide in favour of Napoleon. The French may well have been more advanced, due to Larrey's particularly enlightened attitude for the time, but the battle itself was still a terrible business. Mick Crumplin pictures the battle at the end of the day:

'It's hard for us today to picture the battle as it would have been after such a hard, heavy and densely-packed action. The ground would be covered with wounded horses. Limbless or disembowelled men would be crying and screaming into the night, men suffocating under comrades wounded on the field. It must have been a very dismal sight.'

Unfit For Command?
But what has surprised most historians of the battle is not so much the landscape, the weather, the artillery or the medicine. What intrigues them is the behaviour of the leaders – and in particular, the behaviour of Marshal Ney and the Emperor Napoleon.

Ney was the hero of the rank and file, the bravest of the brave. He had held high command, in particular when he controlled the French rearguard as it retreated from Moscow. Yet at Waterloo he made the most extraordinary errors of judgement.

And if Napoleon was really the greatest military genius since Caesar or Alexander, how could he have thrown away such a seemingly equal contest? Was it all in the mind?

At his court-martial in November 1815, Ney proudly listed his rank and honours: 'I am the Duke of Elchingen, Prince of the Moscova and Marshal of France, a Chevalier of the Order of St Louis; I wear the Grand Cordon of the Legion of

Honour and the decorations of the Iron Crown of Italy and the Order of Christ.'

His personal bravery was not in question. He was so courageous that contemporaries compared him to the knights of the age of chivalry. 'A Marshal of France never surrenders. One does not parley with the enemy,' he said during the desperate retreat from Moscow. After Waterloo, Ney was sentenced to death as a traitor. He gave the final command to his own firing-squad.

But this brave man was a disaster in command at Waterloo. Soon after d'Erlon had lost 5,000 men when his unprotected column had been smashed by the withering fire of Wellington's lines, Ney received the order from Napoleon that he must immediately take the strategically important building at La Haye Sainte.

Ney attempted to do so with a small force at about 4 pm, but was beaten back. Turning away, he spotted British troops returning to the shelter of the reverse slopes, and others – probably wounded men – heading into the distance.

As we have seen he immediately ordered a brigade of cavalry to attack. Soon 5,000 were moving against the Allies. Historian David Howarth described the astonishment of Wellington's command as they realized what was about to happen: 'It looked as if Napoleon was planning an attack by cavalry alone. But nobody had ever heard of an unsupported cavalry attack against an unbroken line of infantry. All along the British line people discussed it in amazement, and everyone who knew the rules of tactics, from the generals down to the sergeants, formed the same opinion: Bonaparte was trying it too soon; he could not hope to break the line like that; it was suicide for his cavalry.'[11]

But, of course, it wasn't Napoleon who was trying it: 'It was Ney, who was now preparing the attack, and people ever since have wondered why he did it.'

It wasn't merely against the rules: it was a catastrophe for the French, riding into battle five hundred abreast. They were mown down in rows by the British defensive formations – the squares – which they discovered, too late, on the far side of the ridge.

Ney's second enormous tactical error occurred in the final phase of the battle, when Napoleon finally threw his precious Imperial Guard into the fray. Rather than leading the attack past La Haye Sainte, which had at last been taken by the French and from which he would have had support, he led the Guard up across those very open fields where the cavalry had so many times charged and failed. 'Nobody knows why he did so,' wrote David Howarth succinctly.

In fact, most of the evidence points very clearly in one direction. 'Ney had been suffering from a form of battle fatigue' writes David Chandler in *Waterloo, The Hundred Days*. 'This made his actions unreliable – periods of almost total lethargy alternating with periods of great and often rash activity.' [12] Historian Geoffrey Wooten is no less direct: 'This officer had almost manic tendencies.'[13]

Did Ney have what we now call post-traumatic stress disorder; and if so, why?

Two factors are significant. Firstly, Ney's appalling experiences in Russia when he had cajoled, threatened and pushed the freezing, starving remnants of his army back through the winter away from Moscow. It was this heroic struggle which established Ney's legendary heroism. Historian Mike Robinson: 'The courage which is spoken of so frequently is here shown in its greatest light. Here is the rearguard of the army. By his sheer force of charisma, his personality, his determination not to be beaten, he manages to defend the Grande Armée from thousands and thousands of Russian troops and doggedly walks back over a thousand miles of territory under the most extreme conditions imaginable –

seeing men dying all around him, freezing to death, dying the most horrendous deaths – and yet he's there: he is the constant, he is the centre around which the resistance of the French army is built.'

Most of those who returned owed their life to Marshal Ney. The others had died of starvation and hypothermia. Every morning on that nightmare retreat they rose from their bivouacs leaving a circle of dead around them on the ground. When at last Ney reached East Prussia, he burst open the door at General Dumas' headquarters. A 19th-century historian tells the story:

'There stood before him a man in a ragged brown coat, with a long beard, dishevelled and with his face darkened as if it had been burned, his eyes red-rimmed and glaring. Underneath his coat he wore the rags of a discoloured and filthy uniform.

"Here I am, then," the newcomer exclaimed.

"But who are you?" the general cried, alarmed.

"What – don't you recognize me? I am Marshal Ney: the rearguard of the Grande Armée!"' [14]

The second factor is simpler: on 18 June 1815, Marshal Ney had had five horses shot from under him. To lose one horse in battle must have been at the very least distressing, but to lose five in a single day must surely have been almost overwhelming.

Mike Robinson thinks Ney lost control of the battle. 'We see repeated flashes of immense frustration. One French witness sees him standing beside an English cannon beating the barrel with his sabre in rage. His uniform is in tatters; he's covered in blood. Musket-balls have gone through parts of his clothing. He's hatless. Here was a man who was in a storm of violence. He's lost his grip on what's going on. He doesn't know quite what to do. He can't see anything that's going on outside his immediate area: he can't see the land, he can't see the enemy, he can't see what's going on behind him. And in this sense you can argue that Ney has completely lost control of the battle – he's no longer able to make rational decisions, he's far too involved, he's far too close to the fighting. He just doesn't know what Napoleon wants him to do.'

What exactly is post-traumatic stress disorder?

Stephen Davies explains that the syndrome has been called various things over the centuries, and that post-traumatic stress disorder is 'a fairly recent psychiatric invention, which has a very long history'. There are three main elements:

- *Re-experiencing*, in which the person who has had the traumatic experience relives it in some way, usually in the form of nightmares or flashbacks.
- *Avoidance*, where the person avoids painful reminders or things which might remind them of the events they had gone through. This is often associated with a degree of numbing or disassociation.
- *Chronic physiological over-arousal*, in which brain and body are actually changed fundamentally by traumatic experiences. The body's normal ways of reacting to stressful events becomes changed in the long term. People become very nervous, and can be easily upset by everyday, common events.

Battlefield Detectives convened a panel of experts. Taking part were historian Mike Robinson, clinical psychologist Stephen Davies, Lt Col Ian Palmer, Head of Psychiatry for the armed services, and psychiatrist Morgan O'Connell, a former Surgeon-Commander in the Royal Navy.

Stephen Davies believes that 'Marshal Ney was not fit for

duty on the day of the battle of Waterloo. He had had a very
difficult time. He'd also shown some quite serious errors of
judgement for the previous few days – it may be that the
Battle of Waterloo is one battle too many for him. It seems
both at the beginning of the battle and towards its end that
he retreats into a situation where he takes enormous
personal risks, but at very little benefit either to his own
soldiers or to the battle.'

Morgan O'Connell also wondered whether Ney had taken
on one battle too many. But the panel was not unanimous,
Ian Palmer believing that Ney was still functioning as a
leader, but O'Connell insisting that if he did so, it was only
as a very junior leader indeed. Ian Palmer emphasized what
he considered the central question: 'The point, from a military point of view, is whether they can continue to function.
Well, he functioned, but he reverted to type.'

For Mike Robinson, the ill-fated cavalry charge was
significant. 'When he orders a limited cavalry charge by a
single brigade of heavy cavalry, and when that order is
disobeyed by the general commanding, something goes.
And not only does he commit the brigade: he commits the
entire division.'

Stephen Davies argues that Ney was retreating into the
role he knew best – that of the man of action – dealing
with the accumulation of years of combat stress by
becoming super-active and behaving in a near-suicidal
manner. 'One can never be certain, but it's my opinion
that Marshal Ney would not have been fit for duty on the
day of the Battle of Waterloo. He'd had a very difficult
time for a number of years with chronic battle stress, and
he was showing some of the signs of that quite clearly by
the time of the battle.'

But Ian Palmer was not convinced by the arguments: 'I
think he was fit. I don't think it's a psychiatrist's job to say

otherwise. He was one of those men who was used: a man for all seasons. Perhaps we should question whether Napoleon was fit to serve.'

What of Napoleon? Distracted, dilatory and indecisive, he had hardly acted as the military genius of old. Was he ill?

Mick Crumplin is unsure whether Napoleon's health could have affected the outcome. He regrets that 'one is totally at the mercy of people who cannot describe illness accurately,' but he does believe that Napoleon too was under great stress. On the day of the battle, 'Larrey let him sleep between 4 am and 6 am, and that must have been for a reason. He was subject to intermittent abdominal pain and fatigue, and he suffered with haemorrhoids which troubled him between 16 and 17 June – Larrey treated him with leeches for that. It is very likely that he had an attack of a urinary infection, making him slightly unwell on the day of Waterloo.'

It's been argued that Napoleon may have been suffering from epilepsy, and there certainly were reports that at other times in his life he had suffered from convulsions, but there is no absolute proof. Ironically, both the military geniuses with whom he is compared, Caesar and Alexander the Great, are said to have been epileptic too.

So did Napoleon's luck run out that day? The weather obviously wasn't his fault, and he did what he could to counter it. He couldn't have known about the effects of powder, smoke and humidity, pollution factors which science is only now beginning to understand. These factors contributed to his inability to see what was actually happening. Not enough was known about stress for him to have been able to predict Marshal Ney's condition, and he himself seemed to be subject to various conditions which would have been debilitating.

In the end, though, Wellington took advantage of his

good luck and Napoleon didn't do enough to counter his own bad luck. It must surely be seen as a failure to have spent all day outside a valley he could not see into, while delegating command to a man who could not see out.

Balaklava – 1854

Introduction

The Crimean War of 1853–56 was the first serious conflict to take place in a Europe recovering from the war-weary years leading up to the Battle of Waterloo in 1815 and the end of the Napoleonic Wars.

Today, the war is probably best remembered by the street names of countless cities throughout the world. There's Balaclava Street in Vancouver; Alma Terrace, San José; Raglan Road, Dublin; Inkerman Way, Huddersfield, and so on. The story behind these incongruous pairings is one that led to at least half a million unnecessary deaths.

In terms of tactics and strategy, the Crimean War began as if nothing had changed in the generation of peace which followed the day Napoleon had been packed off to exile on St Helena.

Many officers still paid for their commissions – and for their promotions, if they were unable to rise through connections alone. Rich young men would land on foreign shores accompanied by their personal strings of horses. Ladies and gentlemen would set off to watch a nearby battle bearing picnic hampers. Medical services were practically non-existent and command structures were a labyrinth of competing forces and uninterested institutions.

The war was fought between unlikely allies in what was then – and, to most people, still is today – a very obscure place. Then it was part of Russia: today, it is within the Ukraine. Located on a map, the Crimean peninsula hangs down into the Black Sea, attached by a very narrow isthmus to the rest of mainland Europe.

The British and the French had declared war on Russia in support of Turkey: in 1855, Sardinia joined in with 10,000 troops, and then Austria too threatened to take up arms. It looked set to become a war which would engulf Europe. Deaths were to be pretty evenly matched – each side probably lost a quarter of a million men – and, as in all wars until the 20th century, most of them would die through disease, not through enemy action.

In any list of pointless wars, the Crimean War comes close to the top. Within that conflict, Balaklava was a needless battle and the engagement for ever known as the Charge of the Light Brigade a pointless and disastrous waste of lives.

The Crimean War Research Society is a well-respected association of professional historians and enthusiastic amateurs who are devoted to the study of the war. The editor of its journal, *The War Correspondent,* is Major Colin Robins.

'The Crimean War ought to be over by the time anybody starts to fight at Balaklava,' he says. 'The Battle of Balaklava wasn't important. The Battle of Balaklava doesn't decide anything. It doesn't change the shape of Europe. The war was largely settled on the west coast of the Black Sea long before anybody gets to Balaklava. The Battle of Balaklava is a series of nasty little engagements in which there's a great deal of sound and fury but there's not a lot of result.'

One of those 'nasty little engagements' was what became known as the Charge of the Light Brigade, a tale of 600 men who rode through 'the jaws of Death.' What set the engagement apart was the poetry:

When can their glory fade?
O the wild charge they made!
All the world wonder'd.
Honour the charge they made!
Honour the Light Brigade,
Noble six hundred.[1]

If the battle wasn't important and the war shouldn't have started, why does either the battle or the war hold any interest at all? Colin Robins explains:

'The Crimean War is extremely important to anyone who studies military history. It represents the change from an almost mediaeval form of warfare to modern war. It actually happened during the war. At the battle of Alma, the British infantry went forward in lines of two, in scarlet tunics, led by – note, *led by* – their general officers, on horseback, with swords raised, saying – for perhaps the last time – "Follow me!", not "There you go, boys!"

'Within weeks we had trench warfare which was uncannily like the warfare of the Western Front in the First World War. We'd gone from warfare which would have been familiar to Marlborough, let alone Wellington, to modern warfare where suddenly artillery became more important. We'd done that in three weeks. Almost everything changed. The medical services, the administration, the transport and the purchase system weren't to last much longer: the system in which staff appointments were always to your sons, nephews and friends or sons and nephews of friends – all of those things changed as a result of the war. So it represents – to me anyway – the dividing line between old war and modern war, and that makes it really fascinating.'

But to non-military minds, it was the events of that morning of 24 October 1854, rather than any advance in military thinking, which still fascinate. It was a day on which the British and their allies were lined up against the might of the Russian Imperial army; and it turned out to be one of the most infamous days in British military history. By noon that day, the flower of the British cavalry would have been sacrificed in the so-called Valley of Death – the result of blundering commanders and misunderstood orders. It was a heroic and wasted charge against overwhelming odds – and it was a military irrelevance.

But there was a force in that battle, on that day, which fought against even greater odds, and which held out for far longer. That force, too, was probably about 600 strong.

They have been airbrushed out of history. They were not cavalrymen, dressed in gleaming scarlet and gold. They were not even British.

They were Turks. And their story is one which our battlefield detectives can reveal.

The Background to the War

Europe, after the fall of Napoleon, was in the midst of a quiet revolution. It was not a violent upheaval marked by wars and strife: rather, it was an all-encompassing transformation in which society itself was changing. 'There is a dynamism about 19th-century Europe that far exceeds anything previously known',[2] wrote historian Norman Davies. 'Europe vibrated with power as never before: with technical power, economic power, cultural power, intercontinental power. Its prime symbols were its engines – the locomotives, the gasworks, the electric dynamos.' He highlights the new social, commercial, industrial and technological forces, and reminds us that 'its leaders were, in the first instance, Great Britain, "the workshop of the world."'

This exciting new era, however, may not have been

apparent to everyone involved in it. A boy born in Salford in the 1850s had a life expectancy estimated by some to be as low as 17, and even in the countryside it was still startlingly low – in 1842, for example, a rural child had, on average, a mere 38 years of life to look forward to.

On the European stage, the so-called Great Powers were jostling for position. Russia wanted to expand – indeed, had been expanding for centuries. For decades it had concentrated on the Middle East, the Caucasus and the Far East. But Europe interested Moscow too – especially that part of Europe forming the Ottoman Empire. In 1783 the Russians had conquered the Crimea, and soon they were making inroads westwards towards the Danube.

Turkey – regarded by Tsar Nicholas I as 'the sick man of Europe' – was nervous. For just as Russia itself was expanding, it seemed likely that the Ottoman Empire would continue to contract. In 1829 Russian troops came within striking distance of Constantinople, and only turned back in the face of international pressure.

But Russia did not give up: it harboured designs on the narrow waters of the Bosphorus and the Dardanelles, because only if it achieved control of the Straits would it gain free access to the Mediterranean, and to the world, with its Black Sea Fleet. This very possibility worried the rest of Europe, especially Britain and France, who saw the prospect of Russian influence in the eastern Mediterranean as a threat to their interests and their empires.

In 1841, an international convention had allowed the Straits to be closed to the warships of all foreign countries – an intolerable restriction to Russia, whose powerful Black Sea Fleet would be effectively bottled up.

Meanwhile disputes about access to, and control of, holy sites in Turkish-controlled Jerusalem resulted in tensions between Russia, which supported Orthodox Christian claims; France, which supported Catholic claims and Turkey itself. The stakes were raised when Russia insisted it held a right to establish spiritual guardianship over the millions of Christians then living in the Ottoman Empire, and threatened that if this principle was not accepted it would both occupy Constantinople and split up all of Ottoman Europe – which included present-day Bulgaria, Romania, Albania, Yugoslavia and much of Greece.

This proved too much for Britain and France, and in 1853 their fleets sailed towards Turkey in a show of strength, at which Russian forces moved into Ottoman Romania on their 'protective' mission.

In October that year, Turkey had had enough and finally declared war on Russia. By itself, this should not necessarily have precipitated a major European conflict, were it not for two new factors. The first was to signal the end of a maritime principle which had stood the test of time since before the days of the Roman Empire. The second was an entirely new concept in world affairs – the power of the press and the resulting tide of public opinion.

At the end of November, the Russian fleet demonstrated its strength with manoeuvres in the Black Sea. It was this fleet which took action against the Turks at Sinope, an important naval harbour on the southern Black Sea coast some 350 miles to the east of Constantinople.

Six Russian ships sailed quietly into the harbour under the cover of fog. The Turks were taken by surprise and soundly defeated by the more powerful Russian force. But it was the nature of its power, and the scale of the defeat, which took the naval world by surprise. The Russian ships were armed with guns which fired explosive shells. Russia was not the first to use them, but hitherto they had been clumsy and particularly dangerous to use on board ships. The guns which did such damage at Sinope were an advanced design with a far greater explosive force than had hitherto been possible. Previously, cannon-fire had seldom actually sunk ships, but the injuries caused to their crews by flying splinters had rendered them incapable of fending off boarders.

The carnage which resulted from these new explosive shells, however, stunned both the world's admirals and the public abroad: all but one of the wooden Turkish ships sank, and nearly 3,000 Turks were killed. Russian casualties amounted to 37. The days of the wooden warship were at an end.

Almost immediately after Sinope, the world's navies turned to a new technology to protect themselves against explosive shells: new ships were designed, developed and put into use which were sheathed in metal – the ironclad.

The second effect of the battle of Sinope was unforeseen. The press, especially in Britain and France, took up the plight of the poor and defenceless Turks, and created a climate of public opinion in which it was suddenly not only feasible to issue a joint declaration of war but politically acceptable, not to say necessary, to do so. This new empowerment of the people through an increasingly popular and available press was to prove a two-edged sword for governments from that moment on.

The press, too, had a new tool which was to revolutionize their own ability to report the news: the 'electric telegraph' meant they would be able to receive news from the Mediterranean battlefront instantly. It was a tool which they were to prove quicker in exploiting than the military. Although at the time of the battle at Balaklava the nearest telegraph connection was in Belgrade, it was only a matter of months before the new-fangled professional 'war correspondent' was able to rely on a connection from the Crimea itself.

The War Begins

And so it was that in January 1854 the allied fleets of Great Britain and France entered the Black Sea, and soon British troops were being embarked for war. On 14 February, thousands of well-wishers packed Trafalgar Square in London to wave off the Coldstream Guards as they marched down the Strand on their way to board the trains which would take them to Southampton and a passage by sea to the staging-post of Malta and beyond. On 11 March the British Baltic fleet sailed to patrol Russia's northern waters. Russia broke off all relationships with Britain and France, and on 28 March the Allies declared war.

By now the British and French forces were in Turkey, and already dying of cholera.

Although Britain's initial objective had been the defence of Constantinople, the idea of moving on to the Crimea, in order to neutralize the Russian fleet by capturing the fortress and harbour at Sevastopol, had been outlined by the Prime Minister, the Duke of Newcastle, to the Commander-in-Chief, Lord Raglan, even before the troops set sail.

In fact, to many in the British expeditionary force, moving on from the vicinity of Constantinople must have seemed a relief. Historian John Sweetman describes the conditions: 'Arriving at Gallipoli on 8 April, they found a distinct lack of accommodation and food. The French had beaten them to the best areas. By the end of May some 18,000 British and 22,000 French troops were crowded around this tiny town, condemned by the disillusioned as "rickety, dirty and dilapidated [with] abominable collections of stagnant filth, reeking with unbearable odours." To their relief, early in June most of the British sailed north to Constantinople and Scutari – but there conditions were, disappointingly, no better, and extreme heat added to the troops' discomfort. Many took solace in alcohol: one night, 2,400 British drunks were reported.'[3]

Soon the Allies moved north inside the Black Sea to Varna, where conditions were just as bad and the means to combat them just as inadequate. By now, Russia had withdrawn from the territory it had earlier invaded, and there seemed to be no reason why the Allies should persist. But the genie of public opinion was out of its bottle, and reacting to the views of public opinion had become politically expedient, just as they would when British and American forces sped into Afghanistan in the 21st century: they couldn't come home without at least the appearance of a fight.

At dawn on 14 September, the exhausted and depleted Allies dropped anchor on the western side of the Crimea, near Eupatoria, in the aptly-named Calamita Bay. It took them all of five days to get ashore.

A week later they arrived outside the small port of Balaklava. They had circled round Sevastopol in order to attack the Russian defenders from the south. On the way, they had suffered from exhaustion, illness and – for the first time – battle: they had defeated a Russian army which had tried to stop them at the Alma River, suffering more than 350 deaths. The French and the British set up siege lines on the heights above Sevastopol, but took control of separate nearby ports, the British occupying the tiny harbour town of Balaclava. They would be there for two years; but only four weeks were to elapse before the events which would make the name of their small harbour reverberate throughout the world.

To protect the Allies from a Russian flanking movement, on the hills above the harbour, the Turks constructed defensive redoubts – fragile earthworks on knolls rising above a low ridge. The ridge lay between two valleys, up one of which the Light Brigade was later to charge.

By now the war was more than six months old. The bulk of the Russian army had left Sevastopol just before the British and French arrived, but continued to pose a threat to the Allies – the possibility that they might get between the besieging forces outside the city and the harbour. Colin Robins explains: 'Balaklava was extremely important for its ready-made, working harbour, albeit very, very small and long and narrow. It was chosen by Raglan as the British base, and from then on all the British supplies came in through that harbour. For the first year or more, the only real base was Balaklava harbour.' If the Russians were to cut the British off from their supply chain – or, even worse, capture Balaklava itself – it would be a disaster for the Allies.

The Leaders

The time for battle was fast approaching. The British at Balaklava numbered some 13,500 men – of whom 1,500 or so were cavalry. Together with their French and Turkish allies, they numbered perhaps 20,000 men with 40 or so guns.

The leaders – on the British side, at least – were an unlikely group. Lord Raglan had first achieved fame as the Duke of Wellington's military secretary in the Peninsular War: he was eventually to become one of the Duke's right-hand men. At the Battle of Waterloo, while riding shoulder-to-shoulder with Wellington, Raglan had been hit by a shot and lost his right arm. Since Waterloo he had been passed over for the supreme command but now, at the age of 66, he was preferred to the other possible candidates because, it is said, the other candidates were all over 70 years old, and 'youth was on his side'. He had never commanded in battle before.

Raglan's cavalry division was led by the Earl of Lucan. Aged 58, Lucan was obsessed with discipline and with uniforms. Ruthless and humourless, he wanted his men to look the part and play the part. Mark Adkin, in his account of the battle, *The Charge*, describes Lucan as 'harsh, bad-tempered, arrogant, vindictive and unpopular', which seems pretty all-encompassing until he continues by adding that Lucan was also 'obsessional, seemingly unable to distinguish between the trivial and the important. Parades, inspections and drills followed one another in a remorseless, unending cycle.'

Lucan's force was divided into two brigades of horse, the Heavy Division and the Light Division. The latter was commanded by his brother-in-law – whom he detested – the Earl of Cardigan.

Cardigan, who had bought his way into – and up – the chain of command, was also a strict disciplinarian; a man who, earlier in his career, had been deemed unfit to command. At 57, he was handsome, brave and subject to rapid mood changes, especially if he felt he was being slighted. He always believed he was right. He kept his own yacht in Balaklava harbour, to which he repaired for a good night's sleep leaving his fellow-officers and troops in the field.

The battle was to be fought against the Russians under Prince Menshikov. He controlled an army of 65,000, of whom 25,000 men and 78 guns were available at Balaklava.

The Turks landed 7,000 men with the Allies. They were commanded by General Omar Pasha, who had been born a Christian – Michael Lattas – in Croatia and had served in the Austrian army before converting to Islam and joining the Turkish army in the 1830s. At Balaklava they had just over a thousand men in the field.

The Battle
The events of that morning of 25 October can be simply told. There were four distinct phases.

- At dawn, the Russians launched their attack against the rudimentary earthworks – the redoubts – on the heights

The Charge of the Light Brigade

Top: Military historian and battlefield guide Richard Rutherford-Moore walks across the Valley of Death – now a vineyard. Redoubt number one would have been in the top right-hand corner, the Russian battery to the left.
Above: Among the enormous amount of World War Two debris littering the Balaklava battlefield, metal detectorist Simon Richardson finally discovered grapeshot on Canrobert's Hill.

Top: Lorraine McEwan (Glasgow University) and field technician Leia Meistrup-Larsen surveying at Balaklava for Battlefield Detectives. Above: Our re-enactment of the Turkish redoubt. The three cameramen include producer Jeremy Freeston (right).

The Battle of the Little Bighorn

Joe Medicine Crow, grandson of Custer's Crow Indian scout White Man Runs, knew many who had taken part in the battle.

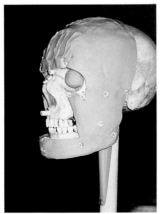

Top: Douglas D Scott, (left) with a Henry Repeater rifle, as used by many Indians, and Steve Aldeson (right) with a Springfield Carbine, as used by the Cavalry, compared the relative speed of fire of each weapon. Douglas fired thirteen shots in the time it took Steve to fire four.
Above: Identifying the dead: facial reconstruction expert Betty Pat Gatcliff produced this bust from a Little Bighorn skull cast. Her evidence helped to identify the remains as those of farrier Vincent Charley.

The pioneers of battlefield archaeology, Richard A
Fox and Douglas D Scott, at the Little Bighorn National Monument.
Inset: Just one cartridge case can help build a picture of the battle.

Each year, the Battle of Little Bighorn is re-enacted by descendants of
both sides of the original battle.

Gallipoli

Top: Geologist Peter Doyle at the site of the British landings.
Above: North Beach, photographed after the August offensive. In the foreground are the tents of No. 1 Australian Stationary Hospital.

Top: Anzac Cove looking south, probably taken on 25 April. Men were safely ashore, but were still easy targets for enemy guns.
Above: Turkish historian Ken Çelik at the site of a Turkish trench.

Top: Peter Doyle in a replica Turkish trench wearing a solar topee – helmets as we know them were not introduced until later in the war.
Above: The original caption in the Illustrated War News reads, with misplaced jollity: 'British troops "ditch" sleeping in "rest troughs"'.

above Balaklava. After between one and two hours, the Turks were driven back from Redoubt No. 1 – there were six redoubts, although only the first four were occupied – just as Lord Raglan arrived at his vantage-point on the Sapoune Ridge, three miles to the west.

- Sir Colin Campbell's 93rd Highlanders, together with the Turks, formed a defensive line behind a bank, in the face of the Russian advance. They were now the only troops between the Russians and the harbour of Balaklava, a mile or so downhill to the south. The Russians were beaten off by musket-fire in a defence immortalized by *The Times* correspondent William Howard Russell as 'a thin red streak, tipped with a line of steel' the ringing phrase later to be remembered as 'the thin red line.'

- As a second Russian cavalry force approached, the British cavalry's Heavy Brigade moved in and – charging uphill – drove them off. Meanwhile the Russians were removing the British guns which had earlier been abandoned at the redoubts.

- Lord Raglan sent an order to the cavalry to protect the guns. The officer who carried the order down to the field, Captain Nolan, had an acrimonious conversation there with Lord Lucan. The cavalry then charged into the wrong – northern – valley, which was lined on both sides and at its head by Russian artillery. The Heavy Brigade turned back, but the Light Brigade charged right down the north valley to engage the Russian battery. Then they charged back again. As Lord Raglan, his staff and the correspondent from *The Times* watched, more than 100 men of the Light Brigade died.

Nothing had been achieved by the Light Brigade's sacrifice. 'Someone,' wrote the poet Tennyson, 'had blundered'. But who?

The 'thin red line' had, indeed, managed to hold off the

Russians. The port of Balaklava, and the entire Crimean campaign, had been saved. But by whom?

The Turks

The Turkish army was one of the oldest standing armies in Europe, and very many of its members were not Turkish at all: they came from all over the Ottoman world. In 1854 Turkey was suffering from very high inflation, and the army's budget was over-stretched, which meant they were forced to rely on poor arms, few uniforms and scant supplies. The western authorities had a very low opinion of their capabilities. The British chargé d'affaires in Constantinople, Colonel Hugh Rose, described them as 'vicious, corrupt, lethargic and timid.'

Dr Feroze Yasamee, Director of Middle East Studies at the University of Manchester, puts the conditions in which the Turkish troops were living into perspective: 'They weren't Turkish regulars; they were militia from North Africa. The previous three or four weeks, the total ration issue that they had been given to eat was two biscuits, and they'd [been] living off what they could find lying around on the ground. There wasn't much left for the poor Turks – they were starving, ill-equipped, under-appreciated – and they're under attack.'

Major Colin Robins of the Crimean War Research Society believes that for years historians have ignored and misunderstood the role of the Turkish army at the Battle of Balaklava. 'The Turks managed to keep firing and managed to hold out for about an hour against the full armed might of one-third of the Russian army, which is all anybody could expect of gunners under those circumstances,' he says. 'At Redoubt No. 1 they fought very bravely and resolutely, and did themselves great credit.'

There are many more who also credit the Turks with an hour-long stand against overwhelming numbers of Russians, and who believe part of the reason why history has misjudged the Turks is because the British didn't seem to be in any hurry to help their allies.

Colin Robins is sure not only that history has denied the Turks the honour due to them, but that the British were guilty of not coming to their support during the first stage of the battle. 'In my view the contribution by those Ottoman troops in Redoubt No.1 on Canrobert's Hill was absolutely vital,' he says. 'Without it, there would not have been time for the defences of Balaklava to be assembled behind them. A grave injustice has been done to the Turks who fought at Balaklava. They fought very resolutely against overwhelming odds without any kind of proper support from the British.'

When the Allied commander-in-chief, with his staff officers and *The Times* correspondent in tow, finally reached their position above the battlefield – overlooking the plain, the valleys and the ridge – the engagement between the Turks and the Russians at Redoubt No. 1 was nearly at an end. Major Robins explains: 'Because Raglan was so late – and so were people like William Howard Russell – in arriving at the viewpoint, they only saw the Turks withdrawing. What he sees, and what the people with him see, is a dysfunctional army just legging it.' They looked through their spy-glasses at people scurrying down the hillside away from the Russians. Colin Robins points out that 'Balaklava was in complete turmoil. The ships there really did think the Russians were going to get through. There was a frantic effort to try and get those ships out of harbour, and if the Turks had not first of all delayed the Russian assault with their gallant defence of Redoubt No. 1, I think there's quite a good chance that the Russians might well have got through.'

Such was the ingrained contempt in which the Turks were held that those who were there didn't for a moment ask themselves just why the Turks were withdrawing. Fanny

Duberley, wife of a British officer, who had followed her husband to the wars, recorded in her Balaklava journal: 'The road was almost blocked up with flying Turks, some running hard, vociferating, "Ship, Johnny! Ship, Johnny!" while others came along laden with pots, kettles, arms and plunder of every description, chiefly old bottles, for which the Turks appear to have a great appreciation.'

The Times, when the first full reports of the battle arrived in London, grudgingly allowed that the Turks had once shown bravery, but that on this occasion they had fled from their defences and 'seem to have abandoned them at once in some unaccountable panic.'[4]

A few days later, William Howard Russell's full report was even more damning. He describes the scene after the Russians had overwhelmed the first redoubt: 'The enemy advanced his cavalry rapidly. To our inexpressible disgust we saw the Turks in Redoubt No. 2 fly at their approach. They ran in scattered groups towards Redoubt No. 3, and towards Balaclava, but the horse-hoof of the Cossacks was too quick for them, and sword and lance were busily plied among the retreating band... Again the solid column of cavalry opens like a fan, and resolves itself into the 'long spray' of skirmishers. It laps the flying Turks, steel flashes in the air, and down go the poor Muslim quivering on the plain, split through the fez and musket-guard to the chin and breastplate. There is no support for them...'[5]

The small Turkish force was certainly under attack – by a formidable foe. Dr Yasamee calculates: 'A rough appreciation of the figures shows that perhaps 5,000 to 6,000 Russian troops were making a beeline straight for Redoubt No. 1, where about 500 or 600 Turks were defending – which they continued to do from about 5.30 am until Lord Raglan finally got up to his viewpoint and looked out across the valley.'

So the famous 'noble six hundred' of the Light Brigade weren't the only group to face overwhelming odds that day. But the Turks' contribution was ignored. Dr Yasamee: 'Raglan, when he came to write his report, and Russell when he came to write his despatch, didn't want to point out that they'd taken three hours to get to the battle, and so those three hours got truncated down to a few minutes. Those redoubts weren't there to be defended – they were to draw a line in the sand and say, "You can't come past here without a fight." They were to give advanced warning of a Russian advance.

'In fact, the Turks had done their job, and done it extremely well.'

The evidence that the Turks were either ignored or slandered at the battle of Balaklava seems clear. Feroze Yasamee graphically describes what it must have been like: 'Hell on earth. They were all North African, so they were used to sunny weather and a warm climate. Here they were, dumped in the autumn of a particularly miserable climate. It was cold, it was wet and they weren't used to it. They hadn't been fed, there was no firewood, they were starving, they were freezing, and then they were under fire – they were under heavy fire – from two different positions. They'd been flanked and they had an advance coming straight at them.'

In the Valley
Battlefield Detectives went to the Crimea.

Richard Rutherford-Moore, battlefield guide and military historian, has made 112 visits to the site of Balaklava. 'I still consider it a very special place,' he says. 'The loss of life here was terrific. Sometimes it brings up deep emotions – you've just got to try and come to terms with them.'

One of the problems all battlefield archaeologists have to face is the shortage of accurate maps. In the case of the

Crimea, the problem had been compounded because it was a closed military area, home of the Soviet Black Sea Fleet; it was off limits to all foreigners and even many Russians. The majority of the historians who had written about the Battle of Balaklava had never visited the site. But now, with the opening-up of the Ukraine, it is possible for detailed archaeological research to be carried out.

Dr Phil Freeman, of the Department of Archaeology at the University of Liverpool, has a particular interest in the archaeology of battlefields, and in Roman imperialism. When he visited the Crimea in 1998, he became fascinated in what archaeology might be able to reveal about the war. Returning in 2002, he's concentrating on developing an accurate map.

Another team – from the Institute of Classical Archaeology at the University of Texas – is excavating nearby. This part of the Crimea is the best-preserved example of the classical countryside on earth, where many of the stone farmhouses and much of the dense grid of country lanes still exist. It was the bread-basket of the ancient Greek world – the core of our democracy. The Institute has NASA funding to use multi-spectral digital data, and satellite and space shuttle imagery, together with aerial photography, to investigate this archaeological realm. With the aid of their sophisticated geographic information systems, there's a chance to answer some of the riddles about the battle.

Dr Freeman, together with consultant metal-detectorist Simon Richardson, hopes to create an accurate map of the Turkish defence site at Redoubt No. 1.

'We're trying to do a topographic survey,' he explained. 'We're going to map the hilltop with all the features and then we can start playing around with the data. We can stretch the information to accentuate the differences, because one of the tendencies of the eye as you're looking across the ground is to smooth it out, and with the vegetation obscuring things it can give a wrong impression.'

But on the site there's a problem.

Phil explains: 'We're getting things like clips. Simon's found shells, webbing, clothing lying around – a piece of cannon shell. There's a strap with a hanger on it – a piece of leather attached for a water bottle or a gas mask. There are bits of human up here as well – bones. But it's all World War Two.' And Phil was angry – he discovered that people had been hacking into the ground, without respect for either the dead or the history, to find souvenirs to sell on the black market.

He believes that 'by carefully mapping the site in some detail, we should get a fairly good idea of patterns and shapes, contours and alignments, which will allow us to filter out the Second World War material from the mid-19th-century material.'

Richard Rutherford-Moore visited the location of the first action of that October morning: the bombardment by the Russians of the 600 or so Turks guarding Redoubt No. 1. At Kamara, the Russians assembled more than two dozen heavy guns and about 3,500 infantry.

At 6 am they opened fire on the Turks in a continuous cannonade.

'Once all the guns had got the range, it would then simply have been an act of just sitting there and sticking it out. It would have been very easy for these Turks – these hungry, emaciated, probably frightened soldiers – to simply run away. Well, they didn't do that. Towards the end of the bombardment the battery here would be a wreck: there would be dead and wounded soldiers, pieces of soldiers lying all over the place, broken artillery gear – and this is exactly what the Russian artillery intended – to clear the way for the infantry. For an hour they had endured this terrible bombardment of shot and shell raining down on their position.'

For over an hour, then, the Russians shelled the Turks. And then they went in: about 1,200 infantry scrambled up Canrobert's Hill towards the redoubt.

By the time the Russians arrived at the crude defence work, those Turks who could do so would have fled. The Russians literally tossed many of the survivors over the edge of the redoubt.

The Turks had lost an enormous number of men in their gallant delaying action. Colin Robins: 'There is no doubt in my mind that a grave injustice has been done to the Turks who fought at Balaklava. They did fight very resolutely against overwhelming odds without any sort of support from the British, because Raglan was so late.'

Although most of the official reports, histories and private letters refer to the Turks as cowards (or 'confounded cowards', according to a letter by Lieutenant-Colonel Calthorpe, which describes them as having run 'as fast as their legs could carry them towards the town'), there were a few with a better understanding. Historian Mark Adkin quotes Trumpet Sergeant Major Smith's recollection: 'As the last of them came over the parapet, I noticed the Russians were hard at their heels... As they gained the plain, a number of Cossacks swept round the foot of the hill, killing and wounding many of them. Some of them, being unarmed, raised their hands imploringly, but it was only to have them severed from their bodies... had a dozen or two of us been sent out, numbers of these poor fellows might have been saved.'[6]

Dr Phil Freeman, despite the problems of the Second World War debris, feels that his and Simon Richardson's surveying work has been successful. 'When we arrived at the hill we had a number of objectives in mind,' he says. 'We wanted to do a topographic survey; we wanted to do a metal detector search and bring the two sets of data together, and we've managed to achieve it. We've been able to map most of the earthworks, and in the process have been able to filter out some of the Crimean material from the Second World War. Simon has been pulling his hair out trying to make sense of it, and he's had some success.'

On the southern side of Canrobert's Hill, Simon found 21 large, spherical projectiles close together which probably originated as canister shot. This possibly indicates that Russian skirmishers attacked from the southern side of the hill – to the rear of the redoubt.

'When we get out of the field, all the survey data that we've taken will be loaded into a computer with a software package and we'll produce a 3D image of the hilltop. In addition to that, we can also then plot in the finds that we've had from the metal detector survey and we can start to think about what it all means. I hope at least that we've created a body of data and a line of interpretation which scholars of the Crimean War campaign could use in the future.'

The First Encounter

Those Turks who could do so retreated towards Balaklava; and, as they did so, their compatriots who had been left in the three other redoubts nearby decided that discretion was the better part of valour. But this was not to be the end of their contribution to the battle. Although they had already lost more men than the Light Brigade was to lose, many of them now joined the defence being organized by Brigadier Sir Colin Campbell with his 93rd Highlanders and two battalions of Turks. They were the last obstacle to a Russian swoop on the port of Balaklava, and disaster for the British.

Richard Rutherford-Moore investigated. 'Their commander

fully understood the power of the infantry rifle,' he says. 'This position commands a great field of fire.' This was to be the engagement which became famous as the 'thin red line'.

The Russian cavalry had arrived.

'The Russians', wrote Russell in *The Times*, 'drew breath for a moment, and then in one grand line dashed at the Highlanders. The ground flies beneath their horses' feet – gathering speed at every stride, they dash on towards that thin red streak topped with a line of steel.'

Russell had dismissed the Turkish contribution to this engagement, but Rutherford-Moore reminds us that Sir Colin already had two battalions of Turks. Any Turk being pursued down the hill by the dreaded Cossack troops would head towards Balaklava, but would find himself running towards Sir Colin's line. Rutherford-Moore: 'No doubt if they saw their own countrymen there, still standing and willing to fight, it would have been an incentive to join them and perhaps try to get a little revenge for what had happened to them.'

Historian John Sweetman estimates that there were 700 British and some 1,000 Turks in this encounter. Sir Colin Campbell deployed his men in two ranks rather than the more conventional square and, just as Wellington had done with his troops at Waterloo, concealed them on a reverse slope. He reminded his men: 'Men, remember; there is no retreat from here, men! You must die where you stand!' They did not retreat, but fired off a volley at the charging Russians who, taken by surprise, faltered, promptly received a second volley – and retired in disorder.

Raglan, who had been watching the battle from his position on the Sapoune Ridge, now ordered his heavy cavalry to attack. Led by Brigadier General the Honourable Sir James Scarlett, the Heavy Brigade moved towards the Russian cavalry. When the two forces were only 100 yards apart, the Russians again paused, allowing the British to crash into a stationary target. Historian John Sweetman summarized the result: 'The whole action from the time that Scarlett started his charge to the enemy retreat took a mere eight minutes. It cost the Heavy Brigade 78 casualties; the Russians suffered 270... the inner defences of Balaklava remained intact. A watching French general declared, "The victory of the Heavy Brigade was the most glorious thing I ever saw."'[7]

The View from the Heights

What people actually saw is crucial to any understanding of what happened at Balaklava.

We know that the British could see the Turks. But what could Lord Raglan see of the battlefield? And – especially – what could the British cavalry down in the valleys see of the Russians and their guns?

The next area our detectives would investigate was the Sapoune Ridge on the Chersonese Uplands. It was from these heights that Raglan's party gained their insight into the battle, and it was from here that the orders were despatched.

Jessica Trelogan from the Texas team is conducting the first inch-by-inch survey of the area and *Battlefield Detectives* arranged for her to investigate both Lord Raglan's position overlooking the battlefield, and the position at which those bickering brothers-in-law Lucan and Cardigan received their final, fateful order.

Raglan had been watching events unfold from on high. He had become impatient – as well he might – at the slow progress of his infantry, who still had not arrived on the scene. What we know he could see happening was the removal of the captured guns by the Russians from the redoubts they had seized earlier. To Lord Raglan, the removal of guns was more than an inconvenience – it was a question of honour.

His own personal hero, the Duke of Wellington, would

not have countenanced such a thing. He dictated a fateful order to his senior staff officer.

'Lord Raglan wishes the cavalry to advance rapidly to the front – follow the enemy and try to prevent the enemy carrying away the guns – troop artillery may accompany – French cavalry is on your left. Immediate.'

It was, to say the least, ambiguous. Rather than sending the junior duty officer, Raglan ordered another man nearby, Captain Lewis Nolan of the 15th Hussars, to deliver the message to the plain below. As he left, Raglan called out to Nolan his second ambiguous order: 'Tell Lord Lucan the cavalry is to attack immediately'.

Nolan was probably the best horseman on those heights that day, and it may well have been this skill which led Lord Raglan to choose him to carry his order – riding down the precipitous slopes at speed was no easy task. But whatever the motive, it was to have serious consequences.

Nolan was more than just a dashing young cavalry officer – he was a cavalry tactician and had written books on the subject. He had a quasi-independent role at Balaklava, having been suggested for service to Lord Raglan by the Secretary of War, no less. Nolan was a fervent believer in the power and strength of the cavalry, and in their ability to conquer any foe. He was brave and did not suffer fools gladly. It hardly needs adding that he and the Lords Lucan and Cardigan all regarded each other with unswerving contempt. As he watched the dithering and inaction from his position on the heights, a fellow-officer assessment was that Nolan, 'under the stress of some great excitement had lost self-command'.

Some seven or eight or so minutes later, Lord Lucan took delivery of the order. It was an order he found pretty baffling. Which front – and which guns? Lucan began to ask for an explanation, but Nolan cut short any argument.

'Lord Raglan's orders are that the cavalry are to attack

immediately,' he stated peremptorily – and even insolently, according to all witnesses.

'Attack, sir? Attack what? What guns?'

'There, my Lord, is your enemy; there are the guns.' And Nolan waved his arm. But at what?

In the summer of 2002, Jessica Trelogan went to the Sapoune Ridge with Richard Rutherford-Moore. The first task was to pinpoint their own position. Rutherford-Moore was armed with an old map, a compass and photographs which had been taken by Roger Fenton in 1855. Jessica Trelogan had satellite imagery, and her laptop loaded with a sophisticated geographic information system. By comparing the old photo graph with their position – looking in particular for rocks in the foreground and the Woronzov Road snaking to the north-west towards Sevastopol – and by checking with satellite imagery, they were able to fix Lord Raglan's position precisely.

Rutherford-Moore, not quite trusting computers, also took compass bearings from the two old Genoese Towers still visible above Balaklava, just as they had been in 1854. Both agreed they had achieved a good match, but Jessica Trelogan's computer had more to offer than the compass: 'I think it would be really neat to see what this would have looked like without trees in it. You know we can't do anything about it now, but we can take it virtually… we can look at the computer, do a little line-of-sight analysis and see if they would have been able to have a clear view through here.'

What Trelogan could do was to recreate the view Lord Raglan would have had on the morning of 25 October 1854.

Then they repeated the exercise down below the ridge, by Redoubt No. 5, where the same procedures were used to establish the positions where Lord Lucan and Lord Cardigan had received the message to charge.

Back at Jessica's research centre, she entered all the infor-mation she had gathered into the system. She was able to demonstrate that from where he stood, Raglan would have enjoyed a commanding view of the battlefield, and in particular would have been able to see all six redoubts. He would have been able to see the Turks being bundled out of Redoubt No. 1; he would have been able to see the Russians taking his precious guns; he would have been able to see the Russians in the north valley. Rutherford-Moore was in no doubt that Raglan had been in the right place: 'It's a pretty good place to stand to see this chain of redoubts.' He likened the commander-in-chief's position to 'the royal box in the opera house: we could see this battlefield unfolding beneath us.'

The View from Below

But if Raglan could see what was going on, what about Lords Lucan and Cardigan, waiting down near Redoubt No. 5, and their cavalry? Rutherford-Moore and Jessica Trelogan discovered that the view would have been blocked in several directions. The visibility at Redoubt No. 5 was blocked in three places. Would Lucan and Cardigan have been able to see the gun battery at the end of the north valley – the eventual target of the Charge of the Light Brigade?

Jessica Trelogan's software provided an unequivocal answer. Richard Rutherford-Moore: 'Could we see it from there? No.'

The British down in the valley would have been unable to see the Russian guns. 'In terms of battlefield administration it would be a very, very bad place for a commander to stand anywhere in this area, because all he could see in front of him is nothing but those places that have already fallen to the enemy – he can see those quite clearly.'

Has the Texan technology helped to confirm what the battlefield commanders could see? Rutherford-Moore: 'This science has actually confirmed everything I always thought about this part of the Battle of Balaclava – in that you can't see where you're going. You can point to where you think a man ought to be going, but you can't see exactly where he is. And the people that you're going to send there can't see it either. The machine is telling us that he couldn't see the target that they went after. It's also confirmed that anywhere round Redoubt No. 5, where the conversation traditionally took place, the visibility was very, very poor.'

Was Lord Raglan's written message sufficient for Lord Lucan to understand what was meant? Rutherford-Moore again: 'It would have to be a verbal exchange, I think, to clarify what this man up here [Lord Raglan] is trying to get across to this man down there [Lord Lucan]. And we know that the only man to offer a verbal explanation [Nolan] was the man who despised Lord Lucan.'

So what was the value of this experiment in battlefield detection? Richard Rutherford-Moore was impressed with Jessica Trelogan's technology: 'It's a wonderful machine – it's telling us that the commanders in the field are standing in the worst possible places to see the enemy. It's also telling us that when an order came down here and was delivered by Captain Nolan to Lord Lucan, he couldn't point at the target because you can't see it from anywhere in this position. However, the man at the top of the hill could see most of everything: any confusion that ensued lay in the passage of orders. It's clear to see why it happened – they're talking about somebody they can't actually see.'

Captain Nolan's wave, then, could only have been an indication of a general direction – not specific advice about where the guns actually were.

'It's also telling us that the troops who attacked this battery, the Light Brigade, moving along this line, couldn't see it when they started off: in fact, they couldn't see it until they were pretty close to it.

'It's a remarkable piece of technology because it's

confirmed everything I've always thought about the evolutions of this part of the Battle of Balaclava. Having tramped over the area for ten years and made over 112 visits, we've now confirmed this!'

What, though, of the charge itself? Richard Rutherford-Moore saddled up and rode though the North Valley, taking the route the Light Brigade followed.

The Charge of the Light Brigade

> 'Forward, the Light Brigade!'
> Was there a man dismay'd?

'A very evocative place to ride', said Rutherford-Moore. 'A very beautiful spot. But at the time of the battle, the troopers and the horses would have had much more to think about than the beauty. There were exploding shells; they were under fire, cannonballs bouncing through the ranks. Increasingly they came under Russian fire, but they were trying to keep together, above all to keep the formation, keep their measured pace, to do it by the drill book. ' Cardigan would have no suggestion of an increase in pace.

> Not tho' the soldier knew
> Some one had blunder'd.

It must have been a terrible experience both for men and for horses: some men had been with their horses a long time.

The projectiles fired by the Russian guns caused ghastly wounds in flesh and bone. If a horse were struck by a cannonball, it would be literally blown to pieces. There was devastation in the ranks of the Light Brigade.

Theirs not to make reply,
Theirs not to reason why,
Theirs but to do and die:

Rutherford-Moore: 'It's a silly thing to do to say you have
to ignore it – you obviously can't ignore it – but you had to
come to terms with the fact that the target is still many
metres away: it's got to be reached and it's got to be reached
in a military formation.'

Into the valley of Death
Rode the six hundred.

It was a massacre.

Lord Raglan never commanded troops again.

The pointless sacrifice of the 600 came to embody all that
was glorious and heroic about the cavalry and the British Army.

But was the Light Brigade annihilated as popular legend
suggests?

Crimean War enthusiast Ken Horton, who sadly has died
since filming *Battlefield Detectives*, had spent nearly 30 years
tracking down what actually happened to the men of the
charge. He had scoured the pension records and the
gazetteers of Queen Victoria's army to track down the individual cavalrymen who took part.

'I was fortunate,' he explained. 'My hobby was family history,
and I use my expertise in trying to locate the men of the Light
Brigade, searching the records, births, marriages and deaths –
deaths in particular – and in the local cemeteries where they
may have been buried. I did a lot of writing, a lot of searching
official records – and located most of the names I wanted.'

He came up with a few surprises. He believed that as many
as 670 people took part in the charge – and that more than
450 of those survived.

'There were 102 killed outright, and 56 were taken prisoner, of whom about half died in captivity. About 450 of those original men did return to the United Kingdom.'

For Ken Horton, his hobby as a battlefield detective had turned into a labour of love. Ken had personally visited more than 300 graves. Often, he discovered graves which no one cares for any more, but because Ken has grown to know each individual life, and because he had recorded all his information over the years, he felt he knew them all and his work allowed others to know those long-dead human beings too.

The Battle of Balaklava was a waste of young men's lives. But although even one life is too many to lose in such circumstances, it's worth remembering that more people from the Ottoman Empire died defying – or at least delaying – the Russian attack on Balaklava. And what was their reward?

Richard Rutherford-Moore tells the distressing story: 'The Turkish troops who survived were then withdrawn back to Balaklava. They were used to haul supplies up from Balaclava up the supply road and in carrying wounded soldiers back to the transport vessels. It wasn't a very nice reward after what they'd done, and the winter saw the end of them. By the end of that winter there were probably none left: they died along with the horses which survived the Charge of the Light Brigade. Their bones are still underneath that long road that climbs up the mountain. It was a miserable end.'

The French General Bosquet, watching the Light Brigade's charge into the valley murmured: '*C'est magnifique, mais ce n'est pas la guerre*' – 'It's magnificent, but it is not war.'

The British, of course, have a heroic poem to honour their dead. But why do we still venerate those 600? Might it be because it helps to avoid having to admit that the British imperial army owed its survival to the troops of the Ottoman Empire?

The Turks have nothing to remember it by.

People will remember the Charge of the Light Brigade for what they think it is. But it is unlikely they will remember the Turkish flesh and blood which was sacrificed on that heroic day.

The Battle of the
Little Bighorn – 1876

Introduction

On 25 June 1876, about 600 men of the United States 7th Cavalry Regiment met a combined force of about 1,500 Lakota Sioux and Cheyenne Indians. The battle on that sultry afternoon lasted for two hours at the most.

Almost half of those cavalrymen were killed, including every single one of the 210 people in Colonel George Custer's battalion. The Indians escaped to the south, having lost an estimated 50 warriors.

The Battle of the Little Bighorn took place in what is now southern Montana, in the Black Hills overlooking the Little Bighorn river. The Black Hills were regarded as sacred by the Sioux.

It is possibly the most famous conflict ever to have taken place on American soil, probably the most controversial and certainly one of the most tragic battles in American history. The events surrounding the battle, the armies who took part, the fame and charisma of the leaders on each side and the mystery surrounding the eventual outcome have secured it a place in the American soul.

The largest American Indian force ever to have been assembled had taken on the 7th Cavalry. And the Indians won.

It was the last great battle between the American Army

and the Indians, and marked a turning-point between those fighting to retain their traditional way of life and the new white forces intent on expanding their empire. The times were changing: the American nation was rapidly expanding to take control of all the lands from coast to coast, the last remaining herds of buffalo were fast dwindling and, on the very day of the battle, a young Scots inventor was giving the first public demonstration, in Cincinnati, of his latest invention – a device called the telephone.

The outcome of the Battle of the Little Bighorn stunned a confident and proud nation just at the moment it was celebrating the hundredth anniversary of independence.

It was a tragic, if simple tale, and for many years it went something like this:

Lieutenant Colonel George Armstrong Custer, a dashing young cavalry officer, an impetuous and popular veteran of the Civil War, had been dispatched in command of the 7th Cavalry to subdue a growing rebellion by the Sioux and Cheyenne under the leadership of Sitting Bull and Crazy Horse. Deep in the isolated Black Hills of the Northern Plains, Custer and his men were surprised by a powerful and savage enemy armed with bow and arrows, lances, tomahawks and clubs. Thousands attacked the column of weary men and horses. The troops were thrown on the defensive and desperately fought their way uphill to form a redoubt. A heroic defence took place on Custer Hill as the Colonel and his men fought to the death against an overwhelming foe. They fought to the last man, to the final bullet, to the last remaining cartridge. But they were annihilated, and Custer himself was the last to die, falling to the ground among the corpses of his men.

For more than a hundred years, this battle – better known to many as 'Custer's Last Stand' – reverberated through the Western world as a tale of pure and unadulterated heroism.

It was a story of legendary defiance against seemingly impossible odds. Within a few years 'Custer's Last Stand' became an iconic symbol of the American West, featuring in everything from Buffalo Bill's *Wild West Show* of 1883 to Errol Flynn's portrayal in *They Died With Their Boots On* in 1941. An 1884 painting of the battle by Cassily Adams – which shows Custer standing almost alone among the bodies of his comrades while befeathered braves close in – was distributed as a print with a first edition of some 15,000 copies. Since then, more than a million copies have been sold.

But though the myth has endured, so have the questions:

- If everyone died, how does anyone know – how does anyone *really* know – what happened?
- Were they really wiped out by thousands of savages as they stood together on the hill-top now known both as Last Stand Hill and as Custer Hill?
- Why were they scalped and mutilated: and above all, did they hold their heads up high, fighting until they ran out of ammunition before succumbing to a hero's end?

Over the last two decades, the battlefield detectives have been finding out. They have applied the techniques of the forensic anthropologist, the archaeologist, the psychologist and the metallurgist to the mystery of the Battle of the Little Bighorn. And a completely different picture is emerging of what happened on that sweltering hot June day of 1876. The myths have begun to crumble.

The men who led the way in this new research, the instigators of much of the battlefield detective work at Little Bighorn, are American archaeologists Richard Allan Fox and Douglas D. Scott. They are in no doubt about the value of archaeology. On the basis of their hard-won evidence we now know about the kinds of weapons used against the

Cavalry, and against the Indians. We know exactly where many of the men fought, how they were deployed and how they died.

So were they able to work out what led one side to victory, the other to defeat?

Background

The Great Plains of the United States form the archetypal Big Country.

Horizons are big here. In the early years of the 19th century, vast buffalo herds stretched as far as the eye could see. But by the middle of the century expansionist pressures were forcing the native Indians westwards, the Sioux and the Cheyenne among them. The lure of gold, the hunger for land and the needs of an expanding population were drawing more and more white settlers out of the east and into these vast and unexploited lands. The young United States government built forts along trails. In the 1860s, Sioux were attacking these and interrupting the trails. Meanwhile, competing railroads were pushing onwards through the American heartland.

A treaty signed with the Indian chief Red Cloud at Fort Laramie in 1868 was designed to bring peace: it set aside land for reservations in which Indians could be supported by federal agencies, but allowed those Sioux and others who wished to roam free to remain in what was known as Unceded Territory. Here they would be free to hunt buffalo and follow their old customs, and here a spiritual leader – Sitting Bull – became the focus of those Indians who were dissatisfied with the new ways.

This uneasy peace was not to last long. Gold was found in the Black Hills in the centre of the Sioux reservation, and before long mining towns had been established, in contravention of the treaty. But the Sioux refused to sell their land. What was more, many of those Sioux living on the reservations were moving off to join Sitting Bull in the Unceded Territory.

The United States government viewed the flight of the Indians as 'hostile' and decided to force the issue and bring those Indians living outside their control back on to the reservations. They were ordered to return 'on penalty of being considered hostile'. They refused, and the government ordered the army to act against them. The stage was set for a confrontation – the last big confrontation between the forces of these two distinct American peoples. It was to be a battle to the death, one which would lead to a triumph in battle for the Indians, but also to the eventual loss of their war against the white man.

On 17 May 1876, General Terry began his campaign and led his Dakota Column westward towards Sitting Bull's last known camp. He had with him cavalry and infantry, scouts and more than 150 wagons, loaded with ammunition, supplies and three ponderous Gatling guns. He even had a river ship at his disposal – a paddle-steamer called *The Far West* which, appropriately, was to sail westwards along the Missouri and towards the Bighorn River. Other columns of troops were moving towards the Indians – from Dakota in the west and from Wyoming in the south. It looked as if there was no way out for Sitting Bull and his people.

On 22 June, Colonel Custer was detached from Terry's main column and sent forward with orders to search for the Indians. With him went all 12 companies of his cavalry, 175 mules and the best scouts from the column. By the evening of 25 June they had travelled 70 miles and, although they had little inkling of it, they were approaching a camp which we now know contained perhaps 7,000 Indians, an estimated 1,500 to 2,000 of whom were fighting warriors. The scouts in

Custer's column reported finding a fresh trail. Custer decided to follow it quickly and marched through the dark until 2 am.

The Protagonists

Who were the leaders of the battle which was about to unfold?

George Armstrong Custer, aged 37, who was to become an American legend, was a flamboyant character, almost larger than life, and already well known to the American public. In May 1876, the *Bismarck Tribune* portrayed him as a dashing young hero: 'General George A. Custer, dressed in a dashing suit of buckskin, is prominent everywhere. The General is full of perfect readiness for a fray with the hostile red devils, and woe to the body of scalp-lifters that comes within reach of himself and his brave companions in arms'.[1] Despite an unpromising early military career – he came last in his class at West Point and was lucky to escape a court martial for failing in his duty a mere few weeks after graduating – he made a name for himself in the American Civil War, during which he rose in rank from second lieutenant to major-general, the youngest in American history. But he was a strict disciplinarian and made himself many enemies. In 1867 he was court-martialled again, for shooting deserters without trial, but escaped with a year's suspension. He was a brutal commander in earlier Indian wars, attacking and massacring a Cheyenne camp at the so-called Battle of Washita.

Chief Sitting Bull, his principal opponent, was a Hunkpapa Sioux. Sitting Bull was a charismatic spiritual leader, a shaman rather than a warrior, who advocated a return to the old life of the Indian hunter. But as a fighter, he was uncompromising. Even after Little Bighorn he responded to a conditional offer of amnesty: 'This country is my country now, and I intend to stay here and raise my people to fill it. We did not give our country to you; you stole it. You come here to tell lies; when you go home, take them with you'. Legendary for his courage, Sitting Bull was a veteran of many wars, having first fought in a battle at the age of 14. Before Little Bighorn, he had a vision in which he saw American soldiers falling into his camp 'like grasshoppers from the sky'. At the age of 45, he was considered too old to fight, and his place on the battlefield was taken by Crazy Horse, Gall and Spotted Eagle. Indian battles were not fought under the same sort of tactical command systems as the US Army employed. They depended on mobility, daring and individual acts of bravery.

The Battle

On the morning of 26 June, Custer's scouts reported large numbers of 'hostiles' in the vicinity. Reluctantly, Custer allowed himself to be persuaded that he had lost the element of surprise, and he decided to attack at once. He resolved to split his regiment and mount a three-pronged attack. This decision has been the subject of continuing debate ever since. He sent his second-in-command Major Marcus Reno, who was fighting his first Indian campaign, forward on the west bank of the Little Bighorn with 175 men. Another officer, Captain Frederick Benteen, was ordered to scout to the south with 120 men and orders to 'pitch into' anyone he encountered. Custer himself followed the east side of river, with 221 men. The pack train of mules was left to follow, with yet another part of the force in support.

Shortly after noon that day, the four groups parted as they deployed under separate commands and descended towards the river valley, the horses and mules sending clouds of dust

into the air as they advanced towards what they still believed
– despite the doubts and suspicions of their scouts – to be a
small and poorly armed foe. For much of the time the
different columns could see each other. Benteen's force met
no one, and turned towards the pack train. A band of
perhaps 100 Indians was reported to Custer and he sent his
adjutant to Reno with instructions. Reno recalled a few days
later that the messenger had told him 'to move forward at as
rapid a gait as prudent, and to charge afterward and that the
whole outfit would support me. I think those were his exact
words'.[2] He was not to hear from Custer again.

Reno ordered a charge – when suddenly, to his astonishment, he discovered that far from the hundred or so
warriors he had expected, he was riding towards an enormous camp of several thousand hostile Indians. 'The very
earth seemed to grow Indians,'[3] he wrote in his official
report.

Reno called a halt to the charge and instead employed a
standard manoeuvre as outlined in the manual of tactics:
ordering his men to dismount and send their horses to the
rear, he had them form skirmish lines which fired towards
the enemy. Soon, however, in the face of tremendous odds,
he withdrew to the cover of nearby woods.

Meanwhile, high up on the valley side, Custer for the first
time seemed to get some inkling of the size of the Indian
encampment and sent a note back to Captain Benteen:
'Benteen come on. Big village. Be quick. Bring packs. PS
Bring packs.'[4] But was it a request for ammunition and reinforcements, or was it a confident Custer trying to regroup his
forces before approaching a vulnerable quarry – the non-
combatant Indians? Custer's plan – the accepted strategy of
the time – would have been to capture these non-combatants
and hold them hostage, but he may have realized that his
small, divided force could not control a vast crowd of

hostages. Custer seemed still to be planning an offensive; but from this point on, both his actions and he himself disappear in the swirling mists of war.

Shortly afterwards, down by the river, Reno seems to have panicked and retreated to the farther bank with his dwindling command. His forces scrambled and kicked their way up hundred-foot bluffs towards a nearby hilltop. By the time they got there, his force of 175 men had been devastated. Some 40 men were dead, three were wounded and 37 were missing. Soon he was joined by Benteen's column. Benteen had just received Custer's message, but on discovering the disaster which had befallen Reno – who seemed to be in shock – his men set about preparing a defensive position while they waited for the mule train to catch up.

Those warriors who had harried Reno up the hillside seemed to have retreated, and when the ammunition reached Benteen he moved on to a high point from which he could see the Indian village below. The hills to the north were obscured by smoke and dust in the late afternoon light. There seemed to be no sign of Custer and his men. One officer later recalled: 'We saw a good many Indians galloping up and down and firing at objects on the ground.'[5]

The Indians started drawing near, and Benteen and his men retreated towards Reno's position.

And in the distance, Custer and his men – all 210 under his command – lay dead.

What had happened? And how had it happened so quickly? How was it possible that the best of the United States Cavalry had been wiped out by what they regarded as a band of semi-civilized hostiles? The only witnesses to the massacre were the Indian warriors themselves, and nobody was to pay much attention to them.

Military investigators and later students of military history had very little to go on. Reno and Benteen had held out against the warriors through the evening, when the Indians seemed to lose interest and drifted away. The next day, relief arrived as General Terry's column caught up with them and the horror of what had occurred became apparent.

Perhaps surprisingly, not everyone immediately assumed that Custer was a hero. The *New York Times* in its report on the massacre on 6 July reported 'So far as an expression in regard to the wisdom of Gen. Custer's attack could be obtained at headquarters, it was to the effect that Custer had been imprudent, to say the least.'

Yet in the very same edition, and without a single shred of proof, there is an early indication that Custer's death was to be mythologized: 'Custer was surrounded on every side by Indians, and horses fell as they fought on skirmish line or in line of battle. Custer was among the last who fell, but when his cheering voice was no longer heard, the Indians made easy work of the remainder'. It was this view, rather than any 'expression of wisdom' that was to reverberate through the annals of the West.

The New Research

And then, over a hundred years later, in the summer of 1983, a bushfire swept through the Little Bighorn National Monument. The Visitor Centre and the white marble markers dotted across the hillside which purported to show where men had fallen were spared, and at first it seemed to have been a disaster narrowly averted. In fact, it was to provide the impetus for an astonishing revision of accepted history and the means of a new interpretation of the iconic story of American valour.

Like most bushfires, the cause was probably a carelessly discarded cigarette: the effect was that the thick sagebrush, grasses and prickly pear covering the battle site were burned away, laying the soil itself bare. Before long, a visitor stumbled across human remains: a single tooth.

The superintendent of the Custer National Park, curious to have been handed such a direct link with the battle, wondered if the fire might reveal more secrets. He was keen to have new material to help interpret the battle site at the Visitor Centre. He invited archaeologist Richard Allan Fox to have a look.

Richard Fox, a young veteran of a more recent American war quickly realized that the physical traces of the battle could lead to far more knowledge of what actually happened. Battlefields, he believed, were the laboratories of war. With enough evidence from bones and bullets, clothing and cartridges and all the other debris which might be located from what was, after all, a relatively recent conflict, Fox believed that he could perhaps solve some of the mysteries about the Battle of the Little Bighorn.

By the winter of 1983 Fox had persuaded the National Parks Service's research chief Douglas D. Scott and his colleagues that serious excavation work should be undertaken. They had few funds, and like most battlefield detectives they planned to use volunteers to do much of the groundwork. They decided that first they would survey the battlefield to record and collect everything they could find.

The first stage in the investigation was to arrange for five to ten people to walk across the site in a straight line and place flags whenever they could see an artefact. People with metal detectors were interspersed in the lines to locate material which was buried. The metal detectors sounded whenever they sensed a metal object and each object was then marked with a flag. With an electronic surveying instrument positioned at a fixed location, the team accurately gauged the distance and bearing of every artefact. A catalogue number, description and the direction which the artefact faced when discovered was recorded before any excavation was undertaken.

Secondly, they planned to excavate around the marble memorial stones which were scattered across the battlefield. These had been placed in position in 1890, supposedly to record the precise spot where each soldier had fallen. Fox and his team hoped to solve the first mystery – why there were more marble memorials than there were deaths at the battle.

'By the end of the first day', wrote Douglas Scott, 'more than one hundred artefacts had been located, recorded and collected, including the backstrap to a soldier's Colt revolver.'[6] They were astounded. Fox was delighted – the archaeological material, he believed, would reveal new evidence to help interpret a controversial and recent battle in a society which is now home to the descendants of both victors and vanquished. Inanimate objects don't lie, and Scott considered them to be material evidence of what occurred.

Soon the team of detectives had to be expanded. A third archaeologist joined the dig, and then – and over successive excavation seasons – more and more experts joined the search or were consulted – authorities on firearms, forensic anthropologists, geomorphologists, historians, osteologists, psychologists. Nobody can say when the search will end, but to date they have recovered more than 7,000 artefacts including bullets, cartridges and cartridge cases, human and equine remains, buttons, coins, jewellery and much more. These objects – the silent and simple debris of battle – were to produce an astonishingly detailed picture of what actually occurred.

Armed with these clues, Fox and Scott were to undertake research which they both liken to detection. They did it by combining the historical record with the archaeological evidence. Scott likens it to police work: 'In solving a crime, police rely upon two disparate classes of evidence. Witness testimony is important, but so are clues provided by the physical evidence of a crime. Detectives interview witnesses while other investigators gather fingerprints, blood samples and other physical evidence, the latter addressing different types of evidence using unique methods. Working together, the two types of investigators form a partnership that enhances the likelihood of solving the crime.'[7]

Richard Fox agrees: 'A battlefield site is like a crime scene; on the one hand you have the physical evidence, on the other the eye witnesses.

'Imagine a murder: detectives come in; they gather the fingerprints, the hair samples, the blood samples and they also gather eyewitness statements: "What did you hear? What did you see?"

'By putting both categories of evidence together, the detectives are more likely to solve the crime – and that's what we do with historical archaeology.

'In a nutshell: archaeology provides the material evidence and history provides the eyewitness evidence. The two together help us understand far better than can either discipline alone.'

So by combining the archaeology – the bones, the bullets and other artefacts – with the history – the army reports, oral histories, photographs and maps – the battlefield detectives hoped to reconstruct the events of the past in a far more detailed and more accurate way than anyone had achieved so far.

At first sight, some of the surviving evidence reinforced the myths about encounters between the Indians and the Cavalry. The bodies of the fallen had been reinterred together in a central grave five years after the battle, on Custer Hill. But many bodies had not been located by that 1881 burial party, and the archaeologists found an almost intact skeleton some distance away. He was a white male aged between 19 and 22. He was five feet seven inches tall and had been shot through the ribs. Both his thighbones showed three parallel cut-marks close to the groin, and he also appeared to have been clubbed in the head. Was this not evidence of a savage and uncivilized enemy who tortured and mutilated their foes? In the bitter warfare of the Plains the dead were often mutilated, perhaps to impair the enemy's spirit in an afterlife so that he could not draw a bowstring or ride a horse, or for revenge, or even as a marker of ethnic identity.

But Richard Fox and his colleagues were investigating much more than the bones in the ground. They were hoping to answer the last of the four major issues in what has become known as Little Bighorn Studies. Historian Robert Utley defines these as:

- Was Custer a fool or a hero?
- Did Custer disobey orders?
- Was Major Reno's withdrawal responsible for Custer's death?
- What did happen on the battlefield?

To learn about out what happened on the battlefield, the detectives focussed on several objectives:

- The weapons and equipment involved. Who was armed with what, and how were these weapons used?
- The chronology of the fight. Would the excavations be able to work out the order in which things happened?
- The Cavalry themselves. Were these fit young troopers? Would it be possible to identify anyone?

What could the battlefield detectives uncover?

The Evidence of the Memorials

The first, most obvious and most moving clues to strike the eye of a visitor to the Little Bighorn Monument are the marble markers scattered across the battlefield on Custer Hill, each one said to denote the position where a cavalryman fell in battle. There are 252 markers, yet only 210 people died on this site. This difference epitomizes the confusion and controversy that surrounds the battle. How could such a basic mistake have been made?

Fox turned to the history books and reports, relying as much as he could on primary evidence. He discovered that there had been no fewer than three separate burials and reburials over several decades. The first burial was completed by Major Reno and his troops on 28 June, three days after the battle. This was a hasty and extremely unpleasant business, and generally consisted of little more than covering the almost unrecognizable, bloated and in many cases mutilated bodies with earth and dust. Carried out in an atmosphere of horror and despair by exhausted and demoralized men, the procedure was little more than a token of respect.

Their remains were not to lie in peace for long. In 1877 troops were sent back to the battlefield to bury the soldiers' remains properly, and Custer's body was removed for burial at West Point – although there is much doubt as to whether they took the right bones. In 1881, as many of the bodies as could be found were exhumed again and reburied in a mass grave on the top of Custer Hill. It was not until 1890 – some 14 years after the event – that marble memorials were positioned where it was believed individuals had fallen, although it is clear that markers were placed for more men than fell in that 'last stand' location. The disparity can be traced, Richard Fox has deduced, to the fact that the 1890 detachment incorrectly placed 42 markers which were intended to commemorate those who died in Reno's battle in the valley.

Many of the markers are placed in pairs, perhaps because they thought that men fell in pairs. A more prosaic explanation is that when the 1890 memorial detachment found were pairs of shallow depressions they assumed that these represented graves, rather than the indentations formed when earth had been scooped up on each side of a fallen body in attempts to cover the dead quickly on that stifling day in June 1876.

As the discovery of the tooth in 1983 had demonstrated, none of the interments had been thorough, and Fox expected to find further remains near the markers. The archaeologists recognized that if the pairs of markers represented a single soldier, they would only find the remains of one individual nearby – but if they found the remains of two individuals, it would tend to support the 'Last Stand' theory of buddies living and dying together.

They consulted the records: they located all the reports, maps and photographs of the battlefield which described the markers or showed where they were placed. A Government Geological Survey map of 1891 showed the location of 244 markers – so only one year after they were erected, there was already a discrepancy.

Detective work about marker placement was not a minor issue. Many of the stories about the battle, and indeed the work of many scholars and military historians, use the position of the markers to visualize the battle and to determine where and how men died. And since 1891, markers have been replaced and moved without formal records being kept. Many more records were consulted, and more anomalies spotted: it was clear that excavation would be necessary.

Over the first two excavation seasons, 26 marker sites were investigated by Clyde Snow and John Fitzpatrick. Clyde

Snow is the most eminent forensic anthropologist of the present day, known as 'the detective's detective'. He studied both zoology and physical anthropology before a career which has included detailed investigations of victims of serial murderers, Dr Joseph Mengele, King Tutankhamun, the Disappeared of Argentina, the victims of the Oklahoma City bombing, the mass graves in the former Yugoslavia and many more.

'There is', he says, 'a brief but very useful and informative biography of an individual contained within the skeleton, if you know how to read it.'[8]

The Evidence of the Bones

Bones, Dr Snow believes, are very good witnesses, but in this investigation he also used historical records to help confirm many of his findings. Among other factors, these showed that the Cavalry troopers of 1876 were a disparate group. Forty-two per cent of the dead in the Custer fight were of foreign birth – 28 from Ireland, 27 from Germany, 16 from Great Britain and the rest from Canada, Denmark, Switzerland, France, Greece and Russia. Like the early United States themselves, it hardly seemed a cohesive group.

Of those born in America, all but six were from the eastern United States. Although the investigators were only able to discover bones from 34 individuals, Snow and Fitzpatrick considered that bone fusion development showed a 'considerably larger number' of under-age troopers than the records suggest. Fourteen of the deaths involved 'massive blunt force trauma', which 'was probably inflicted as a means of dispatching the wounded'. Eight of them had incised wounds from arrows or axes. Three had been shot. 'It appears', Snow and Fitzpatrick summed up, 'that the majority of the troopers were still alive, but more or less helplessly wounded when resistance ceased and that many were finished off with massive, crushing blows to the head'.[9] And when they reported on the site which was alleged to have held the body of George Custer, they noted that 'the description of the grave and its contents is at odds with the account of the original burial.'

But what of the mystery of the extra markers – those set in pairs which suggested that troopers fought together in a last stand? Of the eleven double markers investigated, one pair had no remains, one held both human and horse bones, and all the rest contained the bones of a single individual. In several cases, the individual's bones lay between the double markers.

So this evidence did not support the Last Stand legend. It was not conclusive, of course: would other evidence support the same hypothesis?

More recently Pete Willey, Professor of Forensic Anthropology at California State University in Chico, has been able to investigate more remains, including almost complete skeletons which had been buried outside the mass grave – and which were later reburied there. He discovered that Custer's force were not the fit young men of the romantic paintings or the later Hollywood legend. Most had dental disease, four showed evidence of trauma brought on by horse-riding, many had back problems and joint problems – surprising, given the young age of the soldiers. One trooper had a congenital defect of the lower spine. These were men who spent long hours in the saddle. Using army medical records to supplement the archaeology, they discovered that the men of the 7th Cavalry had been treated in 1,721 instances with 76 different diseases from abscesses and boils to venereal disease and gunshot trauma. Willey's work demonstrated that the frontier was anything but romantic. The troopers were demonstrably not noble warriors at the peak of mental and physical health. Willey and Douglas Scott had discovered, they said, that 'they were simply people of their time with their own aches, pains, broken bones and a myriad diseases brought on by a rugged lifestyle.'[10]

Willey examined the remains of a young man whom they identified through forensic analysis as Trooper Vincent Charley. Charley was 27 years old, yet had lost perhaps a dozen of his adult teeth. He had lived what Willey describes as 'a tough life, with a bad diet, and in that way he is probably very typical of most of the troopers who fought at the battle.' One of the indications of the lives these men endured 'involved their backs. They had ridden long, long miles over tough trails and on saddles that weren't much better than a granite boulder – and each time the trooper came down on the saddle, the inner vertebral disc would collapse like a shock absorber and that shock-absorbing property starts to wear out. That's the first stage. The second stage is that it protrudes out through the fibrous core that surrounds it and impinges on the vertebral column: it can cause pain, it can cause a lack of feeling, even a lack of motor control in some of the lower limbs.'

Altogether they weren't in the best of health. Willey deduced that the troopers were 'in terrible shape that morning in June – they'd ridden all night long; they'd been riding from Fort Abraham Lincoln since May. They hadn't had any rest, their backs were hurting, their teeth were aching. They were in bad shape.'

The Evidence of the Guns

Fox and his colleagues spent many seasons excavating the battlefield, investigating it with the same detail a detective gives to a crime scene. Over the years, their metal-detecting teams located an enormous amount of evidence about the weapons used in this 1876 battle.

Most objects located were found between three and six inches below the surface. The use of metal detectors is regarded with some suspicion by many archaeologists, and is normally banned in such sites – but they proved themselves ideal for this project. In the first two excavations alone, some 4,000 artefacts were discovered. Crucially, in this study, each find – every arrowhead, piece of wire, metal button, bullet, cartridge case – was logged, mapped precisely and entered into an electronic surveying instrument. The results were transferred to a computer which created maps.

When all the cartridge cases and spent bullets were positioned on a map of the battlefield, they revealed the main areas of fighting. When a gun is fired, the spent cartridge is ejected from the firing chamber and left on the ground, so an empty cartridge case signifies that someone has fired from a particular spot.

A spent bullet will reveal – obviously – where a bullet ends up. So an accumulation of lead bullets in an area would also help to define position. Indian bullets, for example, would accumulate around Cavalry targets and Cavalry bullets would accumulate around Indian targets.

But dots on a computer-generated map are useless without context. What the archaeologists were looking for were patterns, and in order to establish a meaningful pattern – to investigate what they call 'pattern analysis' – Richard Fox and his investigators first had to identify clearly which weapons were used to fire the bullets and who fired them. Different weapons use different ammunition, so it was a relatively easy matter – given the right firearms expertise – to identify the weaponry used in the battle.

The detectives knew from the historical record which weapons the U.S. Cavalry used: government troops were issued with the single-shot .45 calibre Springfield carbine and the six-shot .45 calibre Colt single-action pistol. But they were surprised to discover the vast range of guns used by the opposing warriors, especially considering the official policies restricting firearms sales to Indians.

Douglas Scott identified some 47 different types, from ancient muzzle-loaders to the latest state-of-the art repeating Winchester and Henry rifles.

By using modern crime laboratory firearms identification techniques it was possible to discover that a minimum number of 415 guns were used by the Indians. As many as 220 of these were the Henry repeating rifles.

Because Custer had divided his command so much, that by the time he found himself surrounded – he was down to about 210 men – the hapless troopers were, in fact, outgunned by a factor of about four to one and outnumbered by about seven to one.

The Indians had access to the latest technology – and it was more suitable weaponry than the Cavalry's. They also had more firearms than the army. These were hardly the tomahawks and arrows beloved in depictions of the Wild West. Douglas Scott explains how the Indians came by their guns: 'The Indians acquired weapons just like anybody else did. They could go to the trading post and purchase them or trade for them. The government gave firearms and ammunition to the Indians as part of the trading annuities: they were used for hunting – but in this case they were used for hunting white men. And they would take them from the dead – they would take them during the raids or from other tribes – so firearms were acquired any number of different ways. But they were readily available all through the frontier.'

The Cavalry's main weapon, the single-shot Springfield, was not nearly as fast as the repeating rifle, and the army in 1876 did not issue repeating rifles. Rounds had to be loaded into the breech one by one, and the spent cases were ejected one by one. It was accurate: it had an effective range of about 500 yards, and it was designed to kill at a distance. But even the best-trained cavalryman found it hard to discharge more than four rounds a minute. The Springfield was not designed to be used when mounted and it required great skill to use effectively. It was a very useful weapon for concentrated volleying fire which would keep an enemy at a distance, but it was designed with a regular army enemy in mind, rather than the rapidly moving targets presented by Indians on horseback.

Battlefield Detectives drew on the skills and insights of Mark Bohaty, a ballistics expert with the Nebraska State Patrol Crime Laboratory who has made a special study of the Battle of the Little Bighorn. He thinks the Springfield was 'difficult to use accurately. In an experienced, trained person's hands... a very accurate firearm', but its usefulness depended on the circumstances: 'If you have smoke and dust, people running about, and you're trying to take a steady aim – it would be difficult. They were not in a stable, stationary position to take careful aim. I would say that to shoot this particular type of firearm under those conditions it would have been very, very difficult to shoot accurately out to 400 yards.'

The Indians, on the other hand, had large numbers of the Henry repeating rifle. Mark Bohaty described how simple this type of weapon was to use when compared to the Springfield, and how it automatically reloaded each cartridge: 'It's compact in size, and the lever action means that by operating the lever you're actually cocking the hammer and bringing a cartridge up from the magazine. The bolt will pick up that cartridge off the carrier and slide that cartridge into the chamber, preparing the firearm to be fired.'

The Henry's magazine could hold 15 cartridges and the weapon could be fired rapidly, without needing to reload manually for every shot. Although these rifles had a range far shorter than the Cavalry's single-shot Springfield – effectively about 200 yards – they were ideally suited to close combat, and the volume of fire they could lay down created a dramatic and frightening effect. If the exhausted troopers were surprised on horseback by a large force of Indians at close quarters, armed with perhaps 200 repeating rifles, it is not difficult to imagine what the result could be, especially if those same troopers could only fire one bullet every 15 seconds or so.

One persistent rumour maintains that the Cavalry's carbines jammed – even Major Reno referred to this problem. The particular problem was said to be the failure of the Springfield to eject spent cartridges. But extraction failure could be tested by the battlefield detectives, by examining cartridge cases for torn or severed edges or by microscopic inspection for the scratches or marks made by the knives which would be used to free such jams. There were indeed some such marks – but only in 6 out of 1,625 cases examined. 'Extraction failure', Fox concluded, 'was not a significant factor in the defeat of Custer's battalion, at least from the traditional perspective of masses of men rendered helpless.'[11] But still the tale persists: the history Internet site Kronos claims in 2002, 'When placed into a hot, fouled, chamber, the soft copper casing used in the Springfield's ammunition expanded, and as a result it tended to jam the weapons, thus hindering reloading and firing. Originally soldiers were told to extract jammed cartridges with their knives, but after the Little Bighorn battle in 1876 the shell was redesigned, and thereafter the carbine proved quite satisfactory in combat.'[12]

Whether the Cavalry's carbines had jammed or not, the Indians already held the advantage. Mark Bohaty has no doubt that the Indians could fire five to six shots for every one that the Cavalry could manage. 'The weapon made the difference. The amount of firepower that the Indians had, and the types of weapon that they had, were the key in their defeating the U.S. Cavalry in that particular battle – no question about it.'

Tracking the Dead

The archaeologists, then, could identify where people were when they were firing, and they then realized they could also work out who was doing the firing.

But they could go one step further: they knew that in the laboratory they could not only identify the type of weapon being used, but they could also identify each Springfield carbine individually: every cartridge bore a 'signature'.

Richard Fox believes this discovery provided the crux of his research: 'The most important evidence at this battlefield site is, of course, the cartridge cases, and in particular the firing-pin signatures imprinted on the bases of cartridge cases, and the bullets. They tell us two things – the static and the dynamic.

'On the one hand, we can work out where combatants were on the basis of the bullets and cartridge cases and, on the other hand, how the fight progressed on the basis of tracking firing-pin signatures or firearms across the battlefield.'

These signatures were formed at the moment of firing and of ejection of the empty case. Firing the Springfield involved pulling a trigger which released the firing-pin – it then struck the primer at the end of the cartridge, which exploded the charge and fired the bullet. When the ejector mechanism then expelled the empty cartridge, it left distinct marks on the case. The marks on the case from both the firing-pin and the ejector are unique to the individual gun – and the bullet itself will also have a 'signature' as a result of groove marks caused as it travelled up the rifled barrel of the gun.

Mark Bohaty explained: 'When a bullet is fired from a firearm it travels down the barrel, and it's marked by the rifling characteristics that are placed in that barrel.' The barrel and the spiral grooves of the rifling inside it possess 'certain unique imperfections, produced during manufacture, which scratch the bullet in such a way that it can be identified back to that barrel or that firearm.'

Cartridge cases produced even clearer evidence: 'When a cartridge is fired in a particular firearm, it's housed in the chamber of the firearm. When that cartridge is fired, it is struck from the rear by a centre-fire firing-pin, or around the rim. That firing-pin impression has great value in identification. You also have an extractor that grips the rim of the cartridge which leaves an area of potential identification under the rim, and in some cases you can even have breech-face marks where the bolt is holding the cartridge – analogous to a fingerprint. In the case of the cartridge casings, there was some success with identifying cartridge casings with being fired by the same gun. There was much better success with the cartridge casings than the bullets.'

This was crucial. It meant that the battlefield detectives 'could determine Indian positions and movements by groups of casings fired from the same gun, indicating that he was static in that position. Then they located cartridge casings along the same ridge from the same gun, indicating movement of the firearm. It was the same gun that was moving on the ridge, giving them more insight into how the battle actually progressed.'

So our battlefield detectives could identify ejected Springfield cartridge cases and bullets and link them directly to a particular weapon. With a comparison microscope – essentially two microscopes connected by an optical bridge – they could view cartridges side by side simultaneously, as if each casing had been cut in half, and compare them easily.

Because Richard Fox was also using very precise computerized mapping techniques, recording where every cartridge case and bullet was found, they could connect individual positions on the battlefield.

Fox was gaining new insights into battle positions. By looking at the groupings of Indian cartridge cases he discovered seven Indian fighting positions, six of which had not been known before his work.

He could also identify a trooper's position from ejected cartridges left on the ground, and the accumulations of lead bullets could also define positions: Indian bullets would accumulate around a Cavalry position, and Cavalry bullets would accumulate around Indian targets. By colour-coding his finds, Fox was able to draw up clear indications of who was where.

These static views were not enough. Soon Richard Fox and his colleagues were drawing up maps showing what he calls 'pathways' – indicated by connecting lines on the maps – which, while not necessarily showing the routes taken by Indians or troopers, nevertheless show changes in their positions. Once Fox could demonstrate that a particular weapon was discharged in two separate places – which he was able to do as a result of individual 'signatures' – he could track movement.

It was painstaking research. Douglas Scott recalls: 'I believe I looked at somewhere in the neighbourhood of 1,500 cartridges and it took hundreds of hours. But the benefit was remarkable: we were able to literally trace the movement of individual weapons across the battlefield.'

The detectives were close to knowing what happened on that desperate afternoon in 1876.

Patterns and Tactics

Faced with patterns of cartridge cases and bullets, even with connecting pathways, the archaeologists were still left little the wiser. They could see patterns showing clusters of bullets, they realized there were distinct areas where there were groupings of cartridge cases – but how could that information improve our knowledge of the battle itself? Could their archaeological work reveal much more than what types of weapons were being used and where people were positioned? Was there something hidden in the patterns which might reveal how the battle was lost?

Fox needed more understanding of the historical context. What might Custer's troops be up to? What was one supposed to do if one was a cavalryman in the 1870s? Finding answers to these questions required an understanding of military theory.

The answer lay in the tactics: and the tactics they meant to follow are on the historical record. Tactics, at their simplest, are the arrangements made, and the methods followed, in order to achieve a particular objective. They are the framework for military operations. If a military force plans to capture a building, defend itself against an opposing force or infiltrate a border – it applies tactics. Military tactics have evolved over the years as circumstances changed and developed. The tactics used by a tribal group armed only with spears are obviously different from the tactics used by an air force with heat-seeking missiles. They instil order. They are useful because, as Richard Fox emphasizes, battles are often very confusing events.

The U.S. 7th Cavalry used the newly formulated 1874 *Cavalry Tactics* devised by Emory Upton. Upton was a brilliant young commander who had been at West Point in the same year as Custer. Although his manual did at least codify and standardize cavalry tactics, it has been argued that the tactics themselves were at least ten years out of date at the time they came to be issued. They were, in fact, based upon infantry tactics. U.S. Army historians, writing in 1969, noted that 'the foundation of all the rules was the basic thought that cavalrymen must be drilled as infantry and must at all times be prepared to fight on foot. A rather startling alteration occurred when the Cavalry in 1873 adapted the *Infantry Tactics*, accepted by the infantry in 1867, as its drill manual. This system, prepared by Major General Emory Upton, altered previous teaching because it based troop evolutions upon movements by fours. These movements were suited to drill with horses since they allowed room for the mounts to maneuver where earlier ones had not.'[13]

This rule of four, and the dismounting of horses to form what are known as 'skirmish lines' is crucial to understanding what happened in the Battle of the Little Bighorn.

There were 12 companies to a regiment; two platoons in a company, and each platoon was divided into squads of four men. The manual describes skirmishing procedure as the standard organized fighting method. Troops formed lines – 'skirmish lines' – with a distance of five yards between each man and 15 yards between squads. If they dismounted, one man out of each squad took control of the four horses and moved to the rear, or at any rate out of the line of fire.

The effect of this was – at a stroke – to reduce the fighting capability of a cavalry force by 25 per cent.

It also took time and effort to arrange, and it wasn't a particularly easy manoeuvre to undertake while being fired upon.

With hindsight, of course, one can find much to criticize about the U.S. Cavalry's tactics. John McDermott in a 21st-century comment writes: 'One major shortcoming of the United States Army in the 19th century was its failure to develop a course of instruction to train its rank and file in methods of Indian warfare,'[14] and quotes a 19th-century critic, Captain Charles King, who had pointed out that the manuals in use had been prepared by four officers who were 'eminent for everything but Indian fighting.'[15] As an illustration of this, McDermott notes the account of one Cavalry sergeant, James McClellan, of the 3rd Cavalry, who described what the tactics demanded of troopers who were ordered to deploy on a skirmish on foot: 'As the troop halts, the Nos. 1 and 2 link their horses to the No. 3s, who pass their bridle reins to the No. 4s. The Capt., 1st and 2nd Lts., and R and L guides also pass their bridle reins to the nearest No. 4s, who (remaining mounted) lead the horses to the rear as directed by the Captain. Nos. 1, 2, and 3 dart through the horses and form on what was the right flank of the column on the march. Officers and guides take position... then the Captain deploys the troop and directs the attack.'[16]

It was a complicated business, and one which it is hard to imagine being followed to the letter in the face of an attack by hundreds of armed warriors with superior firepower. Certainly the modern reader, in the light of these tactics, will find it easier to sympathize with Major Reno's position as outlined in his official report: '... they were running towards me in swarms, and from all directions. I saw I must defend myself and give up the attack mounted. This I did. Taking possession of a front of the woods, and which furnished, near its edge, a shelter for the horses, dismounted and fought them on foot, making headway through the woods. I soon found myself in the near vicinity of the village, saw that I was fighting odds of at least five to one, and that my only hope was to get out...'[17]

But the archaeologists were not seeking to criticize the 1874 tactics, merely to understand them and to work out whether what they had discovered on the battlefield could be more readily understood in the context of the tactics being deployed.

Richard Fox has found, in the archaeological record, plentiful evidence of these tactics. The language of the archaeological record may be necessarily dry, but nevertheless one can picture the battle: 'Physical evidence from an episode in this region includes combat action... a concentration of Indian bullets indicates that government forces came under an undetermined volume of fire. The linear patterning of unique cartridge case signatures (on .44/55 casings) suggests that some soldiers in the sector deployed in skirmish formation... four individual trooper positions are spaced at nearly regular intervals. A fifth position is some distance to the south. The line, judging from extant evidence, may have been as much as 60 yards in length. Adhering to prescribed tactical intervals, it seems to represent something less than company strength... quite clearly, warriors at some time also occupied the Henryville position where there are numerous expended Indian cartridges...'[18]

So the archaeological record confirmed that the Cavalry were following the tactical manual and forming skirmish lines. Linear skirmish lines left behind them linear evidence. But it showed something else: some of the patterns didn't make sense. There were many cases where the evidence – the Cavalry's spent cartridges – were tightly grouped together, or simply scattered, seemingly randomly. Sometimes the connecting pathways Fox had drawn up seemed to show that individuals had moved from a linear skirmish line to an area of confusion.

Disintegration

Fox believes that battlefield archaeology requires new methods of study and new applications. What would his pattern analysis show if he combined it with a study of tactics? Fox himself knows about war. He flew with the United States Air Force during the Vietnam War. He knew that tactical frameworks were necessary to maintain order, and that if tactical unity broke down – if it disintegrated – then it would be more likely that defeat would ensue.

He could see from his patterns that skirmish lines of troopers changed: that clusters of cartridge cases were often in tight groupings, smaller than the prescribed five yards' distance prescribed by Upton. And he knew that as fear grows in a unit, the participants instinctively tend to draw closer together. This is called bunching. If the commander is unable to restore order, bunching can turn to panic. When panic sets in, men cease to fight according to the tactical framework – they usually attempt to flee. As men flee, they usually don't fight back. Sometimes they throw away their weapons.

Fox was struggling with the problem of understanding what he could learn from the artefacts: 'I was sitting at my ranch in the Wolf Mountains in the middle of a blizzard, trying to figure out how we could put the artefacts to work, and it struck me that we could use modern forensics to track battlefield combatants. These soldiers were here, those soldiers were there, the enemy was there…'[19]

It was clear to Richard Fox that knowing where people actually were on the battlefield was the key to understanding it, 'because, after all, that's the way battles are fought. So I struck on the idea of using modern forensics to move people around – to put the dynamics into the artefact patterns.'

Fox began to study the literature of combat behaviour and the tactics manuals of the time 'in order to fully understand the patterning that emerged on my map. I had to understand the behaviour of men under combat stress and the tactics that they used.'

The pattern showed that the Cavalry had followed the manual. They had deployed in skirmish lines, but then tactical disintegration had begun – they had bunched together, not just on one place but in several places. Then panic had set in and they fled. They ran without putting up much of a fight – they operated on their own, and some fired and some did not. Fox found paths connecting identical signatures in which men abandoned positions and moved to areas where there were, the archaeologists found, few government cartridges but many Indian bullets. Fox pieced together the record to achieve what he described as a bare-bones picture of the behaviour of men during the battle. The process of transition from tactical stability to disintegration 'which peaked at Calhoun Hill, seems to have signalled the beginning of the end. Bunching and flight evidently developed from tactical failures at the Calhoun Coulee and Calhoun Ridge sectors... the first battle line had, until the western threats materialized, encountered nothing too serious in the way of enemy action. Redeployment, however, allowed the Indians to seize advantages and move closer... ultimately command discipline eroded, men tended to bunch together, and flight ensued.'[19]

Fox now knew that under immense duress, men often rushed to where other comrades still survived.

He found no evidence of plan and order. Clustered together, 'men found themselves virtually surrounded by Indians, many apparently close at hand.' His archaeological analysis did not support the conventional view of disciplined and organized cavalry banding together in a last stand. 'The enemy seems to have induced disintegration. Thereafter, troops evidently struggled against their foe in confusion and disorganization.'[20]

The Last Stand?

So what had happened? The final moments took place in a small area: just two little hillocks, Custer Hill and Calhoun Hill, and a gully. The archaeology suggests the following chronology.

Custer wasn't intending to attack armed Indians, and probably wasn't even aware that there were very many in the area. His strategy, which had proved very successful in the past, would have been to destroy Indian homes, capture the non-combatants and hold them hostage. He hadn't realized how many of those there were, so he divided his force again, leaving some companies on Calhoun Hill while he went to find a ford to cross the river and reach the Indian village.

Reduced to a force of some 80 men under his personal command, he then spotted the many thousands of fleeing non-combatants and realized his force would be too small to control them. He decided to turn back and wait for Benteen with his troops and supplies. But he didn't know that Benteen and Reno were trapped. When the Indians realized that there was a completely separate force of troopers which they had not yet confronted, they rode north in their hundreds to find them.

They attacked the companies on Calhoun Hill, who broke ranks and panicked. 'The white men acted as if they were beside themselves, shooting wildly in the air', an Indian later recalled.

Custer had now reached his hilltop with his small section, and was on the defensive for the first time. The well-armed Sioux swept down on him. He probably saw the chaos and slaughter on Calhoun Hill. More and more warriors arrived and many of his soldiers had dismounted.

But the final act did not take place on Custer Hill.

Richard Fox: 'We often think of Custer Hill as the last-stand hill where the last fighting took place – where the last soldiers died. The common perception is that the last fighting took place on Custer Hill. The archaeology and analysis indicates otherwise. In fact, there was a deployment off Custer Hill which was initially successful, but the Indians counter-attacked and broke their cohesion and they fled down into a deep ravine area – and that's where the last fighting took place. This is indicated by a handful of government cartridge cases and quite a number of Indian bullets.'

It was all over very quickly.

The Reaction

Just how different from the myth this evidence is, of men instinctively cowering together and then fleeing into a gully, becomes clear from any reading of the traditional story. Peter Panzeri, a serving officer in the U.S. Army and a writer with a passionate interest in American-Indian wars, very bravely quotes his own earlier flawed hypothesis in his most recent and very detailed account of the battle,[21] an account which credits Fox's groundbreaking archaeological discoveries. 'Encountering an overwhelming number of hostiles at the centre of the village', he had earlier written, Custer's 'soldiers desperately fought their way uphill, racing on their tired horses for a defensible hilltop, pursued by thousands of hostiles who all jumped on their horses and immediately counter-attacked... eventually Custer and his immediate command was annihilated, fighting to the last man and the last cartridge, at the Little Big Horn.' These are words which Panzeri now gracefully disowns, 'It is a sensational and fatalist account, fostered mostly by Elizabeth Custer [Custer's widow] and those who sought to cover mistakes or further glorify the disaster as inevitable fate. The fatalistic theories are untrue, unfounded and readily disproved.'

So why had everyone got the story so wrong for more than a hundred years? Partly it was a need for heroes in a country struggling to form itself, but it also seems to have been an attempt to hide the incompetence of a government and of a military force which set out to enforce policy. Not unnaturally, Custer's widow Elizabeth was a tireless campaigner for her husband to be seen as a hero. Speaking in 1923, she said that she hoped that the 45th anniversary celebrations might 'serve to dispel every last, lingering doubt or criticism that might even tend to dim the glory of that band of troopers and their beloved general, heroes all, who went to their death with the imperishable valor of the American soldier – fighting a hopeless fight to the last man and the last cartridge, at the Little Big Horn.'[22]

But in fact, not everyone had got the story wrong. As we have already noted, that early report in *The New York Times* made it clear, a mere few days after the massacre, that there were those who felt that the politicians had been guilty of a grave error, and so had the army, and so had Colonel Custer.

Of the politicians and the army, the newspaper reported: 'The reason for an expedition against the Indians this Summer is not well understood, nor has any satisfactory explanation been published. The wild Sioux had never been willing to live upon the reservations marked out for them, and the understanding has been that they were to be whipped into submission...The question of the policy and right of the war will now be renewed and discussed, and, indeed, is discussed today. Those who believe in the policy of the extermination of the Indians, and think the speedier the better its accomplishment, look upon the condition of war as inevitable, and are for pouring thousands of troops into the Indian country and giving them a terrible punishment. This class is small, even in the Army... The invasion of the Black Hills has been condemned over and over again by the peace party, and there are very many who can truthfully say, "I told you so."'[23]

And of Custer: 'THE ATTACK CONDEMNED AS RASH BY OFFICERS OF EXPERIENCE... So far as an expression in regard to the wisdom of Gen. Custer's attack could be obtained at headquarters, it was to the effect that Custer had been imprudent, to say the least. It is the opinion at head-quarters among those who are most familiar with the situation, that Custer struck Sitting Bull's main camp... no doubt, Custer dropped squarely into the midst of no less than ten thousand red devils and was literally torn to pieces. The movement made by Custer is censured to some extent at military headquarters in this city. The older officers say that it was brought about by that foolish pride which so often results in the defeat of men...'[24]

But *The New York Times* was not a witness to history. Thousands of people were, however; and until now, their history has been ignored. They were those 'red devils' of the newspaper report.

The 'jumble of recollections', as Fox terms them, were complex and often contradictory. No Cavalry trooper saw the events that have been called 'The Last Stand', although they gave many accounts of the events leading up to it and to the other fighting that took place at the Battle of the Little Bighorn. But many Indians recorded their impressions and memories of the battle in which they took such a devastating part – the battle they know as 'The Greasy Grass.'

And many of the Indian accounts have been questioned by Fox. For example, Cheyenne oral history refers to Cavalry officers committing mass suicide, but Fox's teams found no evidence at all that this occurred, and no Sioux accounts refer to such behaviour. On the other hand, many accounts, specifically the testimony of warriors who took part in the battle, ring true in the light of the archaeological record. Here, for example, is Low Dog's version of Custer's retreat when he first realized the strength of his foe: 'I called to my men: "This is a good day to die: follow me."'... As we rushed upon them the [soldiers] dismounted to fire, but they did very poor shooting. They held their horses' reins on one arm while they were shooting, but their horses were so frightened that they pulled the men all around and a great many of their shots went up into the air and did us no harm.'[25]

And White Bull reported: 'I charged in. A tall, well-built soldier... saw me coming... when I rushed him, he threw his rifle at me without shooting... We grabbed each other and wrestled there in the dust and smoke... He hit me with his fists on the jaw and shoulders, then grabbed my long braids with both hands, pulled my face close and tried to bite my nose off... I yelled as loud as I could to scare my enemy, but he would not let go. Finally, I broke free. He drew his pistol. I wrenched it out of his hand and struck him with it three or four times on the head, knocked him over, shot him in the head and fired at his heart... *Ho hechetu*! That was a [good] fight, a hard fight. But it was a glorious battle; I enjoyed it.'[26]

Joe Medicine Crow is aged nearly 90. As the grandson of one of Custer's Indian scouts, he is the closest living witness the *Battlefield Detectives* team could consult. 'I have heard my grandfather telling about his experiences with Custer, and the rest of the military people who were here at that time,' he told the team, 'he was only seventeen then.' Joe believes that there's always been a bias against the Indian version: 'My grandfather, White Man Runs, says it was such a huge battle, covering a huge area and no one man was able to see it all. So that's why there are so many different versions of the battle. It is the same way with the Sioux and Cheyenne, they didn't see the whole, they see just the part that they were involved in. For some reason the white man doesn't like to hear the Indians tell it the way it was. They don't want to hear the Indians' story. They don't like to hear the truth. Sometimes the truth is too terrible, too sad – like Custer's death.' In the final analysis, he believes that Custer was at fault for not listening to his scouts: 'According to my grandfather he was a darn fool for not listening to their warnings

– that it was too big a camp for him to attack. They told him to wait but he wouldn't do it.'

It was a disaster for the U.S. Cavalry, and it was to lead to the end of the Sioux way of life.

Archaeology alone cannot answer everything about Custer's decisions. But Fox and Scott believe that a good detective will place reliance on the witnesses as well as the inanimate clues. Contemporary documents refer to Custer as a glory-hunter – he was trying to make a name for himself. Many believe that Custer badly underestimated the Indians' strength. Crucially, we know that Custer divided and then divided and then divided again his command.

From the archaeology, Scott shows that the Cavalry moved from a state of controlled tactics, to bunching together, to tactical disintegration and flight. He dismisses the argument that Custer's guns were mechanically suspect, and that he ran out of ammunition.

The troopers were young men, but not necessarily fit and healthy young men.

He is critical of the guns the Cavalry used, which took far too long to reload in the circumstances, particularly compared to the Indians' weapons: 'The effect of repeating rifles on the soldiers... lay not only in the killing but also in the shock that such weapons can deliver at close range... coupled with the liability of the single-shot carbine in close-in fighting, probably contributed significantly to demoralization [of]... the entire battalion. The shock effect was magnified by the likelihood, based on archaeological data, that the Indians had at least 200 repeating rifles.'[27] He also shows that the Indians became better armed as the battle progressed, as they gained possession of even more weapons from the fallen cavalrymen.

He has shown that many of the Indian testimonies are accurate. He believes that shock was the major factor leading to tactical disintegration. Shock was induced by the suddenness with which the troopers found themselves under attack, by the closeness of the enemy and by their overwhelming numbers.

Let Joe Medicine Crow have the last word about the battle at Little Bighorn: 'The Indians', he asserts, 'were being pushed out of their land, and massacred here and there. It was Sitting Bull's last stand. Not Custer's last stand.'

In the end, there is still much which is unknown about the Battle of the Little Bighorn. But Fox and his colleagues have shown that history and archaeology together bring us new insights. Some ancient battles have left so little surviving physical evidence that we cannot even be sure where they took place. But where a physical record does exist, the history is incomplete – without taking full account of the archaeological record and the battlefield detective.

Gallipoli – 1915

Introduction

One thing about the Dardanelles campaign, which unfolded over nine months of 1915 on the Gallipoli peninsula of Turkey, is beyond dispute: it was the scene of the most appalling loss of life. Around 130,000 men – Turkish, British, French, Australian, Indian, Canadian, New Zealander and Gurkha – died during the campaign. They were contesting a tiny portion of dry and rugged Turkish land and, when the Allies withdrew, it was universally admitted that the entire nine months of fighting and death had gained them absolutely nothing.

Many legends have grown up around the Gallipoli campaign. Universally admitted to have been an absolute disaster for the Allies – indeed, one of their costliest blunders of the entire First World War – the blame for failure at Gallipoli has long been laid at the doors of incompetent commanders and a failure of political will in London and Paris. The story has become one of troops, especially the colonial troops from Australia and New Zealand – the Anzacs – being pointlessly sacrificed by callous imperial authorities.

Indeed, in many ways the Allied commanders on the ground *were* old-fashioned and out of their depth. They were men used to fighting small colonial wars, not an intensive campaign of modern warfare. The attack on Gallipoli was also disastrously disorganized. The (true) story is often repeated of how no one had informed those responsible for loading the ships that this was to be an amphibious assault, and therefore supplies needed to be stowed in a particular order with that in mind – with the result that all the stores had to be unloaded and then packed all over again once the ships reached the eastern Mediterranean. There were other significant – and almost unbelievable – failures in communication. It is true for example that General Sir Ian Hamilton, in charge of the operation, did not call for reinforcements at a crucial moment, with disastrous results, because he had been told at the outset by his superior, Field-Marshal Lord Kitchener, that none could be spared. What no one had informed him was that Kitchener had subsequently changed his mind, and had ordered the British general in Egypt to provide Hamilton with any reinforcements he needed. But because Hamilton never asked, his opposite number in Egypt never offered.

However, examining the Allied defeat from the point of view of the political and military leadership and their obvious failings is only one way of explaining what happened. Recent work by battlefield detectives taking a rather different approach has shown that, even had the campaign been excellently led and the logistics organized down to the final detail, the Allies would still most likely have been defeated. For this battle – if so it can be termed – did not hinge on strategy and politics. Success or failure here was all about terrain, and so about geology. These twin enemies added immeasurably to the difficulties the Allies faced.

Contemporary analysts are also showing that it is possible to look at this battle another way: not so much as an Allied defeat – the consequence of a catalogue of Allied mistakes –

but more as a Turkish victory. And nowhere was Turkish skill shown to such excellent effect as in their understanding of the terrain and their use of it in their own defence.

The Battlefield

The Gallipoli peninsula is a beautiful place. A long sliver of land, it lies on the northern, European side of the Bosphorus. This extremely narrow sea channel winds eastwards from the Mediterranean, through the Sea of Marmara, past Istanbul, and links the Mediterranean with the Black Sea.

Villages dot the peninsula. Around the coast, and on the gentler slopes, there are farms and cultivation. But most of the land here is steep, rugged, bare, dry and utterly inhospitable. Very narrow beaches are backed by crumbly limestone cliffs, beige and white in the bright sun. Inland from the shore rises an impressive landscape of razor-backed hills, badly eroded by severe rainstorms and cut into by steep-sided ravines and gullies. Underfoot the ground is rocky, with a very thin layer of loose, dusty soil. The only vegetation is the kind of low scrub which can survive in such harsh terrain: thorny, barbed, with an aromatic smell in the shimmering heat haze, the kind which snags clothing and scratches bare flesh. All the long summer days there is the continual buzzing of insects and the popping of hot seeds.

From the heights, the view of the Mediterranean is spectacular – a glittering turquoise blue, dotted with the distant shapes of Greek islands.

Over nine months in 1915, this unforgiving land became a bitterly-contested battlefield where the horrors suffered by the troops simply defy description. Today, there is something exceptional about this place. There are 31 cemeteries on

Gallipoli, where row upon row of low headstones name the tens of thousands of young men who were killed here. But it is not just these graves which make it such an affecting place to visit. It is the fact that unlike Hastings or Waterloo, for example, or certainly any of the battlefields on the Western Front, the landscape here has barely changed. It is possible to come close to imagining what it was like in 1915.

Of course, this feat of imagination is made easier by the fact that this 20th-century battlefield – and the men who inhabited it – were documented by war photographers. In hundreds of photographs, we can pick out the mundane details of how they lived and died here, and scrutinize the faces which stare back at the camera for clues to what they were going through. But more than this, in so many places the precise location of photographs taken so long ago can be pinpointed and matched.

Today, a visitor can go to a remote gully, the rocky slopes rising on either side, and find it deserted. A photograph taken in 1915 shows exactly the same gully during the Dardanelles campaign, an ant-heap of activity, home to dozens of men. Countless beaten footpaths snake between bell-tents and khaki ridge tents painted with crosses, and between the shacks and defensive earthworks, reinforced with wood, which scramble up the steep sides of the ravine. Clinging to the hillside, these are built one above another, like flats in a tenement block.

And the soldiers themselves can be glimpsed sitting on camp chairs outside these shacks, almost like flat-dwellers sitting on their balconies. Trains of mules disappear up the gully which leads away from the coast inland, while at the beach end – the beautiful blue Mediterranean is behind the spot where the photographer must have been standing – men in a motley collection of bits of army uniform sit, stand, lounge – eating, drinking, smoking, playing cards.

Though at first sight this deserted gully today may seem to hold no traces of the thousands of men who once passed through it – just the ghosts of the figures in the photograph – the peninsula is in fact covered by the more solid debris left behind by nine months of battle. On the narrow beaches are rusting pieces of metal, huge gun barrels and stretches of barbed wire. Snaking out into the sea are the rotted stumps of what were once wooden jetties built to land supplies for the troops. Gun emplacements and shelters are cut into the cliffs. Well-heads still stand where they were sunk nearly a century ago.

Up on the heights trenches still exist, hacked into the pale yellow ground, and holes in the ground give access to the collapsing network of tunnels which Anzac and Turkish troops used to lay mines to undermine their opponents' trenches. Embedded in rocks and poking out of the ground are bullets, shrapnel fragments and spent cartridge cases.

But most evocative of all – perhaps because they tell of everyday life, and so provide an all-too-comprehensible connection with the men who fought here, even for those who have never been in battle – are the prosaic remains of these soldiers' rubbish. There are scattered bits of tin can which once held corned beef and jam rations; and broken fragments of rum bottles. There is less of this rubbish among the Turkish soldiers' lines, for they had less to throw away, but all over the peninsula can be found the very human evidence of the lives lived here: a dropped button, a regimental badge; a bit of a broken belt-buckle – and, sticking out of the ground, pieces of human bone.

The Plan

The Dardanelles campaign, as conceived in London in early 1915, had a number of objectives. It was intended to secure the seaway from the Black Sea to the Mediterranean so that the Russian Black Sea Fleet could come to the assistance of the Allies and Russian grain could reach the hungry tables of western Europe. It was also thought that such an attack on the Ottoman Empire would quickly knock this ally of the Germans out of the war and, by opening up a second front, would prove a useful way of breaking out of the deadlock on the Western Front.

The campaign was devised as a naval one. Allied warships were to use their big guns to demolish the Turkish forts which controlled the Dardanelles and the approach to Constantinople, now Istanbul. Small numbers of troops would be landed to take the forts and destroy any mobile gun batteries, but it was never expected that large numbers of soldiers would be engaged. Russia would then press on Constantinople from the east as the French and British navies approached from the west.

However, things went wrong from the start. At its widest point the Dardanelles sea passage measures just over two miles; at the 'narrows', less than a mile. At no point was an Allied ship attempting to advance on Constantinople out of range of Turkish forts, or mobile gun batteries, on the shore. The latter proved much more effective than the Allied commanders had expected.

British trawlers had been brought in to act as minesweepers ahead of the warships, but no one seemed to have realized that the current in the Dardanelles was swift. Working in pairs, linked together with minesweeping gear, the trawlers could make little progress upstream and were sitting ducks for the shore-based Turkish gunners.

The Allies had some success in capturing the Turkish forts, but very little against the mobile gun batteries. Turkish reinforcements were quickly rushed to the peninsula. By early March 1915 it was finally appreciated in London that no progress would be made this way, and the decision was made that an expeditionary force would have to be landed on the Gallipoli peninsula to secure the land overlooking the Dardanelles passage. This seemed to be the only way to get the warships through to Constantinople.

As plans were being finalized for the expeditionary force, a final attempt by the Navy to break through was made, on 18 March. It ended in total disaster, with the sinking of three Allied battleships. The projected 'small expeditionary force in support of a naval attack' transmogrified almost overnight into a major amphibious landing of infantry.

Back in London, command had been given to Sir Ian Hamilton. The orders Kitchener gave him have always been cited as symptomatic of everything which was wrong with the Gallipoli campaign from the point of view of the Allied command. They have been seen to epitomize, in micro-cosm, the reasons for the campaign's failure. Hamilton was initially told he would have fewer troops than had been planned and no chance of any air support. It was clearly indicated that he should have no flexibility in what he was to do, for he was told that failure was not to be contem-plated: the political ramifications with Britain's friends and allies in the Middle East would be too damaging. As for intelligence about the place he was to attack, he was given a 1912 Turkish army handbook, a tourist map of the area and a single page of instructions.

His troops were to be a mixture of many nationalities, mostly inexperienced, none of whom had any experience of amphibious landings. Indeed, this was to be the first amphibious landing in history against a defending force armed with the weapons of modern warfare.

From the beginning, it seems, the Allies underestimated their enemy. Just as in the Crimea, when the Turks were Britain's allies, racist sentiments were widespread amongst

British commanders and men. The Turkish army was a conscript one, and generally poorly equipped. It did, however, have some well-trained gunners, and artillery which proved more effective than that of the Allies. Turkey also had a small number of very well-trained officers, among them the brilliant and inspirational Mustafa Kemal Bey, who would go on to be the first leader of modern Turkey. They were also fighting to defend their homeland, on territory they knew well.

Whether from some kind of deep-seated contempt for non-Western troops or simply from carelessness, throughout March and April the British command gave away any advantage of surprise by continually announcing its intentions. The address for the field post office for the campaign was given out as the 'Constantinople Expeditionary Force.' The planned quantity of troops to be landed was telegraphed to any local spies by the giving of numbers to a meat contractor on the Greek islands which would serve as bases for the campaign.

It did not take a brilliant commander to realize that the Gallipoli defences needed strengthening against a likely attack. Under the command of the German Liman von Sanders, the Turkish troops spent the next month doing just that – improving the roads, practising manoeuvres and covering many of the beaches with tangles of barbed wire.

The Commanders

In command on the Allied side was the 62-year-old Scot, General Sir Ian Hamilton. Condemned in many histories of Gallipoli as weak, disorganized and lacking in dynamism, Hamilton was a complex mixture of elements. A Presbyterian from Argyll, he had lost his mother as a child and, after his father's posting to India, had been brought up by aunts. Indeed, he listed the chief influence on his child-hood not to be any member of his family, but his aunts' Swiss maid. He was a professional soldier, but also an intellectual who loved poetry and wrote beautifully. Courteous and respectful of other people's feelings – to a fault, perhaps, given his position – he was also extremely courageous, and was twice recommended for the Victoria Cross for personal bravery. In the years after the First World War he campaigned for reconciliation with defeated Germany.

Before he received his command at Gallipoli, Hamilton had served with honour in South Africa, Russia and India, but nothing could have prepared him for what he had to face at the Dardanelles, where he had to command an enor-mous multinational force under extremely difficult circumstances. In addition, the colleagues and senior commanders upon whom he had to rely were not much help. With a couple of notable exceptions, the descriptions of his team in a recent history of Gallipoli paint an accurate group portrait: one was said to be 'devoid of imagination and apparently unable to learn from his mistakes', another was 'a kindly man but patently inept', a third 'irresolute and unfitted to command', while another is dismissed as 'a stupid pessimist.'

Hamilton's opposite number on the Turkish side, Liman von Sanders, was a German cavalry officer nearing retire-ment who knew his troops well. He had been intimately involved with the modernizing of the Ottoman army before the war and the introduction of German officers to key posts and the removal of some of the least effective Turkish offi-cers. He proved to be both more decisive than Hamilton and more in touch with his front-line troops, but perhaps his most decisive contribution to Turkish victory at Gallipoli was the way he facilitated the activities of a fiery and insubordi-nate young Turkish colonel called Mustafa Kemal Bey.

Mustafa Kemal Bey, who came to be known as Atatürk and led the modernization of his country in the 1920s, was a professional soldier, a colonel of only 34 years of age at the time of Gallipoli. He was a brave and inspired leader of his men. He knew the Gallipoli peninsula intimately. He never waited for orders, but brilliantly took the initiative, and on more than one occasion during the campaign his actions proved decisive in holding back the Allies.

Western histories have always emphasized the failings on the side of the Allied command. The Turkish perspective is, not surprisingly, somewhat different. Turkish academic Kenan Çelik explains that while the British were still commanded by men of an older generation, in Turkey the older generals had been blamed for the Ottoman Empire's prewar defeats in the Balkans and had been swept aside, to be replaced by younger, more forward-looking commanders. The British always waited for orders, says Çelik, 'not like Mustafa Kemal. He acted always on his own initiative and he encouraged his men to do the same. Gallipoli was not old man's war. It was young man's war. Young man can update very quickly. Old man is hard to change.'

The Landings

The date for the Allied landings was set for 23 April 1915, but it was delayed by bad weather and finally took place at dawn on 25 April.

In the dark, the soldiers came ashore at five different landing beaches (codenamed S, V, W, X and Y) at Helles, on the tip of the peninsula, and further north at what became known as Anzac Cove. In almost every case the sites selected were totally unsuitable for a landing. Some beaches were so narrow and the cliffs so steep that the soldiers were trapped without anywhere to take cover and unable to move inland as planned. Some soldiers were landed in deep water and drowned before they could get ashore; others struggled to swim through submerged rolls of barbed wire and were cut to pieces.

There were no proper landing-craft. As soldiers, weighed down with kit, tried to totter down precarious gangplanks, they created perfect targets for Turkish marksmen; others were rowed or towed ashore in long lines of small boats. Steel helmets were not yet in use, so the men sat in these little open boats with nothing but cloth caps or solar topis on their heads – sitting ducks. The sea, it was said, was soon red with blood as far as fifty yards off shore as Turkish soldiers with machine guns sprayed the Allied troops with bullets from above.

Eyewitness accounts written at the time capture some of the horror and chaos of the landings. An officer of the Dublins wrote home: 'I jumped out at once into the sea (up to my chest) yelling at the men to make a rush for it and to follow me. But the poor devils – packed like sardines in a tin and carrying this damnable weight on their backs – could scarcely clamber over the sides of the boat and only two reached shore un-hit...' Another officer, who would be killed later in the campaign, wrote of a moment when he had successfully negotiated the barbed wire entanglements on a landing beach and came under fire from a line of Turkish soldiers in a trench. 'I looked back. There was one soldier between me and the wire and a whole line in a row on the edge of the sands. The sea behind was absolutely crimson, and you could hear the groans through the rattle of musketry. A few were firing. I signalled to them to advance. I shouted to the soldier behind me to signal, but he shouted back, "I am shot through the chest." I then perceived they were all hit.'

The intention had been to gain the high ground – a low

hill called Achi Baba. It was in the centre of the peninsula, just eight kilometres from the shore. The battle plan envisaged taking Achi Baba within 24 hours. In fact, it was never captured, despite nine months of attacks and battle, interspersed with periods of stalemate. The troops dug in, built trenches which in many ways resembled those of the Western Front, and proceeded to fight over territory which could be measured in yards rather than miles. Disastrous offensives in which troops of the Allied or the Turkish side went 'over the top' in massive numbers and died in equally massive numbers further adds to the impression that this campaign, planned as an alternative to Flanders, ended up sharing many of its characteristics.

Kenan Çelik, who now works as a battlefield guide at Gallipoli, paints a terrible portrait of the aftermath of one such battle when, over eight days, 16,000 Turkish soldiers died. Eventually there were so many dead of both sides lying on the ground between the lines that they looked, one Turkish officer wrote in his diary, like lines of worshippers in the mosque on a Friday, lined up in rows and rows, apparently praying.

The young officer wrote: 'I went through the battlefield. It was disgusting. All the dead men lying line after line, wave after wave. And maggots coming out of mouths and noses. Worms. Flies in their millions. It was disgusting. For days and days, it was in my dreams. I couldn't get it out of my head.'

The Turkish commander asked for a truce so that all the bodies could be buried but, Çelik explains, the senior British officer refused, fearing that the Turks, who were short of weapons and ammunition, would use the truce to gather weapons from the dead. So the bodies were simply left on the ground, in the heat, to putrefy.

A new Allied offensive in August, with additional troops being landed at Suvla Bay, further north up the peninsula, was as unsuccessful as the original landings. Through the autumn the stalemate continued, broken only by an appalling storm in late November which brought frostbite and deaths from hypothermia. In late autumn the decision was made by the Allies to withdraw, and by the first week of January 1916 every last soldier had been taken off the peninsula.

While the landings have come to be seen by the British army as an example of everything done wrong, the evacuation is viewed as something of a textbook success. Enormous efforts were put into fooling the Turkish defenders that it was business as usual. Empty supply boxes continued to be landed, with troops being evacuated at night. Shells continued to be fired and the same number of cooking fires lit each night. Heath Robinson contraptions were set up so that firing went on from empty trenches.

However, given that rumours of a likely evacuation were rife throughout the Allied camps on the peninsula and on the Greek islands from November, and that the evacuation itself took place over more than three weeks, it seems unlikely that the Turkish command had not got wind of what was planned. Çelik claims the Turks realized the Allies were evacuating – and simply chose to let them go.

The Battlefield

Geologist Peter Doyle from the School of Earth and Environmental Sciences at Greenwich University, Chatham, in Kent, is fascinated by the way the conflict at Gallipoli unfolded. But unlike more conventional students of the Gallipoli campaign, he is not looking at the issues of political disagreement, contrasting personalities and styles of leadership or logistical failings. He is examining the ground beneath the soldiers' feet and trying to establish how important this was in determining what happened.

When he visited the peninsula for the first time, Doyle was bowled over by what he could deduce just by looking at the landscape.

'You don't have to be a military man to appreciate the difficulties of the terrain', he says. 'For instance, on 'W' Beach at Helles, you say, "How the hell did they attack that?" From a geologist's perspective, it's a gift: rather than the difficulties of reconstructing terrain from maps on land which has often changed beyond recognition – as on the Western Front – the terrain at Gallipoli really hits you straight on. It's stunning, for instance, to look down from the Turkish-controlled heights at Anzac Cove and see the obvious advantages of terrain: it's moving, yet beautiful – amazing.'

By studying the geology and hence the terrain, Doyle is able to work out exactly what difficulties the troops would have encountered on the peninsula. The landscape determines so many things about a battle: where, and if, soldiers can shelter; where the dominant ground is and how many aces are handed to defenders, how many to those who attack. Where will the going be easy or hard for men, animals and vehicles? Will the rock type make digging trenches, gun emplacements, shelters and even latrines easier or more difficult? What will be the availability of water? Every one of these factors was to prove crucial in Turkish success and Allied failure at Gallipoli.

The Intelligence
Doyle has examined the campaign, and the difficulties the terrain created for the Allies from the very first moment: the April landings. For the troops who landed on the beaches of Gallipoli in that early dawn in April 1915, the first issue controlled by the terrain would be the ease or difficulty of getting ashore.

Doyle and his colleague Peter Chasseaud have discovered that the difficulties were quite different at the various landing sites. Moreover, these inherent difficulties were further multiplied by the ignorance of Allied commanders about the landscape on which they were to land, and so the troops' lack of preparedness for what they found.

Military intelligence gathered about the peninsula before the landing, it turns out, was extremely poor. This is not a new revelation: the joke has long been told of officers in Alexandria being dispatched to buy copies of Baedeker's guidebooks to Turkey so that these could form the basis of the commanders' plans. But Doyle and Chasseaud are the first to have made a precise study of just what resources the Allies had at their disposal, and what they knew to expect about the terrain on which they were planning to embark. Though the story about them relying simply on guidebooks turns out to be apocryphal, the truth is that they did not know very much.

Prior to the April landings, sketches of the beaches and the outline of the land had been made from small boats sailing just offshore and from aircraft flying over the peninsula. This information was added to a map obtained by the War Office which Doyle and Chasseaud have been able to run to ground.

'The one-inch map was drawn at the War Office before the First World War,' explains Chasseaud, 'but the map it was derived from was a French survey done in the Crimean War, so we're going back to about 1855.'

The age of the map was not the problem, and Chasseaud believes it showed the terrain pretty well. The problem was the carelessness with which it had been redrawn.

'When it was redrawn it was simplified, missing out quite a lot of the contours or terrain information, and it did give the impression that the terrain wasn't quite as rugged or savage as it was', he says.

By analyzing this map, Peter Doyle can see just why the Allies were unprepared for what they found. Not only did it give the impression of a much less rugged landscape, but it was also far from complete. Indeed, whole hills were simply missing from the map, giving commanders a completely unrealistic idea of what could be achieved by troops landing on the beaches. Compare this with the kind of planning which went into the D-Day landings in Normandy when, for instance, commandos were landed on the beaches to collect soil samples to enable estimates to be made of the kind of going troops and vehicles would encounter. Nothing on this War Office map of Gallipoli could prepare the soldiers for the reality they met on the ground.

Bill Sellars is an Australian writer who came to Gallipoli for the first time in the late 1980s. Something about the place – and the ghosts of what took place there – captured his imagination, and he now lives a short drive away from the battlefield, researching and writing about the campaign. He took the *Battlefield Detectives* crew to a spot just above Anzac Cove. It's a graphic illustration of how the maps let the soldiers down.

On the map, a continuous slope is shown from the landing beach up towards the high ground which the Australians were ordered to try and capture. But when the advancing troops reached this spot, they found themselves not on a continuous gentle slope but at a cliff-edge. Between them and their objective is a deep, steep-sided gully, simply absent from the map. Even had they been able to get across this ravine, the only way to reach the high ground they were heading for was to walk in single file – and totally exposed – along the razor-sharp spine of another narrow ridge. It is possible to negotiate that narrow ridge, with the land falling away precipitously on either side – Bill Sellers has done it, though in daylight and in peacetime – but even then, it's not something he'd like to do again.

This example was repeated numberless times, all over the peninsula. Details on maps are not just important for helping troops navigate: they are also crucial in helping soldiers identify the best places for defence, or the best site for a machine-gun post. Without detailed and accurate maps, it's impossible to plot lines of sight. All these critical details were absent from the maps which the Allies used at Gallipoli.

But the inadequacy of their maps was only the first difficulty the landing troops encountered. With topographical and geological maps spread out before him, Doyle looks at how the terrain at 'W' Beach, for example, forced the hand of the First Lancashire Fusiliers, who landed here. Turkish machine-guns occupied the high ground overlooking the beach.

'The cliffs are funnelling the men into a triangular form of beach', says Doyle, 'and the location of the machine-guns on the top of these hills would give direct enfilading fire down on to the men as they came ashore. So the machine-guns are picking them out in this position. As they are getting trapped in the wire, so the machine-guns are taking them out.

'The geology in this region is definitely controlling the way in which the men can travel. They cannot scale the vertical cliffs easily. So there was only one way once you landed.' That was to fight inland at any cost.

The Lancashires faced strong and determined opposition from the Turkish 2nd/26th Regiment on their route off the beach, but two geological factors left them with no choice. The ground around 'W' Beach was almost impossible to dig, so they were unable to establish any shelter on the beaches and it made no sense to stay there. Beyond the cliffs, as they fought inland against variable opposition, the going was relatively easy.

Because of the differing terrain, the problems faced by the attackers were quite different at Helles where the British landed and at Anzac Cove where the Australians stumbled ashore, though the two are only a few miles apart. In fact, conditions for the Australians, New Zealanders and Indians at Anzac Cove were almost exactly the reverse of those encountered by the British.

'The Australians and New Zealanders were arriving at a completely different set of rocks and completely different terrain', says Doyle. 'It was crazy, broken, badlands-type topography which meant it was harder to establish them-selves [inland]: much easier to dig in. It had very dire consequences for the future.'

For though the Anzacs dug in and gained some protec-tion, the local geology determined that there was almost no water at all. At Helles, there was water, albeit at great depth. This lack of water at Anzac would go on to be an absolutely crucial factor in how the campaign developed over the coming months.

Turkish success at 'V' Beach was also thanks to the terrain and their effective use of it for defensive purposes. Here the Dublin and Munster Fusiliers and the 2nd Hampshire Regiment landed from an old colliery vessel, the *River Clyde*. Inspired by the wooden horse at Troy, a hole had been cut in its side and the soldiers came ashore across a pontoon bridge of boats. But the beach is overlooked by cliffs and narrows to a bottleneck. The Turks had placed wire and posi-tioned machine-guns to rake the beach. No more than three platoons and four old machine-guns defended the place: yet they mowed down the Dublins and the Munsters in their hundreds. As Nigel Steel, of the Imperial War Museum, comments: 'If you sit at the top of the beach, you can see how a blind man could hit anyone trying to land.'

The Allied commanders had not just underestimated

how the terrain would assist the Turkish defenders; they had also too easily dismissed the fighting abilities of the Ottoman army. Armed with modern equipment, including highly accurate Mauser rifles and Maxim machine-guns, the Turks showed themselves to be not only disciplined, but well motivated.

But the terrain did not just dominate what went on in the first hours of the campaign. Though the Allies put their efforts into improving maps – indeed, at Anzac Beach cemetery there is a poignant memorial to Major C.H. Villiers-Stuart of the 59th Punjabi Rifles, 'killed on 17 May 1915 by shrapnel while correcting contours on a defective map' – nothing could change the fact that the terrain itself would determine so much of what happened. A better map could have avoided some of the disasters of the early hours of the attack, but it could not conjure water from ground which had none, nor turn a landscape which was good for a defender into one which favoured those on the attack.

Terrain and Defence

The shape of a landscape is, of course, crucial to any battle: and Gallipoli was better suited to defence than attack. As Bill Sellars puts it, 'Two guys with a couple of rifles on the high ground could do a hell of a lot of damage. And they did.'

Doyle puts it more scientifically: 'Terrain is another weapon of war. A good commander understands his or her terrain. Why is that? Because you have got a force and terrain can multiply the effect of that force. If you, for example, only have a few men and you can site those men effectively on high points channelling troops into the intervening space between them, then you are effectively multiplying the action of that force.'

At Gallipoli, all the advantages were in the hands of the

defenders. At Helles, for example, though the attackers could sweep the slope of the land with artillery fire, they also were forced to make their way up narrow gullies to get inland. Defenders, by siting their machine-guns intelligently, could multiply the effect of those machine-guns, as the attacking men were herded by the landscape into these narrow spaces.

'I can say in my mind that terrain lost the battle for the British and French and won the battle for the Turks,' says Doyle. 'There is no doubt about it. And understanding that terrain won it.' For the Turks knew the landscape well and deployed effective tactics to exploit its natural advantages.

Peter Chasseaud has also shown how the lack of accurate maps meant that the Allies were not able to exploit the advantages they did have. The troops needed the support of long-range artillery from the ships offshore. But without accurate height data, it was impossible for these guns to be used effectively.

'You needed very accurate height data, particularly with the rugged terrain at Gallipoli,' says Chasseaud. 'If your angles of sight are wrong, then your shells are either going to sail over, or fall short and hit your own troops. So your contours have to be very accurate on a good artillery map.' Certainly at the beginning of the campaign, no such good artillery maps existed.

Trench Warfare

In other ways, too, the geology of different spots on the Gallipoli peninsula determined the way the nine-month-long conflict unfolded. While the British troops landing at Helles were forced by the lack of cover on the narrow beaches to fight their way inland at whatever cost – and the cost was enormous in terms of lives lost – the troops landing at what came to be called Anzac Cove, coming ashore at a place other than the one they had expected, soon found the geology made the digging of trenches and tunnels relatively easy. It was, therefore, not just the frequently quoted order of Hamilton that the Anzacs should 'dig' which led to them digging in. The British at Helles simply could not have dug, in the rocks on which they landed, the complicated network of trenches that the Anzacs engineered.

Up at Anzac Cove, there soon existed trenches and tunnels which mirrored what was happening on the Western Front – and, as a result, a similar kind of warfare came into being. Long lines of trenches snaked around the hillsides and many men spent months – sometimes the whole campaign – without ever catching sight of an enemy soldier. Bill Sellars paints a vivid picture of this kind of warfare: 'In some case the troops just had to occupy the trench without firing – without seeing a Turk for weeks on end – because to put your head over the parapet was instant death. So in many cases their activity was sitting in extreme heat, with limited food – often very salty – waiting for an attack, but not actually taking part in any action.'

Often there was hardly any no-man's-land separating the two lines of trenches: 'It was a matter of a few metres, a few sandbags and bodies piled in a trench, separating the other line from the Allied line.' Stalemate was interspersed by suicidal missions 'over the top', when waves of soldiers were cut down by machine-guns. Sappers tunnelled out towards enemy trenches and laid mines. Grenades – hand-made out of jam tins by the Anzacs – were lobbed across the narrow no-man's-land between the two lines.

The terrain also encouraged snipers. Snipers worked in a team. Home-made periscopes were used to scan the enemy lines and spot someone who was temporarily unprotected.

Simple ruses such as waving a hat on a stick were used to attract attention from the opposite side and tempt an enemy sniper to reveal himself. The most infamous snipers at Gallipoli could kill a man glimpsed through a tiny loophole at distances of more than 100 metres. Some became so well known that they were given a roving commission. The Australian 'Billy' Sing, for example, had more than 100 confirmed kills as a sniper at Gallipoli.

The complex, confusing, deeply fissured terrain also led to troops becoming disorientated during assaults. Peter Doyle describes how troops, lost in 'the great jumble and complexity of the terrain that the geology there had made' frequently died in confusing incidents of so-called 'friendly fire.'

Health and Hygiene

From the early days of the campaign, the commanders recognized that water was to be a critical element in this battle. Hamilton wrote with frustration on one occasion that half his troops were digging trenches and the other half collecting water, leaving no one available for actual fighting.

The geology, and thus the water it provided, was quite different for the Turkish troops, for the mainly British troops at Helles Point and for the Anzacs. The Turks were generally well provided with water. The British troops could find some water-bearing limestone rocks, though at considerable depth and yielding varying amounts, depending on the season. The Anzacs, however, were able to get almost no fresh water at all, once they had exhausted the small amount present at the beach itself. Water for the Anzacs, perched on their tiny beachhead, had to be shipped from Egypt and then landed under threat of fire.

For most of the campaign, therefore, water was in extraordinarily short supply here and the Anzac troops were restricted to three pints per day, for all purposes including washing and washing-up. With temperatures in the nineties, each soldier could have been losing as much as a litre of water per hour. Even had they been sitting in the shade doing nothing, they should have been drinking at least three litres of liquid a day to avoid dehydration, with its harmful consequences.

But dehydration was not the only problem caused by the water shortage. Colonel Alan Hawley, Commander of Medical Services for the British Army's 3rd Division, has looked at how disease was able to spread so damagingly amongst the Allied troops at Gallipoli. Water was the critical link in the chain which led to disease. The hardness of the ground in many places meant that latrines could not be dug, so men were simply going behind the bushes. With the lack of water, they were not washing their hands afterwards. With such a shortage of water, men could not even keep their cooking and eating utensils clean.

Even when latrines were dug, the shortage of wood to make coverings meant that they were open pits over which flies crawled in their thousands. Graves, too, could not be dug for dead bodies. So there were hundreds of corpses lying rotting in the open.

Flies alighted on everything. It was almost impossible to eat food before flies had landed on it – and these flies were also crawling all over the rotting corpses, the piles of human excrement and the latrine pits. Throughout the summer of 1915, terrible gastro-intestinal problems such as dysentery spread rapidly among the troops.

Lack of water also meant the medical tents and operating theatres were not kept adequately clean, with consequent post-operative complications. Dust got everywhere; and everyone suffered from lice.

The diet was also monotonous, salty and lacking in fresh

fruit or vegetables. Understanding of nutrition was still in its infancy. Many troops at Gallipoli suffered from vitamin deficiency diseases such as beriberi and scurvy which, though not fatal, were debilitating. There was also a neglect of dental problems and a shortage of dentists, so many soldiers quickly became unable to eat.

Gradually bad health came to be a greater threat to the troops than the Turkish guns. Among the Australian soldiers, for example, there were never fewer than 18 per cent sick, and in September 1915 the sick list reached almost one-third of all troops.

Nigel Steel, author of a number of books on the Gallipoli campaign, considers that after May 8 the poor state of health of the Allied troops – a direct result of the terrain and climate – became a major factor in their ineffectiveness.

'Almost all the men were suffering from the effects of the climate – from sunstroke to stomach troubles, dehydration and diarrhoea to full-blown dysentery', he says. 'Soldiers who became exhausted by mere routine tasks could not reasonably be expected to mount vigorous uphill attacks in bad, scrubby terrain against a well-prepared enemy.'

No Way Out

The problems of the Allied soldiers at Gallipoli were compounded by a factor which was perhaps unique to this battlefield. Horrible as soldiers' experiences have been on almost every battlefront in history, at Gallipoli there was something else: no escape from the horror of the fighting. Troops in Flanders could travel back from the front for rest and recuperation. The wounded could be evacuated to hospitals in safe areas. There were meals, starlit walks, skating on frozen ponds, even snatched nights of romance in seaside hotels, all safely beyond the reach of the guns. But at Gallipoli, there could be no escaping – however briefly – into this kind of 'normal' life. Behind the Allied trenches, there was only the sea. Everywhere was within range of enemy guns. Every day, soldiers at Gallipoli were killed off duty, by snipers or by shrapnel, just as their comrades died in the front line. Men died as they swam in the sea, and as they played impromptu games of cricket. Men died squatting over the latrine pits or crouching by cooking fires. Men died unloading crates of bully-beef; and wounded soldiers, waiting to be evacuated, died lying on stretchers on the beaches. The threat of death was ever-present.

It was also true that those who were wounded were not well-placed to survive. The landscape made the evacuation of casualties especially difficult. The shortage of adequate maps meant it was extremely difficult to inform the stretcher-bearers of where an injured man might be lying. The steepness of the terrain meant wounded men often had to be rolled downhill, it being impossible to carry them. Trenches cut in this rocky ground were too narrow for the stretcher-bearers, whose knuckles were raw from knocking against the sides of the trench. The delays in evacuating the wounded meant that gangrene spread and amputation of injured limbs became more likely.

This lack of respite – coupled with the widespread feeling among the troops that this campaign was hopeless and the high command incompetent – made Gallipoli an acutely intense theatre of war. The fact that anyone could be killed at any moment led, observers noted, to a general fatalism amongst the men.

Colonel Hawley reads the medical reports with a modern eye. In such an environment, where the lack of safe 'rear areas' meant there was no opportunity for relaxation, he would expect to see a rise in psychiatric cases. Examining the medical records of units at Gallipoli, what he has found is not a rise in reported psychiatric disorder but an increase in what was then called 'soldier's heart.' In 1915 this was thought to be a physical symptom of cardiac disorder. Now it is thought to be an early manifestation of post-traumatic stress disorder.

Hawley has also noted the first signs of something he calls 'conditional obedience'. Troops follow orders, but with no great enthusiasm or application: on occasion, though they do not refuse to obey an order, they simply fail to carry it out.

The Final Irony

The detective work which has lately been done on the geology of the Gallipoli peninsula has established that the Allies' campaign could probably never have been successful. But there is a further irony for the Allies. The nine-month campaign at Gallipoli, with its tens of thousands of dead, was devoted to the objective of winning the high ground of Achi Baba, from which the Allies expected to be able to dominate the Dardanelles. But what careful analysis of accurate maps reveals – the accurate maps Allied commanders at the time did not possess – is that Achi Baba does not give the commanding position the Allied commanders expected.

'The Allies were transfixed on achieving the heights,' says Doyle, 'but there is evidence that once you get to the heights you are still not going to see your goal: the Narrows.' Though it is possible to see water glimmering in the distance, there are two further ridges between Achi Baba and the sea. There is no clear view at all of the troublesome gun emplacements which had made life impossible for the warships back in February and which had sparked off the entire Gallipoli campaign in the first place.

Nigel Steel is also dubious as to how successful the Allies would have been even had they been able to take the Dardanelles. It is now clear that the Turks would have regrouped and regrouped, fighting and frustrating the Allies every inch of the way. It would not have been the easy fight the Allies anticipated. Given Turkish resistance, he questions whether it is credible that the Allies would really have bombarded the ancient city of Constantinople with its treasures and historical buildings.

So it seems the basic objective was as flawed as the maps with which the troops first stumbled ashore in April.

There is something about all battlefields which draws visitors, students, enthusiasts. Tourists wander between the tombstones, reading the inscriptions, sobered by the youthfulness of the dead. Most visitors to Gallipoli are Turkish citizens, who come with pride and gratitude to honour their dead and enjoy their glorious – though bloody – victory. But Bill Sellars feels it differently. His passion for the place and the stories of what went on here is as strong, but its source is something different.

'For me, it's not the glory of war or anything like that', he says. 'It's the sheer human endurance of tens of thousands of men of both sides pitting themselves against each other in terrain like this. Can I imagine just sitting here with the smell of rotting corpses day after day? Living on no more than a litre of water a day sometimes; whatever scraps of food could be sent up – salty tinned beef; hard biscuits. Could I have done seven months of that? No.

'I don't so much question why – that's the political side. I question how. I just don't know how. We stand here: 20,000 men died over there. A similar number died on the other

shoulder of the hill. It's so peaceful. So beautiful. It's so
bloody. I still don't know how.'

Notes

Unattributed quotations are from *Battlefield Detectives* interviews.

Hastings

1 Elisabeth Van-Houts, *History Today*, October 1996 vol. 46 no. 10.
2 Matthew Bennett, *Campaigns of the Norman Conquest*, Osprey, 2001.
3 Bernard S. Bachrach, 'Some Observations on the Military Administration of the Norman Conquest', in Stephen Morillo, *The Battle of Hastings*, Boydell and Brewer, 1996.
4 David Bernstein, 'The Blinding of Harold', in Stephen Morillo, *The Battle of Hastings*, Boydell and Brewer, 1996.

Agincourt

1 Anne Curry, *Agincourt 1415*, Tempus Publishing Ltd, Stroud, 2000.
2 Matthew Bennett, *Agincourt 1415*, Osprey, 1991.
3 Ibid.
4 Christopher Gravett, *English Medieval Knights 1400–1500*, Osprey, 200.
5 Frank Taylor and John Roskell (trans), *Gesta Henrici Quinti*, Oxford University Press, 1975, quoted in Anne Curry, *The Battle of Agincourt – Sources and Interpretations*, The Boydell Press, Woodbridge, 2000.

6 Ibid.

7 Ibid.

8 Matthew Bennett, op. cit.

9 Matthew Bennett, op. cit.

10 Frank Taylor and John Roskell, op. cit.

11 Anne Curry, op. cit.

12 Anne Curry, *Agincourt 1415*, Tempus Publishing Ltd, Stroud, 2000.

13 Anne Curry, op. cit.

14 Frank Taylor and John Roskell, as above, p37.

15 Matthew Bennett, *Agincourt 1415*, Osprey, 1991.

16 John Carman, *British Archaeology* no. 21, February 1997.

17 John Keegan, *The Face of Battle*, Pimlico, 1991.

18 Anne Curry, *The Battle of Agincourt – Sources and Interpretations*, The Boydell Press, Woodbridge, 2000.

Armada

1 Felipe Fernandez-Armesto, *The Spanish Armada – the Experience of War in 1588, Oxford University Press*, 1988.

2 Colin Martin, *British Archaeology*, April 2002.

3 Colin Martin and Geoffrey Parker, *The Spanish Armada*, Manchester University Press, 1999.

4 Ibid.

5 Ibid.

6 Colin Martin, *An Introduction to Marine Archaeology*, http://www.bbc.co.uk/history/ancient/archaeology/marine_2.shtml

7 George Bass, Interview, *Diving Into History*, 9 June 1999.

Waterloo

1 Elizabeth Longford, *Wellington*, Weidenfeld & Nicolson 1992 quoting Wellington's *Despatches*.

2 David Chandler, *Waterloo: The Hundred Days*, Osprey, 1980.

3 Quoted in Geoffrey Wooten, *Waterloo 1815*, Osprey 1992.

4 Elizabeth Longford, op. cit.; quoting Sir William Fraser, *Words on Wellington*, London, 1899.
5 John Keegan, *The Face of Battle*, Pimlico 1991.
6 David Howarth, *Waterloo – A Near Run Thing*, Windrush Press, 1997.
7 From *The Field of Waterloo*, Unknown officer.
8 Mick Crumplin, *Surgery at Waterloo*, Unknown.
9 Ibid.
10 M.K.H. Crumplin, *Vascular Problems at the Battle of Waterloo*, European Journal of Vascular Surgery no. 1, 1987.
11 David Howarth, op. cit.
12 David Chandler, op. cit.
13 Geoffrey Wooten, op. cit.
14 Philip de Segur, *History of the Expedition to Russia Undertaken by the Emperor Napoleon in the Year 1812*, London, 1860.

Balaklava

1 Tennyson, *Charge of the Light Brigade*, 1864.
2 Norman Davies, *Europe: A History*, Pimlico, 1997.
3 John Sweetman, *Balaclava 1854*, Osprey, 1990.
4 *The Times*, 6 November 1854.
5 *The Times*, 14 November 1854.
6 Quoted in Mark Adkin, *The Charge*, Pimlico, 1996.
7 Sweetman, op. cit.

Little Bighorn

1 *Bismarck Tribune*, 14 May 1876.
2 Major M.A. Reno, *Report on the Battle of Little Big Horn*, 5 July 1876.
3 Major M.A. Reno, op. cit.
4 U.S. Military Academy.
5 Quoted in Peter Panzeri, *Little Big Horn*, Osprey, 1995.
6 Douglas D. Scott, P Willey, and Melissa A. Connor, *They*

Died With Custer: Soldiers' Bones from the Battle of the Little Bighorn, University of Oklahoma Press, 1998.

[7] Douglas D. Scott, Richard A. Fox Jr., Melissa A. Connor, and Dick Harmon, *Archaeological Perspectives on the Battle of the Little Bighorn*, University of Oklahoma Press, 1989.

[8] Current *Biography 52* http://emuseum.mnsu.edu

[9] Clyde Snow and John Fitzpatrick, 'Human Osteological Remains from the battle of the Little Bighorn', from *They Died With Custer: Soldiers' Bones from the Battle of the Little Bighorn*, University of Oklahoma Press, 1998.

[10] Douglas D. Scott, P. Willey, Melissa A Connor, op. cit.

[11] Richard Allan Fox, Jr., *Archaeology, History, and Custer's Last Battle*, University of Oklahoma Press, 1993.

[12] Joseph R. Svinth, 'A Chronological History of the Martial Arts and Combative Sports 1860–1899', http://ejmas.com/kronos/NewHist1860-1899.htm 2002

[13] Stubbs, Mary Lee and Connor, Stanley R., *Army Lineage Series: Armor-Cavalry Part 1*, Office of the Chief of Military History, United States Army, 1969.

[14] John D. McDermott, 'Report Prepared for the American Battlefield Protection Program', Frontier Heritage Alliance, Sheridan, Wyoming, 2000.

[15] Charles W. King, 'Arms and Tactics', *Army and Navy Journal*, March 327, 1880.

[16] James McClellan, *A Day with the Fighting Cheyennes*, Motor Travel 22, p20, January 1931.

[17] Major M.A. Reno, op. cit.

[18] Douglas D. Scott, Richard A. Fox Jr., Melissa A. Connor, and Dick Harmon. *Archaeological Perspectives on the Battle of the Little Bighorn*. University of Oklahoma Press, 1989.

[19] Ibid.

[20] Ibid.

[21] Peter Panzeri, *Little Big Horn 1876*, Osprey, 1995.

[22] Quoted in Douglas D. Scott, Richard A. Fox Jr., Melissa A.

Connor, and Dick Harmon, *Archaeological Perspectives on the Battle of the Little Bighorn.* University of Oklahoma Press, 1989.

[23] *New York Times*, 6 July 1876.

[24] Ibid.

[25] Quoted in the PBS documentary *The West*, 1996. http://www.pbs.org/weta/thewest/program/episodes/six/goodday.htm

[26] Ibid.

[27] Douglas D. Scott, Richard A. Fox Jr., Melissa A. Connor, and Dick Harmon, *Archaeological Perspectives on the Battle of the Little Bighorn*, University of Oklahoma Press, 1989.

Further Reading

Books

General
Keegan, John; *The Face of Battle*; Pimlico, 1991
Keegan, John and Wheatcroft, Andrew; *Who's Who in Military History*; Routledge, 2002

The Battle of Hastings
Holmes, Richard; *War Walks 2*; BBC Books, 1998
Bennett, Matthew; *Campaigns of the Norman Conquest*; Osprey, 2001
Ville de Bayeux; *La Tapisserie de Bayeux*; Artaud Frères
Gravett, Christopher; *Hastings 1066*; Osprey Campaign no. 13, 1992

Agincourt
Curry, Anne (ed.); *Agincourt 1415*; Tempus, 2000
Bennett, Matthew; *Agincourt 1415*; Osprey, 1991

The Spanish Armada
Howarth, David; *The Voyage of the Armada*; Lyons Press, 2001
Martin, Colin and Parker, Geoffrey; *The Spanish Armada*; Mandolin, 1999
Konstam, Angus; *The Armada Campaign 1588*; Osprey Campaign no. 86, 2001

Fernandez-Armesto, Felipe; *The Spanish Armada – The Experience of War in 1588*; Oxford University Press, 1988

Rodriguez-Salgado, M.J., (ed.); *Armada 1588–1988 An International Exhibition to Commemorate the Spanish Armada: The Official Catalogue*; Penguin, 1988

Waterloo

Howarth, David; *Waterloo – A Near Run Thing*; Windrush Press, 1999

Chandler, David; *Waterloo – The Hundred Days*; Osprey, 1997

Wooten, Geoffrey; *Waterloo 1815*; Osprey, 1992

Balaklava

Adkin, Mark; *The Charge*; Pimlico, 1996

Sweetman, John; *Balaclava 1854: The Charge of the Light Brigade*; Osprey Campaign no. 6, 2000

Sweetman, John; *The Crimean War*; Osprey Essential Histories, 2001

The Battle of the Little Bighorn

Allan Fox, Richard; *Archaeology, History and Custer's Last Battle*; University of Oklahoma Press, 1993

Scott, Douglas D. et al; *Archaeological Perspectives on the Battle of the Little Bighorn*; University of Oklahoma Press, 1989

Panzeri, Peter; Little Big Horn 1876; Osprey, 1995

Gallipoli

Rhodes James, Robert; *Gallipoli*; Batsford, 1965

Steel, Nigel and Hart, Peter; *Defeat at Gallipoli*; Macmillan, 1994

Moorhouse, Geoffrey; *Hell's Foundations*; Hodder & Stoughton, 1992

Internet Sites

General
http://www.emill.com/fas/battle.html
Forensic archaeology, especially Little Bighorn.
http://www.bbc.co.uk/history/war/index.shtml
http://www.fordham.edu/halsall/

The Battle of Hastings
http://www.cablenet.net/pages/book/
Site dedicated to theories about William's landing site, but
    contains much more.

Agincourt
http://www.aginc.net/battle/

The Spanish Armada
http://tbls.hypermart.net/history/1588armada/
http://www.newadvent.org/cathen/01727c.htm
http://www.nmm.ac.uk/education/fact_files/fact_armada.
    html

The Spanish Armada
http://www.rbethke.pensacola.com/Armada.htm

Waterloo
http://www.pbs.org/empires/napoleon/home.html
Resource-rich site, includes an interactive battle of Waterloo
    simulator.

Balaklava
http://www.suite101.com/articles.cfm/crimean_war/
Very detailed and comprehensive site.
http://www.hargreave-mawson.demon.co.uk/cwrs.html

The Battle of the Little Bighorn

http://www.custerbattle.com/sub_pages/archaeo_sub/
fieldwork.htm

http://www.pbs.org/weta/thewest/program/

American TV series includes documentary material, background and images of Little Bighorn.

Gallipoli

http://www.iwm.org.uk/online/gallipoli/navigate.htm
The Imperial War Museum's guide.

http://www.nzhistory.net.nz/Gallery/Anzac/galli-poli/
index.htm
New Zealand site.

http://www.canakkale.gen.tr/eng/engindex.html
Turkish site.

http://www.anzacsite.gov.au/
Australian site.